ALSO BY ROBERT BRENT TOPLIN

Radical Conservatism: The Right's Political Religion

Michael Moore's Fahrenheit 9/11: How One Film Divided a Nation

Reel History: In Defense of Hollywood

Oliver Stone's USA: Film, History, and Controversy (editor)

Ken Burns's The Civil War: Historians Respond (editor)

History by Hollywood

*Hollywood as Mirror: Changing Views of "Outsiders" and "Enemies"
in American Movies*

*Freedom and Prejudice: The Legacy of Slavery in the
United States and Brazil*

Unchallenged Violence: An American Ordeal

Slavery and Race Relations in Latin America (editor)

The Abolition of Slavery in Brazil

REPUBLICAN EXTREMISM

FROM JOSEPH MCCARTHY TO DONALD TRUMP

Robert Brent Toplin

CONTENTS

INTRODUCTION 1

1. CONTRASTS IN RED AND BLUE 6

2. PROMISE AND PERIL IN THE FIFTIES 25

3. LESSONS FROM PRESIDENTIAL ELECTIONS 37

4. BOOMING AND CRASHING ECONOMIES 60

5. MOVIES AND POLITICS 69

6. CONSERVATISM TURNS RADICAL 91

7. THE PSYCHOLOGY OF TRUMP AND MAGA 99

8. LITE NEWS ON FOX 109

9. RESPONSES TO COVID 117

10. THE EXTREME COURT 139

11. RACIAL POLITICS 146

12. GUNS, IMMIGRATION, AND CLIMATE 159

13. GLOBAL THREATS 177

14. BIDEN'S PRESIDENCY 201

EPILOGUE 215

15. REFORMING THE GOP 215

NOTES 230

INDEX 244

INTRODUCTION

For decades, American society has been roiled by troubles created by Republican extremism. The GOP is now far removed from the mainstream, center-right organization of the past. Its radical politics have divided the American people, produced governmental dysfunction, and undermined democratic traditions. Early signs of the Republican Party's shift appeared in the 1950s with Joseph McCarthy's red baiting and in the 1960s with Barry Goldwater's defense of extremism. The party's move into radical politics gained momentum in the 1990s under Newt Gingrich's leadership and continued into the twenty-first century.

Donald Trump contributed significantly to this development. When Trump sought reelection as President of the United States in 2023, many Americans worried that his return to the White House could be disastrous for the nation and the world. Pundits, elected officials, and others objected to Trump's incendiary rhetoric and threatening behavior. Numerous Republicans objected, as well. They complained that Trump and his MAGA followers hijacked the party. But their protests had little impact. Donald Trump's influence grew. By March 2024, he was the GOP's presumptive nominee for President of the United States.

Why has Republican resistance to extremism been so daunting and frustrating?

Clues can be found in history. The Republican Party enabled radical politics long before Donald Trump became a dominant figure in its affairs.

Since the 1950s, on numerous occasions Republicans had chances to reject firebrands and commit to mainstream politics, but GOP leaders were reluctant to act. Glittering prospects of electoral victories motivated them to endorse radical ideas and candidates. Republicans that opposed these actions found it increasingly difficult to challenge the party's trajectory. Strident radicals churning out combative rhetoric fared better in the GOP's primary elections than centrists that favored negotiation and compromise. Pressures grew for obeisance to far-right agendas. The party eventually purged numerous moderates from its ranks. Militants denigrated them as RINOS, Republicans in Name Only.

A related pattern occurred in conservative media. Incendiary commentators attracted large audiences on radio and television. Rush Limbaugh showed the potential of aggressive showmanship in syndicated radio and television programs. Limbaugh attacked liberals, Democrats, gays, feminists, and others. Mixing humor with contempt, he achieved fame, fortune, and power. Numerous commentators on the radio imitated his combative style. Celebrities on television did, too, including Bill O'Reilly, Sean Hannity, Tucker Carlson, and Laura Ingraham. In the twenty-first century, feisty entertainers dominated the rightwing communications industry.

GOP leaders might have succeeded in preventing their party from becoming a bastion of far-right politics if they had displayed determination to challenge the agitators. Some courageous Republicans spoke out over the years but lacked support from the party. Senator Margaret Chase Smith boldly criticized Joseph McCarthy's excesses in 1950. Only a few Republicans backed her. Nelson Rockefeller warned about the John Birch Society and Barry Goldwater's extremism in a speech at the GOP's national convention in 1964. Delegates shouted him down. In the 1990s GOP House Minority Leader Bob Michel criticized Newt Gingrich's efforts to commit Republicans in Congress to sharply negative, take-no-prisoners battles against Democrats. Michel lost the fight. Decades later, Republicans Liz Cheney and Adam Kinzinger warned about threats to democracy from Donald Trump and his MAGA followers. Republicans quickly ostracized Cheney and Kinzinger.

By that time, objectors to extremism had little chance of success. Most Republican politicians recognized it was safer to work with the radicals than challenge them. To secure a future in the Republican Party it was essential to go with the flow.

When Donald Trump vied for another four-year stint at the White House, many Americans – Democrats, independents, and some Republicans, as well -- believed a second Trump presidency would become a menace to American democracy. Europeans were anxious, too. They worried that Trump would turn his back on NATO and tolerate aggressive moves by Vladimir Putin.

Extremism was no longer just an internal problem for the GOP and American society. It endangered the international order that had promoted global peace and prosperity for decades.

This book identifies key points in the Republican Party's path toward extremism from the 1950s to the present. The chapters focus on key people and events that affected the party's transformation. The chapters show how the GOP lurched to the right and polarized the nation through its positions on elections, the presidency, the economy, the Supreme Court, race relations, guns, immigration, Covid, crime, the mass media, climate change, international relations, and war-making.

The book does not offer simplistic, partisan rants. It maintains that America needs mainstream political parties. The United States had a moderate Republican Party in the Eisenhower era and to some extent in later years. Presently, many Republicans favor mainstream politics, but they lack influence in the radicalized GOP.

When crafting these chapters, I was not interested in expanding upon ideas already circulating in the mass media. I aimed to create original perspectives. The strategy for generating distinctive interpretations was to seek lessons from history. A comparative framework is evident through much of the analysis. The chapters explore connections between current events and history.

Linking the present and past is an activity that engages several prominent interpreters of American politics. Jon Meachem, Michael Beschloss,

Heather Cox Richardson, Douglas Brinkley, Rachel Maddow, and several other communicators illuminate connections. Analyses in this book are different because they apply lessons from history to a broad range of controversies from the 1950s to the present. The essays focus on specific situations that reveal how the GOP abandoned mainstream ideas and practices.

Comparisons of Republican and Democratic politics appear throughout the book. The analysis challenges claims made by numerous pundits that both parties are deeply troubled by extremism. The historical record demonstrates this is a false equivalency. The Democratic Party has been much more responsive to changing economic, social, and political conditions from the 1950s to the present than the Republican Party. It has been more receptive to debate, negotiation, and compromise. Public opinion polls in recent years indicated that Democrats were considerably more attracted to moderate, mainstream politics than Republicans.

The first chapter in the book provides an overview of major shifts in Republican and Democratic politics from the 1950s to the present. That section creates a foundation for the analyses that follow. The bulk of the book examines controversies that fragmented American politics from the Fifties to the present. Drawing conclusions from that history, the epilogue offers recommendations for reforming the Republican Party.

An examination of the GOP's record of extremism can lead to pessimism about prospects for reform. The growing influence of Donald Trump and his MAGA devotees in Republican affairs in recent years makes the party's radical course seem irreversible.

Evidence from recent history is concerning, but the Republican Party's future may not resemble its past. There have been numerous times in American history when problems seemed inescapable. Many Americans were pessimistic in the 1780s when the new nation's experiment with self-government was in jeopardy, in the 1830s when slavery appeared unassailable, and during the Great Depression when the nation's broken economy seemed unrepairable. Yet those crises passed. Conditions improved.

A note of cautious optimism can apply to the current situation. The GOP may eventually temper its radicalism. The party's adjustment could be modest or major. Reform might come in response to election outcomes. A shift might occur quickly or require years to play out. Whatever the cause, size and speed of the adjustment, change seems likely because radicals gained enormous influence in the Republican Party. They turned their backs on America's mainstream political traditions. Their far-right politicking has alienated many voters.

The return of mainstream conservative politics could be led by the GOP, or it might appear in the form of a new organization if Republicans fail to curb their party's radical course.

ONE

CONTRASTS IN RED AND BLUE

These two overviews reveal that one political party, driven by pressures for conformity, turned increasingly radical. The other, more open to debate and compromise, responded vigorously to changing political conditions and ultimately took a more centrist, mainstream path.

This book focuses on the Republican Party's growing radicalism over three-quarters of a century, but the record of the Democratic Party's evolution during those years is an integral part of the analysis.

Extremist Republican Politics: A Brief History

In recent years, commentators in the mass media have been consumed with questions about the impact of Donald Trump's controversial leadership, but long after Trump is gone from the political scene historians will be asking a different question, one that does not presently receive much consideration. They will ask why Republicans allowed such an incompetent, corrupt, and destructive person to acquire so much power and influence in their party. Why did leaders in the GOP remain generally silent when Trump violated American political traditions, threatened democracy, undermined public health, and put national security at risk? They will ask, too: Why did most Republican leaders in Washington serve as Trump's *enablers* by praising or accepting his leadership rather than challenging it?

Historians can discover roots of the problem in the Republican Party's long-term evolution toward conformist politics.[1] Donald Trump's influence was not simply a product of his drive and personality. Since the 1950s, pressures for fidelity and unity have been building in the party. Leaders tolerated shifts toward extremist politics. They stifled disagreements about policy and candidates, purged dissenters, and promoted ideological uniformity. By fostering an undemocratic political culture, they contributed significantly to the GOP's modern crisis and the nation's as well.

This transformation occurred gradually over several decades. The makeover became notable in the 1960s, turned sharper during Ronald Reagan's presidency, and accelerated from 2000 to 2016. Pressures for unity accentuated notably during Trump's presidency. By the early 2020s, the GOP was far removed from the center-right organization of Dwight D. Eisenhower's leadership in the 1950s. The Republican Party had become a radical-right organization.

How did the change occur? This overview from the 1950s to the present identifies key people and events that affected the transformation.

In the late 1940s and early Fifties, the Republican Party was not exclusively a hub for right-wing politics. There were influential conservatives in the GOP, such as Ohio senator Robert Taft, but prominent moderates and liberals carried weight as well. During the 1950s, President Dwight D. Eisenhower skillfully held these disparate groups together. Arthur Larson, Eisenhower's speechwriter, praised Eisenhower for promoting a moderate, "modern," big-tent party that was receptive to diverse political viewpoints.[2] Both in the White House and in Congress, mainstream conservatives were in the driver's seat.

Evidence of the party's future troubles appeared early in the early 1950s when Joseph McCarthy, a reckless and opportunistic Republican senator from Wisconsin, acquired enormous political influence. He was the most significant Republican fearmonger of the post-World War II era. In dishonest and shameful ways, McCarthy stoked worries about communist subterfuge in the federal government and in U.S. society.[3]

McCarthy exploited fears that were already prominent in American society. When he gave a speech about communist subversion on February 9, 1950, that attracted considerable media coverage, many Americans were anxious about recent international news. The Soviets tested their first atomic bomb in 1949, and that year China fell to control by Mao Zedong and the "Reds." Also upsetting was news about Alger Hiss, a prominent statesman who had been charged with working on behalf of the Soviets. Shortly before McCarthy's influential speech in Wheeling, West Virginia reports indicated that Klaus Fuchs, a scientist involved in the Manhattan Project, had given atomic secrets to the Russians.

Joseph McCarthy did not produce important new evidence about communist subversion, but he *acted* like a crusader who was successfully exposing treasonous activities. In the Wheeling address McCarthy warned that democracy could be destroyed not "from enemies without, but rather because of enemies within." Public concern about disloyalty among individuals holding important positions in the government and public institutions was already growing in the late 1940s. The bombardment of these and other disturbing news stories provided rich opportunities for political exploitation.

In 1950 Maine's Republican senator Margaret Chase Smith bravely asked colleagues to endorse a Declaration of Conscience that criticized McCarthy, although the document did not mention him by name. She said the Senate had become a "forum of hate and character assassination." Smith asked the senators not to seek political victories by riding the "Four Horsemen of Calumny – Fear, Ignorance, Bigotry, and Smear." Only six Republican senators signed the Declaration, and five of the six soon removed their names. Not until 1954, when McCarthy overreached by attacking the U.S. Army, did several Republican senators add their voices to a chorus of criticism. The Republican Party put up little resistance until McCarthy appeared vulnerable. Even President Eisenhower, who despised McCarthy, worked cautiously and mostly out of public view when dealing with the troublesome senator.

Joseph McCarthy's crusade against communism added new elements to the Republican Party's agenda. McCarthy gave Republican politics the appearance of a culture war. Most developments in politics have antecedents, of course. Cultural elements were at play in American politics well before the Fifties. But Joseph McCarthy amplified cultural themes. He exaggerated threats related to minor social tensions in American society.

McCarthy did not just charge individuals with ties to communism. His contemptuous remarks targeted a broad swath of American society. He expressed disdain for Democrats, liberals, well-educated elites, and others. McCarthy lambasted the distinguished Secretary of State Dean Acheson, calling him a "pompous diplomat in striped pants, with a phony British accent." He denounced "egg-sucking phony liberals" and called for investigations of homosexuals.

In 1959 a prominent historian, Richard Hofstadter, related McCarthy's appeal to earlier tensions in U.S. history. Hofstadter noted that in the past Americans worried about the influence of gold gamblers, Catholics, immigrants, Masons, international bankers, and others. Anxious citizens talked about dark conspiracies involving powerful groups that threatened the American way of life. Individuals that supported Joseph McCarthy or the ultra-right John Birch Society "believe themselves to be conservative and usually employ the rhetoric of conservatism," observed Hofstadter, but the main source of their discontent was "restless dissatisfaction with American life, traditions, and institutions." Many of McCarthy's supporters feared social change.

Several GOP politicians in Washington found McCarthy repulsive, but they opportunistically backed him. They recognized McCarthy's popularity aided Republican candidates in national and local elections. In 1954 changing conditions in the U.S. and abroad and personal errors contributed to McCarthy's downfall. But the demagogue's brief time as a GOP celebrity left an impression. The demagogic senator's attack-dog tactics produced electoral dividends.

The demise of Joseph McCarthy made the GOP look again like a mainstream party, yet troubles with extremism resurfaced a decade later. Barry Goldwater, the Republican nominee for U.S. president in 1964, was a militant champion of a laissez-faire, a doctrine opposing government interference in economic affairs. Goldwater said, "I have little interest in streamlining government or making it more efficient, for I mean to reduce its size." He advocated aggressive spending on the military to strengthen defense against challenges from communist countries. Some of his fervent grassroots supporters hyper-ventilated about communist conspiracies inside the USA.

At the national convention, moderate Republicans expressed concern about Goldwater's radical supporters, especially members of the John Birch Society. New York governor Nelson Rockefeller addressed the concern boldly. Rockefeller denounced extremism in a speech at the convention. Boos and catcalls from the galleries drowned out his message.[4] Later Barry Goldwater accepted the nomination and thrilled the delegates with a controversial assertion. He declared, "Extremism in defense of liberty is no vice" and "moderation in the pursuit of justice is no virtue."

Several forms of militant rhetoric found expression at the 1964 Republican National Convention that are now familiar in Republican politicking. Rightwing delegates lambasted the news media. They denounced television reporters as leftwing partisans. Some delegates claimed a cabal of kingmakers in New York City had been manipulating the party's selection of candidates and stealing votes. References to Democratic opponents turned harsh. Barry Goldwater told a reporter that President Lyndon Johnson, who was running that year for a second term as President, was "the biggest faker in the United States," and "the phoniest individual who ever came around."

In 1980 Republicans rallied around a more broadly appealing spokesperson for conservatism, Ronald Reagan. The former movie star was a talented communicator. Reagan was an enormously influential champion of free-market approaches to economic issues.

Reagan championed tax cuts, deregulation, smaller government, and traditional values. He had been enthusiastic about New Deal liberalism in the 1930s and 1940s, but in the 1950s and 1960s Reagan found a new faith, conservatism. When serving in public office, though, Reagan operated like a pragmatic leader. As governor of California and President of the United States, he sometimes compromised with Democrats. Reagan *needed* to cooperate with them to achieve his goals. Democrats had a strong presence in California politics in the late Sixties and early Seventies when Reagan was governor of the state, and they had political clout in the U.S. Congress in the Eighties, when Reagan served two terms as President.

Ronald Reagan made numerous statements about politics, but arguably the most influential comment appeared in his first inaugural address. He asserted, "Government is not the solution to our problem; government is the problem." That message succinctly identified a key idea that affected GOP politics in Reagan's time and beyond. In the twenty-first century, the GOP's references to the federal government turned cynical and damning. Republicans criticized "unelected bureaucrats" and warned about a menacing "deep state" or "administrative state." They often characterized the federal government as an alien force that blocked economic progress and threatened individual liberties.

In the 1990s, Reaganite conservatism, which emphasized economic concerns, received a challenge that later influenced both conservatism and Republicanism. Patrick Buchanan mounted a bid for the Republican Party's presidential nomination in 1992 that placed cultural issues in the foreground. Buchanan was unable to defeat the incumbent U.S. President, George H.W. Bush, in the GOP primaries, but he gave Bush a scare. Buchanan attracted more than two million votes. At the Republican National Convention, he made a provocative statement that undermined Bush's campaign in the general election. Buchanan said, "There is a religious war going on in this country. It is a cultural war, as critical to the kind of nation we shall be as was the Cold War itself, for this war is for the soul of America." Democrats and many Republicans as well criticized the speech as divisive and extremist.

Patrick Buchanan excited some voters in the Republican base with strident denunciations of American politics and society, a strategy that Donald Trump later applied with greater effect.[5] Buchanan's attacks on immigration tapped cultural and racial fears. Buchanan warned that thousands of aliens from Africa, Latin America and Asia had settled in the USA illegally. They were not as assimilable as earlier settlers in American history, he asserted, and their sheer numbers would change the society founded by white Europeans. Buchanan called for a fence along the southern border to block an "invasion." He also promoted nationalism and isolationism. Buchanan attacked "globalists," opposed "free trade," and slammed corporations for importing cheap foreign goods. He said those economic practices undermined U.S. manufacturing and left many Americans unemployed.

Establishment Republicans found Patrick Buchanan's presidential candidacy in the 1992 and 1996 GOP primaries troubling, but they could not reject him openly. Buchanan's aggressive politics attracted a loyal following of grassroots Republicans. Patrick Buchanan slammed "elites" in both parties for betraying ordinary Americans. Leaders in the GOP establishment worried that efforts to denigrate or ostracize Buchanan would lead the firebrand to bolt the GOP and take legions of admirers with him. Years later, Reaganite Republicans faced a related problem when dealing with Donald Trump, a more effective campaigner.

Pressures for fidelity to radical political stands intensified in the 1990s. Congressman Newt Gingrich demonstrated that a militant strategy could yield huge political rewards. He encouraged Republicans to call their Democratic opponents corrupt, traitorous, sick, and radical. Gingrich's combative tactics drew media attention and helped Republicans achieve major victories in the 1994 congressional elections. Many Republicans modeled their politics on Gingrich's style.[6] Their hostility applied not only to Democrats. They expressed disgust for moderate Republicans as well. The epithet RINO (Republican in Name Only) sent a clear message to members that objected to their leadership. Adapt or step aside.

In the early 2000s, a foreign policy issue created additional pressures for unity and conformity. Soon after the 9/11 tragedy, President George W. Bush and leaders in his administration made a case for military action against Iraq. They claimed significant evidence had been discovered connecting Iraq with Al Qaeda's attacks on the World Trade Center and the Pentagon. They also promoted unsubstantiated claims that Saddam Hussein's government had been developing weapons of mass destruction. Commentators on Fox News and Republican politicians cheered President Bush's call for military action against Iraq. They ridiculed journalists and Democrats that questioned the administration's claims. Foreigners, including French leaders that objected, became targets for mockery, too. Republicans renamed French

Fries, Freedom Fries. They bolstered the case for military action through fearmongering. During the leadup to bombing and invading Iraq, party officials sounded like jingoists. Very few Republicans objected to the Bush administration's drumroll for war.

In the twentieth century, single-issue conformity characterized numerous sub-groups in the GOP. Each sought robust, solid party backing for its cause. Each partisan interest group threatened to punish resistors in the primaries. Pressures to give full-throated endorsement to radical positions intensified. Politicians needed to go along to get along.

Grover Norquist, an aggressive promoter of the laissez-faire outlook on economic issues, became a powerful force in these years through his no-tax-increase pledge. First presented in the 1980s, the pledge received considerable support in later years. Norquist pressured Republican lawmakers to sign the commitment to oppose increases on marginal income tax rates for individuals and taxes on corporations. He explained the purpose in dramatic terms: "My goal is to cut government in half in twenty-five years, to get it down to the size where we can drown it in a bathtub." GOP politicians recognized that resistance to Norquist could leave them vulnerable to Republican challengers. In 2012, 95% of Republican legislators in Congress signed the pledge as did all but one of the GOP's presidential candidates.

Opposition to the federal government's regulations became a sine qua non for Republicans in the early twenty-first century. Candidates seeking office needed to support the huge tax cuts that favored wealthy individuals and corporations favored by George W. Bush's administration. The rationale for backing large cuts rested on a false claim. Since the time of President Ronald Reagan's first term, Republicans had been claiming giant tax cuts paid for themselves. In truth, those tax reductions created fiscal crises. George W. Bush's tax proposals spiked the national debt as did proposals of the next Republican president. The Trump administration's large tax cuts, which also favored rich individuals and corporations, added $2.3 trillion to the federal debt. These tax initiatives created major fiscal imbalances, but very few party members expressed concern. They greeted the controversial tax cuts with almost universal praise. Politicians concurred with the party's laissez-faire dogma.

Republican partisans that identified themselves as religious conservatives also exercised influence. The safe position for an aspiring GOP politician was to recite the favorite talking points of evangelical voters. Candidates needed to identify as "pro-life" regarding abortion. Later, a different goal emerged: defending "religious liberty." The term sounded like an ideal that Americans of all political persuasions could endorse, but it proved highly controversial. The religious right's initiatives broke down the separation of church and state that had been enshrined in the First Amendment.

During these decades of radicalization, Republicans understood the importance of identifying as fervent "conservatives." They needed to demonstrate enthusiasm for the concept. Their rhetoric featured numerous references to "conservative" positions, "conservative" values, and "conservative" ideals. "Conservative" became one of the most familiar words in the GOP's political vocabulary.[7]

Mitt Romney's statement during his 2012 presidential campaign revealed the pressures to conform. At a meeting of the Conservative Political Action Conference, Romney described himself as "severely conservative." His purpose was obvious. Having served as governor of Massachusetts, a state many Republicans viewed as a liberal bastion, Romney needed to show fellow Republicans he was on their team. "Severe" was an inelegant term, but it signaled that the candidate was robustly committed to the favored ideology.

Mitt Romney, the CEO of a large private equity investment firm, championed Ronald Reagan's approach to conservatism during his losing presidential campaign in 2012. Like Reagan, he favored reductions in federal programs, reducing government regulations, and cutting taxes on individuals and corporations. Romney's messaging suggested Republicans could stimulate private investment, create new jobs, and lift the U.S. economy to new heights by freeing business from Washington's bureaucratic interference.

The case for laissez-faire had served GOP candidates well for years. In the 2010s, however, that message lost much of its appeal. Many voters were frustrated and angry. They believed they'd been denied the fruits of an expanding economy. Reports appeared in the national media that indicated their assessment was basically correct. The principal beneficiaries of tax cuts and deregulation during Reagan's presidency and in later years were the country's wealthiest families. In the 1980s and beyond incomes of the top 5% of American families increased much faster than the incomes of other families. The share of income going to middle- and lower-income households shrank.

How could Republicans attract support from middle and lower-income Americans in a period of growing concern about inequality? Republicans responded largely with a strategy of distraction. Their rhetoric diminished attention to traditional Reaganite demands for downsizing government. Instead, Republicans stressed emotion-laden social and cultural issues. Exercises in fearmongering helped to retain grassroots support for the party in a time of intensifying economic discontent.

Political analyst Thomas Frank described the tactic in an influential book, *What's the Matter with Kansas?* (2004). He noted that in 2000 citizens in poor counties identified strongly as conservatives and voted Republican even though their economic interests appeared to be better aligned with the Democrats. Republicans frequently campaigned on "explosive social issues," Frank pointed out, yet they did little or nothing about them after winning elections. GOP legislators then concentrated on helping business. "The trick never ages; the illusion never wears off," observed Frank. "*Vote* to stop abortion; *receive* a rollback in capital gains taxes" . . . "*Vote* to screw those politically correct college professors; *receive* electricity deregulation."[8]

In local and national campaigns Republicans often framed hot-button social issues as major problems in American society. They warned about immigration, affirmative action, gay marriage, liberal education, secularism, elitism, feminism, and other supposed dangers. In the 2020s, they added new scare-words such as "woke culture," "cancel culture," and Critical Race Theory.

Republicans that favored Reagan-style fiscal conservatism worried that culture warriors were hijacking conservatism and Republicanism. Those conservatives were trapped in a mess of their own making. For years they had benefited from the social backlash, enjoying its potential for driving grassroots partisans to the polls. Party leaders did not engage in frank and vigorous debates about the wisdom of giving the culture warriors extraordinary influence in GOP affairs. Now liabilities were becoming apparent. Candidates that embraced wild conspiracy theories were coming out on top in the party's primary elections. Many independent voters in the swing states rejected the radicals and voted for Democratic candidates.

Reaganite conservatives were eager to deal with the situation, but managing the enraged masses proved difficult. In the 2010s and 2020s grassroots Republicans demanded action, not just words. Sensing strength in numbers, they wanted the GOP to respond directly to their social and economic grievances.

During Barack Obama's presidency, Reaganite conservatives, tried to channel this anger. They hoped whites' distrust of Obama, the nation's first African American president, resistance to spending on Obama's health plan, discontent over bank bailouts, and opposition to immigration would produce huge electoral gains for the GOP. At first, the strategy seemed to work. Thousands of voters turned up at Tea Party rallies. The GOP sent many new faces to Washington after a strong showing in the 2010 midterm elections.[9]

It soon became evident, however, that traditional conservatives could not control the uprising they had encouraged. A sign of potential trouble appeared in 2014, when Eric Cantor, a prominent Republican leader in the House of Representatives, lost the primary election to an obscure Tea Party favorite who railed against "Washington" and immigration. In subsequent years, other Reaganite conservatives lost elections to ultra-right culture warriors that emphasized social issues. The people's rebellion left the GOP vulnerable to dominance by a rambunctious communicator who could exploit partisan rage for his own advantage.

Donald Trump's presidency seemed at first to provide a solution to the tensions. During the presidential campaign of 2016, Trump addressed the concerns of diverse groups in the GOP's coalition. Reaganites were pleased that he promised tax cuts, deregulation, and a downsized federal government. Trump appealed as well to economically troubled voters with promises to boost manufacturing and slam tariffs on products from China. He pleased the culture warriors with hints about blocking immigration. Evangelicals were enthusiastic about his pledge to appoint justices to the Supreme Court that were critical of abortion. Trump appeared uniquely qualified to combine laissez-faire advocacy with fearmongering.[10]

It became evident during four years of the Trump presidency, however, that the Republican Party had a troublesome standard bearer. Trump, a truth-challenged, reckless, and mercurial leader, showed little respect for democratic institutions and traditions. Exhibiting an enormous ego and lust for power, he acted like an autocrat. Building an enthusiastic cult following among fans that ultimately became identified as the MAGA crowd, Trump created his own base of support. He had only loose ties to the Republican Party. If old guard Republican leaders tried to check his power, Trump could turn his army of backers on them. If resistance grew substantially, Trump might bolt the party and take millions of adoring followers with him. That scenario could severely damage the GOP and open huge opportunities for the Democrats.

If the Republican Party had a vibrant democratic tradition in its internal affairs, its leaders could have been more effective in checking some of Trump's excesses. But for years they had not fostered vigorous internal debates about ideas, positions, and candidates.

Republicans acquiesced to Trump's leadership during abundant controversies about his fitness to lead the nation. The party did not confront Trump strongly when his rhetoric and actions during the 2016 election campaign violated fundamental American political traditions. Republicans remained largely silent when President Trump lied about threats from Covid-19 and promoted bogus health remedies. When Donald Trump spread false conspiracy theories about a stolen election in 2020, many Republicans remained silent or voiced support for the big lie. After President Trump's words and actions appeared to ignite a crowd's assault on the U.S. Capitol, some Republican officials expressed disgust but then quickly reversed themselves. Hours following the attack, 147 House Republicans objected to the official certification of electoral votes.

When Trump began campaigning for president in 2023, most Republican politicians refused to acknowledge that he was likely to undermine democracy if he returned to the White House. Some Republicans tried to avoid taking a stand on his candidacy; others supported him. Even though Trump faced indictments related to serious accusations, numerous Republicans engaged in the politics of distraction. They lambasted the "Biden Justice Department" for attempting to block Donald Trump from campaigning for the presidency.

Years of pressure for conformity and acquiescence to radicals' influence left the party vulnerable to dominance by a reckless demagogue and his millions of doting fans. Traditional conservatives were appalled by the trajectory of the Republican Party in recent years, but they were ill-equipped to deal with the problem. For much too long, they had enabled or accepted extremism.

Mainstream Democratic Politics: A Brief History

Some political analysts complain that the Republican Party is radically conservative, and the Democratic Party is radically progressive. They argue that the nation needs a moderate, centrist, mainstream party. Organizers of the No Labels movement succinctly identified this assessment. They said their organization responded to Americans that were "tired of the extremes of left and right."

Claims about radicalism on both sides promote a false equivalency. American politics have been roiled primarily by one extremist party, not two. The United States already has a centrist-minded political body, the Democratic Party. Its membership includes many progressive-minded Americans that favor moderate, not radical reform.

In recent decades Democrats have been much better practitioners than Republicans of ideas expressed by a figure that traditional conservatives admire. Edmund Burke, an influential Dublin-born member of Britain's Parliament (1729-1797), said, "A disposition to preserve and an ability to improve, taken together, would be my standard of a statesman." Burke understood reform is necessary for progress, but revolutionary change can be dangerous. After praising initial reforms in France, Burke criticized the French Revolution's radical turn. He warned that France's revolutionaries were destroying morals, law, stability, and security. Burke made a case for gradual adjustments based on practical experience.

In 2015 *New York Times* columnist David Brooks, a moderate conservative, offered a Burke-like perspective on Republican radicalism. Brooks's liberal colleague at the *Times*, Paul Krugman, responded with both agreement and dissent regarding Brooks's message. Their exchange drew attention to significant differences between America's two principal parties.

David Brooks, whose outlook resembles traditional conservatism, berated Republicans in the 2015 op-ed for acting like "insurgents and revolutionaries." Republicans "abandoned traditional conservatism, for right-wing radicalism," he argued. They treated "compromise as corruption, ignored inconvenient facts, and characterized Americans who disagreed with them as aliens." Sadly, the modern GOP produced "elected leaders of jaw-dropping incompetence," politicians that were "incompetent at governing and unwilling to be governed."[11]

When describing admirable political qualities, Brooks invoked ideas of Burke. True conservatives, he said, show "intellectual humility, a belief in steady, incremental change" and a preference for reform over revolution. They favor "conversation, calm deliberation, self-discipline, the capacity to listen to other points of view and balance valid but competing ideas and interests.[12]

Paul Krugman suggested Brooks had good reason to lament the decline of traditional conservatism in the GOP but thought his assessment of history was too present-oriented. Republicans exchanged mainstream conservatism for a "radical doctrine" long before 2015, said Krugman. President Ronald Reagan contributed to the shift. He "embraced supply-side economics," which was "not only a radical doctrine but one rejected by virtually the entire economics profession." Later, Republicans attacked Obamacare, yet it was "pretty conservative," because it was "a classic example of incremental change, building on the existing system rather than trying a complete overhaul." If you want traditional conservatism, argued Krugman, "the only people with real influence with anything like that mindset are Democrats."[13]

Krugman's judgment that Democrats promoted mainstream politics, even moderate conservatism, has considerable merit. Democrats, for the most part, acted like they appreciated Burke's insights. They backed incremental reforms that responded to shifting societal needs and changes in public opinion. On virtually every major reform that dealt with challenges in modern life – social security, health care, consumer protection, civil rights, infrastructure development, renewable energy, worker protection, gun safety, and more -- Democrats backed cautious governmental initiatives to improve conditions. They championed measured reform.

The Democrats' commitment to gradual, incremental change rather than radical transformation can be seen in the politics of modern Democratic presidents. Those leaders campaigned and governed as centrists, not flaming liberals. John F. Kennedy, Lyndon B. Johnson, Jimmy Carter, Bill Clinton, Barack Obama, and Joe Biden were mainstream politicians. Kennedy and Johnson advanced civil rights in a time when public concern about racial injustice was growing and news about segregation damaged U.S. relations in global affairs. Carter promoted deregulation of major industries and appointed a chairman of the Federal Reserve that fought inflation aggressively. Clinton responded to conservative political gains by announcing the era of big government was over. Obama called for health care reform based on private insurance. Joe Biden won the Democratic nomination for president in 2020 in large part because he had a stronger reputation as a moderate than the party's other major contenders.

Democrats responded vigorously when their party faced stinging electoral setbacks in 1972, 1980, 1984 and 1988. Groups such as the Democratic Leadership Council, New Democrats, Clinton Democrats, and The Third Way urged greater political moderation. A reset was essential, the reformers argued, to win the hearts and minds of American voters. When Barack Obama began his presidency in early 2009, he met with the New Democrat Coalition.[14] Obama announced he was a "New Democrat" and a "pro-growth Democrat."[15] During the 2016 presidential primaries, the Democratic establishment rallied around Hillary Clinton and strongly opposed the candidacy of Democratic Socialist Bernie Sanders.

On key issues, Democrats often sought bipartisan support for major legislation but received little or no cooperation from Republicans. The Democrats' experience struggling to obtain some Republican backing for the Affordable Care Act is a case in point. Republicans rejected negotiation, unified in opposition to the legislation, and made continued attempts to jettison Obamacare after it became law.

The Obama administration's proposal for expanded health care borrowed ideas promoted earlier by the conservative Heritage Foundation and Republican Governor Mitt Romney when he was governor of Massachusetts. The Democrats' plan included concessions to big pharma, insurance companies, and the health industrial complex, and it maintained employer-provided health care arrangements that had been in place for decades. For several months Democratic managers delayed a vote on the bill in vain attempts to acquire bipartisan support.

Republicans attacked the proposal aggressively. They demonized the ACA, calling it Obamacare, thinking the name would make the legislation appear toxic to voters that disliked the President. When Congress voted on the ACA in 2010, not a single Republican in the U.S. House or the Senate backed it. Senate Minority Leader Mitch McConnell later identified the true purpose of his party's wall of opposition. "It was absolutely critical that everybody be together," said McConnell, "because if the proponents of the bill were able to say it was bipartisan, it tended to convey to the public that it was OK, they must have figured it out."

Over the next four years Republicans in Congress voted to repeal and replace Obamacare 54 times, according to the *Washington Post*'s count. Republicans' promise to "replace" the legislation was deceptive. They had not created a well-defined counterproposal for health care. The GOP's principal purpose was to leave the impression McConnell sought -- that radical Democrats forced hyper-partisan legislation upon the American people. Resistance to Obamacare excited the ultra-conservative Tea Party movement and helped Republicans achieve major gains in the 2010 midterm elections.

The Affordable Care Act represented a moderately conservative reaction to medical insecurity in America. It delivered healthcare to millions of economically struggling Americans, and it supported others that had inadequate health insurance. The ACA was not the radical "socialist" legislation that many Republicans claimed. The act's provisions were much less ambitious in scope than healthcare programs implemented in other advanced societies around the globe.

In the years after Barack Obama left the White House, public opinion polling showed a substantial portion of Americans that identified with the Democrats favored moderate change. A survey conducted by Gallup in December 2018 asked Republicans and Democrats if they wanted their party to be more conservative, liberal, or moderate. Republicans said they wanted their party to be more conservative by a margin of 57 to 37. Democrats wanted their party to be more moderate by a margin of 54-41.[16]

A 2021 analysis published by William A. Galston and Elaine Kamarck of the Brookings Institution provided a related ideological portrait of the Democratic Party. Galston and Kamarck noted that 2020 was the *first time ever* in the surveys that liberals constituted an outright majority of Democrats (51%). The brief surge in liberal identity that year came in reaction to Donald Trump's failed responses to the Covid crisis and his campaign for a second term in the White House.[17]

In October 2023 *Washington Post* columnist Dan Balz reported a recent Economist/YouGov poll "showed more rank-and-file Republicans say they want their representatives to stand on principle 'no matter what' than say they would rather compromise to get things done . . . Democrats, by 3-1, said they favor compromise to get things done."[18]

It would be helpful if Democrats had Republican allies in efforts to create bipartisan legislation that dealt with major challenges of American life. In recent years, partners in crafting legislation have been few or nonexistent. Republicans often took the role of obstructionists when Democrats proposed reforms. The Republicans' enthusiasm for Ronald Reagan's claim that "government is the problem" affected responses. When the GOP turned extremist, hostile rhetoric about the place of government in U.S. society intensified. The party's "war" against the federal government was, on its face, ironic. Republicans campaigned aggressively to win an opportunity to govern, but once in office they concentrated on stripping government of its authority.

The distinction between the two parties turned stark. Republicans lost their activist role in shaping bipartisan reform bills, which had been evident in the 1950s and into the 1960s. When proposals to protect civil rights were under consideration in the Sixties, Republican Everett Dirkson, the Senate minority leader, provided valuable support for defending the rights of African Americans. Later, bipartisan support was unusual. Democrats often promoted new initiatives to deal with the nation's problems, and Republicans mobilized aggressively to block those proposals.

For decades now, Democrats have faced the wearisome, frustrating task of attempting to enact moderate reforms in the face of intense GOP opposition. Some Republicans signaled interest in proposals made by Democrats, especially those in the Senate and those representing states in the north and far-west. But the GOP's growing army of obstructionists often muscled those reformers aside. Democrats had to operate largely without allies when dealing with the nefarious role of big money in politics, the lack of adequate health care for many Americans, the ravages of climate change, the need to rebuild infrastructure, and other challenges.

Policymaking was not high on the GOP agenda, as Republican Mitt Romney noted in September 2023 when speaking to reporters. Senator Romney said his small wing of the Republican Party was interested in real issues and shaping policy, but members of his party's much larger wing was devoted to expressing resentments, getting even, and settling scores. Romney could not undermine his effort to make the Republican Party more responsive to the needs of the American people by acknowledging an embarrassing fact. Democrats had been far more active in creating policies designed to improve the lives of the American people.[19]

Former President Bill Clinton made a related observation in an interview with David Rubenstein on Bloomberg Television in October 2023. When asked about the difference between the two parties, Clinton joked that the GOP was dominated by radicals, with about 90% sounding extreme. Democrats had extremists, too, he acknowledged, but the radicals constituted only about 10% of the Democratic membership. Clinton was shooting from the hip. He lacked statistical data to back up his numbers. Yet his humorous point, delivered with a smile, contained an element of truth. Radical ideas and actions were ubiquitous in the actions of one party. Commitment to moderation was prevalent in the other.

TWO

PROMISE AND PERIL IN THE FIFTIES

This analysis points out that the Republican Party under President Dwight D. Eisenhower's leadership provided a model of center-right politics. Eisenhower encouraged the GOP to become "modern," a term that suggested moderation.

Some important political achievements in the Fifties were bipartisan. The Eisenhower Highway Act of 1956 was a notable example. That legislation stimulated enormous economic growth throughout the nation.

In the early Fifties a problem appeared that polarized American politics. Joseph McCarthy, a reckless demagogue, achieved considerable political clout. In 1954 changing domestic and international conditions as well as McCarthy's excesses led to his demise. There are lessons in this history. In related ways Donald Trump's also weaponized the politics of fear.

Good Old Days: Consensus in the 1950s

Tired of partisan clashes? Weary of seeing pundits of the Left and Right scream at each other on television? Then discover greater peace of mind by looking back to a time when Republicans and Democrats got along much better. At least that is the characterization of U.S. politics in the 1950s presented by Arthur Larson, who served as one of President Dwight D. Eisenhower's top speech writers. In *A Republican Looks at His Party*, an influential book of 1956, Larson describes less angry, indeed, friendlier times. He claims leaders in Washington achieved a form of "consensus"– basic agreement on the major political issues – in the Fifties. Legislators discarded their ideological baggage, says Larson. He identifies a Republican Party that is quite different from the radically conservative organization of today. In fact, Arthur Larson gives the GOP major credit for advancing pragmatic approaches to politics, and he praises the Republican president, Dwight D. Eisenhower, especially, for making that achievement possible.

According to Larson, lots of Americans realized in the Fifties that the old politics of ideological clashes between the Right and Left no longer served the nation well. Before the Great Depression leaders had pushed laissez faire to extremes, Larson notes. That approach was unfortunate, because it produced inequality and left the financial system vulnerable to a breakdown. Then liberals reacted to the economic problems by elevating the position of ordinary Americans through a variety of New Deal programs. But Larson concludes that liberals often made government excessively intrusive in business affairs.

President Eisenhower took the best of both traditions and avoided the extremes, Larson argues. Dwight D. Eisenhower's policies gave both sides lots to cheer about. Liberals appreciated Eisenhower's support for an expansion of Social Security benefits. They also liked construction of the interstate highway system, a vast public works program that stimulated the economy and created thousands of jobs. Conservatives were happy to see that Eisenhower backed pro-business measures. The President recognized that the American people's suspicion of big business had become excessive during the Great Depression. It was time to liberate businessmen from burdensome restrictions established by Washington's legislators and bureaucrats. Private enterprises needed to operate more freely to make the economy dynamic.

Arthur Larson acknowledged the old ideological divisions had not passed away completely Some Americans were still inclined to support radical positions of the Left and Right. But those people constituted "small minorities," he assured readers. Extremists were not a serious threat to the political order because, "they are out of tune with the feelings of the over-whelming majority of Americans." Larson expressed confidence that a new "American Consensus" was here to stay.

We understand now that Larson was much too sanguine about pros-pects for achieving long-lasting agreement on political fundamentals. When he published *A Republican Looks at His Party* in the mid-Fifties, some leaders on the right were already launching a partisan conservative movement (as in the case of William F. Buckley, who began publishing the *National Review* in 1955). Liberals, too, expressed discomfort with the idea of "consensus." In the Sixties many of them claimed the nation needed to battle poverty, inequality, racial discrimination, and other problems more aggressively.

By the late 1960s and early 1970s, the American Consensus that Arthur Larson described so glowingly no longer seemed relevant. U.S. politics became polarized. Disagreements over the Vietnam War, civil rights, black and white protests, crime and violence, women's liberation, abortion, and other issues made "conflict" not "consensus" appear more characteristic of America's political culture.

Later, shifts within the parties widened the ideological divide. Conser-vative Democrats, including many southerners resistant to racial integration, moved into the GOP's camp. Some liberal and moderate Republicans felt uncomfortable within the rightist-oriented GOP. They shifted to the Demo-crats or identified as independents.

Arthur Larson was overly optimistic when he concluded in the mid-1950s that Washington had achieved an impressive degree of harmony and that the Republican Party could lead the nation forward. He did not see that the cooperative spirit could break down quickly, nor did he appreciate how much his own party would soon contribute to the nation's fragmentation.

From today's perspective, Arthur Larson's interpretation appears naïve, but his assessment is important, nonetheless. *A Republican Looks at His Party* reminds us that for a brief time in the 1950s many Republicans and Demo-crats favored pragmatism over ideology. Unfortunately, the spirit of political cooperation and negotiation was not realizable in the long run. Clashes over substantive issues soon disrupted the consensus. Larson's book showed that the dream of an effective centrist order inspired genuine hope in the Fifties about Washington's potential to achieve significant progress.

Productive Bipartisanship: The Eisenhower Highway Act of 1956

In the 1950s President Dwight Eisenhower proposed the largest single infrastructure program in U.S. history – construction of a vast interstate highway system throughout the United States. Congress debated the proposal at length. At first, many lawmakers said the plan was expensive, and they could not agree on how to pay for it. Eisenhower maintained the investment in infrastructure would ignite an economic boom. He was right. That gigantic project fueled prosperity in the Fifties, Sixties and beyond.

In the 2020s, President Biden promoted another huge economic lift through his infrastructure plan. It stimulated new development of roads, bridges, ports, railroads, airlines, broadband, and electric power and it sped America's shift toward clean energy. Many Republicans objected to Biden's proposal. They complained that it cost too much and involved excessive government interference in business affairs. Those critics failed to recognize the value of infrastructure investment stimulated by smart government planning. Republicans could have better appreciated the wisdom of Biden's proposal if they examined the history of the interstate highway construction program of the Fifties. That bi-partisan legislation jump-started vigorous economic growth.

President Dwight D. Eisenhower is often identified as the "father" of America's interstate system because he promoted the idea and construction began under his watch. But the roadway system really had two key "parents," not one.

Back in the 1930s, President Franklin D. Roosevelt called for a related highway program as part of his New Deal commitments to public works. Roosevelt was an enthusiastic champion of superhighways.[20] He believed a web of modern four-lane roads could spark economic development and provide construction jobs for unemployed Americans during the Great Depression. Unfortunately, he pitched this argument in the late 1930s, a difficult time to launch expensive new projects. An economic recession in 1937 and early 1938 diminished support for his New Deal. Furthermore, Republicans won many congressional races in the 1938 elections. Republicans wanted to cut federal spending. In 1939 and beyond, worries about German, Italian, and Japanese aggression led Roosevelt to concentrate on a buildup of America's military. The highway project languished.

It came back to life when Dwight D. Eisenhower was president. Eisenhower had become interested in highway construction in 1919, shortly after World War I ended. At the time he was a U.S. Army officer and directed a large caravan of military vehicles from Washington, D.C. to San Francisco. Traveling across the country took two months. The trip was difficult because of the nation's primitive road conditions. Eisenhower recognized motor transport needed a much better road system. Later, in World War II, Eisenhower served as the Allies' supreme commander in Europe. When Eisenhower entered Germany, he saw that country's modern, high-speed autobahn. These two experiences influenced President Eisenhower's decision in the 1950s to promote a new highway program. [21]

Both Republicans and Democrats were concerned in the Fifties about recessions. They thought an interstate system could build a strong foundation for long-term economic growth. But they were sharply divided about how to pay for such a massive project. Many lawmakers opposed taxation to fund the system. President Eisenhower resisted taxed-based solutions, too. He called for a self-financing highway arrangement that included numerous toll booths. Several leaders in Congress preferred a no-toll arrangement. They eventually agreed to a plan in which the federal government covered 90% of the cost, in large part through a gasoline tax. Democratic Senator Al Gore, Sr., and two Democrats in the House, George Fallon, and Hale Boggs, worked out the details.

Promoters of the new legislation wisely associated it with national defense. The mid-Fifties was a time of anxiety about threats from the Soviet Union. Advocates of the bill claimed a modern highway system would facilitate the movement of soldiers and equipment in the event of war and facilitate the escape of citizens from cities endangered by nuclear attack. By linking the legislation to national defense, the Federal-Aid Highway Act of 1956 received broad support. There was just one vote against it in the Senate.

The legislation's impact on the U.S. economy was enormous. Road construction provided thousands of jobs. Businesses supplied cement, asphalt, and steel. Gasoline production surged. Large trucks were able to move cargo in less time and at lower cost. Numerous restaurants and gas stations appeared at highway interchanges. The highways spurred expansion of the suburbs. Home construction soared.[22]

Change had a downside, too. Major shifts in the economy hurt some Americans. Travelers abandoned the old two-lane and four-lane roads. Communities far from interstate highways and exchanges lost businesses and population. In large metropolitan areas, the highways divided neighborhoods. Population and wealth shifted quickly to the suburbs. Political leaders failed to account for the negative impact of road development on specific segments of the population.

Trade-offs are inevitable when major technological and social transformations occur. History shows that modernization uproots lives, yet the changes often deliver more gains than losses. Technological innovations that brought the automobile into American life damaged the careers of horse breeders, farriers, blacksmiths, and carriage makers. But the automobile improved American life substantially. Construction of the interstate highway system hurt citizens in some isolated rural and small-town communities and residents in the inner cities, yet, overall, that transportation revolution produced broad-based prosperity.

When Donald Trump campaigned for president in 2016, he made huge promises about backing infrastructure development, but Trump and Republicans in Congress did little to advance construction projects from 2017 to 2021.[23] Federal spending on roads and bridges as a share of the U.S. economy did not increase substantially during those years. Nor did GOP legislators provide leadership at a time when the nation's roads, ports, and airports were in poor shape. Federal spending on water infrastructure dropped to a thirty-year low in those years.

In the early 2020s, President Joe Biden and Democrats in Congress offered less rhetoric about infrastructure and more action. Their promotion of future-oriented investments through projects involving both government policy and private enterprise stimulated major changes in Americans society. Spending on infrastructure had the potential to deliver major improvements in Americans society.

Margaret Chase Smith and Liz Cheney Asked Republicans to Challenge Demagoguery. The GOP Ignored Them

On May 13, 2021, Representative Liz Cheney warned Republican colleagues that they were taking the GOP on a dangerous course. At the time, Republicans were removing Cheney from a top leadership position because she dared to criticize President Donald Trump for making false claims about a stolen election. Cheney vowed to continue speaking out because of Trump's "lack of commitment and dedication to the truth and to the Constitution." She appealed to American ideals in a manner that resembled Senator Margaret Chase Smith's "Declaration of Conscience" in 1950. Chase's statement warned about another politician given to conspiracy-mongering, lying, and abuses of power: Senator Joseph McCarthy. Smith, like Liz Cheney, urged colleagues to affirm democratic principles.

In both cases Republican legislators rejected the women's appeals. In 1950 Republicans feared McCarthy's political clout. They turned their backs on Smith. In 2021 Republicans feared Donald Trump's political heft and did the same to Cheney. Reactions to Smith's declaration constituted a turning point for the Republican Party in the 1950s. The GOP became tethered to a reckless demagogue for four more years. Liz Cheney suggested her GOP colleagues were at a turning point as well. The Republican Party and American democracy could be seriously damaged, she warned, if its leaders did not break away from Donald Trump's nefarious influence.

When Margaret Chase Smith presented her Declaration of Conscience on June 1, 1950, Senator Joseph McCarthy was less than four months into his rise as a powerful demagogue. There was an opportunity to check his political momentum. McCarthy had attracted national attention in February 1950 by falsely claiming he had a list of more than 200 people in the State Department that were "known communists." Joseph McCarthy, taking advantage of public fears about communist subterfuge, made several unsubstantiated charges, He damaged the reputation of many innocent people. Reckless fearmongering made him an extraordinarily powerful figure in American politics.

Margaret Chase Smith of Maine, the only female U.S. senator at the time, presented her "Declaration of Conscience" on June 1, 1950. She denounced the "selfish political exploitation of fear, bigotry, ignorance and intolerance." Smith urged Americans to recall fundamental American ideals, including the right to criticize, hold unpopular beliefs, protest, and think independently.[24]

Smith could not rally many Senate colleagues to her cause. At first, she had six backers for the Declaration, but they quickly peeled away. McCarthy's influence strengthened when the Korean War began just 24 days after Smith presented her Declaration of Conscience. The U.S. military commitment to prevent a communist takeover of the Korean peninsula created opportunities for McCarthy's politicking. GOP senators were cognizant of the risk of opposing McCarthy. Only Oregon senator Wayne Morse stood by Margaret Chase Smith (years later Morse was one of just two senators that refused to endorse the Gulf of Tonkin Resolution that gave President Lyndon Johnson authority to take military action in Vietnam). Lacking allies, Margaret Chase Smith recognized the futility of fighting. She moved on.

From the perspective of history, it is evident that the timidity of senators in June 1950 made an unfortunate impact on the Republican Party and the nation. Joseph McCarthy became more irresponsible after GOP colleagues failed to check his lying and bullying. McCarthy wreaked considerable damage in American society over the next four years. His power did not decline substantially until he overreached spectacularly in 1954.

Liz Cheney made her declaration of conscience in a *Washington Post* op-ed (The GOP is at a Turning Point. History is Watching Us").[25] Like Smith, Cheney urged colleagues to confront threats to democracy before it is too late. She said Trump repeatedly claimed the 2020 election was a fraud.

"His message: I am still the rightful president, and President Biden is illegitimate." Trump lied, and his words helped to ignite violence at the Capitol, Liz Cheney argued. Trump sought to "unravel critical elements of our constitutional structure that make democracy work – confidence in the result of elections and the rule of law." The Republican Party was "at a turning point," she warned. "Republicans must decide whether we are going to choose truth and fidelity to the Constitution."

House Republicans abandoned Liz Cheney. Her lost crusade had the appearance of Margaret Chase Smith's unsuccessful summons to principle in 1950. Cheney, like Smith, had only one outspoken Republican congressman supporting her aggressively -- Representative Adam Kinzinger of Illinois.

Kinzinger recognized that he had become persona non grata in the GOP, but he tried to express a degree of optimism. He suggested the Republican Party would someday change. Kinzinger described the present moment as a "low point" for the GOP. Eventually, he argued, Republicans will solidify their position as members of "a once honorable party that was marred by lies."[26]

The Politics of Joseph McCarthy and Donald Trump: Similarities and Differences

There are some intriguing similarities between Trump's activities and those of Joseph McCarthy. Both surged in popularity by accentuating the politics of fear. Yet both lost popular support when their demagogic behavior alienated many Americans. The denouement came quickly for McCarthy. He seemed invincible at the beginning of 1954, yet in a matter of months, he fell from grace. Donald Trump slipped, too, in 2020, enough to lose the presidential election to Joe Biden. When Trump encouraged a march to the Capitol on January 6, 2021, many of his most ardent supporters in Washington expressed disgust. Trump did not fade away like McCarthy, however. Donald Trump reestablished his power base quickly. The differences between their two situations are also intriguing.

Joseph McCarthy, a U.S. senator from Wisconsin, rose to prominence in early 1950 by stoking fears about communism. His speech at an event for Republican women attracted considerable media attention. McCarthy claimed misleadingly that he had a list of 205 names of disloyal officials that were "still working and shaping the policy of the State Department." Journalists and politicians identified McCarthy's lies and misrepresentations, but the senator managed to keep them off-balance. McCarthy often announced new charges about communist influence in America, diverting attention from controversies related to his previous assertions.

When a conservative Democratic senator, Millard Tydings, headed an investigation of claims about communist influence, McCarthy attacked him. Joseph McCarthy's staff promoted a doctored photo that falsely associated Tydings with an American communist leader, and McCarthy aided Tydings political opponent. Millard Tydings had been a popular lawmaker before McCarthy targeted him. Tydings lost his bid for reelection in 1950. His experience demonstrated the perils of resistance to McCarthy.[27]

During a four-year period, Joseph McCarthy wielded extraordinary power. Like President Trump, he bullied and threatened opponents. Many of McCarthy's fellow Republicans were troubled by his behavior, but they kept quiet. They understood that McCarthy's aggressive tactics boosted the GOP's political fortunes. Republicans also recognized the electoral power of McCarthy's loyal followers.

Joseph McCarthy achieved broad public support largely because communism seemed to be expanding globally. In the years after World War II, the "Cold War" began. The Soviet Union tightened its grip on Eastern Europe, Mao Zedong's communist revolution took control of mainland China, the Russians developed nuclear weapons, revelations indicated spies gave secrets to the Russians, and the Korean War dragged on without a settlement. "Reds" seemed to be making substantial gains. Americans wanted tough leaders who would stand up against communist aggression. McCarthy acted like the man of the hour.

In early 1954 Joe McCarthy's popularity ratings were strong. A poll in January reported that 50% of Americans queried approved of him and only 29% disapproved. By late 1954, however, polls revealed a striking loss of support. 35% judged McCarthy favorably in the November 1954 survey, 46% unfavorably.

What caused the senator's fast decline? McCarthy overreached, especially when he attacked the U.S. Army. Newscaster Edward R. Murrow's television program delivered a scathing indictment of McCarthy's tactics, and the Army-McCarthy hearings, broadcast on national television, revealed McCarthy's lies and abuses. Changing conditions also weakened the senator. Dwight D. Eisenhower, a war hero and popular Republican president, restored public confidence. Cold War tensions eased. The Soviet leader, Joseph Stalin, died in 1953, and a few months later fighting in the Korean War stopped. McCarthy's tactic of stoking fear of communism lost much of its appeal in the changing political environment.

Donald Trump's record of grabbing power looks similar in important ways. President Trump also attempted to frighten the public with scary claims about dangerous conspiracies and threats from radicals. Trump pounced on Republicans and former administration officials that criticized him publicly. Using vicious attacks and ridicule, he smashed anyone who betrayed him. Trump learned how to fight critics tenaciously from a disreputable lawyer, Roy Cohn, who had also advised McCarthy.[28]

As in the case of Joe McCarthy, new developments stirred discontent with Trump's leadership. In 2020, Americans became anxious about the pandemic and its impact on the economy. They worried, too, about clashes over politics, culture, and race, divisions that President Trump stoked.

Donald Trump lost the 2020 election, but not by much. Joe Biden's margin of victory in key swing states was small. Trump's influence did not decline as rapidly as McCarthy's did in 1954. Trump's support took a hit after the January 6, 2021, assault at the U.S. Capitol, but his appeal with the GOP's base remained strong and grew in subsequent years.

Trump had many advantages that McCarthy lacked. A large percentage of Republicans still supported him after he left the White House. Politics in the U.S. were much more polarized in the 2020s than in 1954. Party loyalty did not break easily in recent years, a time of strong partisanship. Furthermore, Trump, adept at stagecraft and manipulation of social media, managed to keep his fans engaged. Trump was a much stronger crowd-pleaser than Joseph McCarthy. Trump also held a more impressive title. Donald Trump had been President of the United States, while Joseph McCarthy was only a U.S. senator and a politically damaged one at that by late 1954. McCarthy took to brooding and drinking in the aftermath of his embarrassing performance in the televised Army-McCarthy hearings. Trump responded to misfortune by falsely declaring himself the true election winner and launching an aggressive campaign for a return to the White House. McCarthy lost much of his backing in the national media in 1954, but Trump held on to it in 2021 and beyond. Right-wing celebrities on television, radio, and social media jumped on his bandwagon when he became the leading GOP presidential candidate for 2024.

Joseph McCarthy faded quickly as a prominent figure in American politics. Donald Trump recovered rapidly from setbacks and returned soon to shattering American political traditions.

THREE

LESSONS FROM PRESIDENTIAL ELECTIONS

Journalists and historians have presented abundant commentaries about presidential elections. Can anything new be said? Interpretations in this chapter attempt to do so. The first two identify connections between the 2000 and 2020 elections. Four essays on the 2012 presidential contest draw lessons from Barack Obama's victory and Mitt Romney's loss. Three interpretations of the 2016 election offer clues about Donald Trump's surprising win over Hillary Clinton. One analysis suggests that actions by just five men were critically important in delivering the presidency to Donald Trump.

In 2000 Rioters Tried to Stop a Presidential Vote Count. They Succeeded

On January 6, 2021, a violent mob invaded the U.S. Capitol. Believing Donald Trump deserved the presidency, rioters tried to prevent certification of Joe Biden's victory in the Electoral College. Their vicious attack failed. Twenty years earlier, a group of rioters *succeeded* in stopping the vote count and influencing the outcome of a presidential election. In 2000 Democratic candidate Al Gore had half a million more popular votes than George W. Bush and probably would have finished with more electoral votes as well if rioters had not stopped the ballot count in Florida. Through physical intimidation, a few dozen partisans in the "Brooks Brothers Riot" achieved what thousands of rioters at the U.S. Capitol failed to do. Protesters in 2000 helped secure the presidency for their candidate. In some respects, the "Riot" of 2000 was a prelude to the much larger riot at the Capitol in 2021.

Shortly after the November 7, 2000, election, it became evident that Florida's 25 electoral votes would determine the outcome. Bush's lead in the state disintegrated over days of recounts. It dropped from 1784 to 327 and then to 154. Attention focused on Miami-Dade County, a Democratic stronghold. A recount of thousands of ballots there seemed likely to produce large gains for Gore. On November 22, Miami-Dade's canvassing board was rushing to complete its work before a November 26 deadline.

Strategists for George W. Bush's campaign panicked. Their candidate appeared close to losing the election. Quickly, James Baker, George W. Bush's chief legal adviser, reacted. He spoke frequently to the media, insisting Bush won. Baker claimed any further counting would produce "mischief."[29] Privately, he recognized a predicament. In a conversation with team members, Baker acknowledged, "We're getting killed on 'count all the votes' . . . Who the hell could be against that?"

One of the key players in Republican efforts to block Miami-Dade's recount was Roger Stone, Richard Nixon's "dirty trickster" and an associate of Donald Trump. Stone recruited Cuban-American protesters through warnings on the radio that Gore planned to stage a coup like Fidel Castro attempted in Cuba[30]. Stone also organized phone banks that encouraged Miami Republicans to storm the downtown counting site. On the day of the rioting, he operated a command center from a Winnebago parked nearby.[31]

Other organizers arranged to fly Republican lawyers and staffers to Miami from Washington, D.C. in flights provided by the Enron and Halliburton corporations.[32] Enron later disintegrated in scandal. Dick Cheney, CEO at Halliburton until the summer of 2000, became Vice President in the Bush administration.

The event that stopped vote counting in Miami-Dade became known as the "Brooks Brothers Riot" because the white protesters were well-dressed in button-down shirts and sport jackets. Several "rioters" appeared outside the room where counting was taking place. Screaming, "Stop the count! Stop the Fraud!" they pounded on doors and demanded, "Let us in!"[33]

The county's Democratic Party co-chairman, Joe Geller, was at the scene during the melee. When he procured an Official Democratic Party Training Ballot, protesters accused him of stealing a voter's ballot.[34] They kicked and jabbed him. Geller later reported, "At one point I thought if they knocked me over, I could have literally got stomped to death." He escaped in an elevator, where several protesters quietly joined him. When the elevator doors opened, revealing television cameramen in the lobby, protesters screamed about voter fraud. They performed for the national media.[35]

The Brooks Brothers Riot left three canvassing board members fearful about intimidation and concerned about negative publicity. They decided to cancel the recount.

Leaders from both sides later acknowledged the "riot" played a decisive role in producing Bush's victory. Others disagree, noting that a Republicans in the Florida legislature were planning an unprecedented effort to award all of Florida's electoral votes to Bush, if they were needed. Also, the U.S. Supreme Court took unprecedented action. A controversial interpretation by the Court's conservative majority stopped the recount and gave Bush a 537-vote win in Florida. If three more days of counting in Miami-Dade had produced a substantial lead for Gore, as expected, Florida's Republican legislators and conservatives on the Supreme Court would have found it extremely difficult to reverse the voters' choice.

The events of November 22, 2000, made an impact. Al Gore, who had been at the forefront of publicizing climate change, could have provided a powerful voice for action as President of the United States. George W. Bush entered the Oval Office, instead. Bush and his advisers eventually led the nation into a disastrous invasion and occupation of Iraq. When Hurricane Katrina struck, Bush and his FEMA director, previously a commissioner of the International Arabian Horse Association, responded ineptly. Their flawed leadership in an emergency contributed to the suffering of many citizens.

The Brooks Brothers Riot was a significant event. It had long-term consequences for U.S. and global history.

Democrats' Reaction to the 2000 Presidential Election Contrasts with Republicans' Response to the 2020 Election

A survey released June 1, 2022, by Politifact averaged findings from several opinion polls. It revealed that 70% of Republicans thought Joe Biden was not the legitimate president. The Republicans' erroneous judgment was not just the viewpoint of grassroots members of the party.[36] Numerous GOP leaders in the fifty states backed Donald Trump's claim that he was the true winner of the 2020 election.

The persistence of denial by many Republicans regarding Trump's defeat contrasts dramatically with the Democrats' general acceptance of Al Gore's loss in a presidential election. In 2000 Democrats had much greater reason to protest the outcome than Republicans had in connection with the 2020 presidential election. In 2000 many Democrats – ordinary citizens and party leaders – expressed displeasure over the way conservative members of the Supreme Court prevented a continuation of vote counting in Florida counties. The totals in the Electoral College were close that year; the winner of Florida's electoral votes would be the next president. A 5-4 majority ruling by justices of the Supreme Court nominated by Republican presidents delivered the White House to George W. Bush.

Most Democrats grudgingly assented. In subsequent months they treated George W. Bush as the authentic president. The Democrats' position on the election had been influenced by their presidential candidate. Al Gore announced in a televised speech to the nation, "While I strongly disagree with the Court's decision, I accept it."[37]

Gore responded quickly when the numbers first appeared to favor Bush. When it appeared that Bush had an insurmountable advantage in the Florida electoral count on the evening of the 2000 presidential election, Gore called Bush to concede. Later in the night, however, the Republican's lead in Florida slipped to about 600 votes, and it continued to narrow as counting proceeded. At 3 AM Gore retracted his concession. Later, a machine recount lowered Bush's advantage in Florida to 327 votes. Florida's Supreme Court ordered immediate manual recounts. Officials in specific counties began working to determine voter intent in the case of "hanging chads" and "pregnant chads" on paper ballots.

Ordinarily, determination of election rules and vote counts are the purview of states, not the federal government. Yet in this case, Republicans appealed to the U.S. Supreme Court, seeking a ruling to halt the counting. Their strategy succeeded because justices nominated by Republican presidents ruled in a manner that stopped the recount. The majority reasoned that no satisfactory method could be achieved by the "safe harbor" counting deadline. Four justices in the minority disagreed vehemently. Justice John Paul Stevens identified one of their key concerns: "Preventing the recount from being completed will inevitably cast a cloud on the legitimacy of the election."

The cloud *was* cast, not only through the apparently partisan intervention of conservative justices, but also in the way that strategically placed GOP authorities were able to put their thumbs on the election scales. Florida's governor Jeb Bush was the state leader of his brother's presidential campaign, and Republican Katherine Harris, Florida's Secretary of State and co-chair of Bush's state election campaign, vigorously tried to halt the recount and certify a Republican slate of electors that would give Bush the presidency.

The 2000 election had the stench of scandal. Many Democrats were disappointed and frustrated. Nevertheless, most of them accepted Al Gore's example. When speaking to the nation on national television, Gore announced that he had called Bush and congratulated him on becoming the 43rd president of the United States. "I offered to meet with him as soon as possible so that we can start to heal the divisions of the campaign and the contest through which we've just passed." Urging respect for the law, Gore said, "what remains of partisan rancor must now be put aside, and may God bless [Bush's] stewardship of this country." The election was over, Gore affirmed. It had been resolved "through the honored institutions of our democracy."[38]

Arguably, Gore should have questioned the justices' intervention in Florida's vote count *before* they rendered a decision. It seemed obvious at the time that conservative members of the Court were likely to take advantage of their one-vote majority and rule in a way that smacked of political partisanship. The will of the voters should have determined the presidential outcome, not one person on the Supreme Court. Nevertheless, Gore and the many Americans that voted for him behaved honorably. They accepted the ruling.

The Empty Chair, Starring Clint Eastwood (Produced by Mitt Romney)

During the 2012 presidential election campaign, Mitt Romney constantly reminded voters that he knew how to govern effectively because he was a successful businessman. But during one of the most important evenings of his presidential campaign – the night he delivered an acceptance speech at the Republican National Convention -- Romney fumbled. He allowed Clint Eastwood to address the nation shortly before his own speech. Romney and his top convention aides did not know how the famous Hollywood actor intended to handle the situation.

The events of that night did not inspire confidence in Mitt Romney's skills as a planner, organizer, and leader.

When journalists blasted Clint Eastwood's speech as weird and inappropriate, Romney's aides quickly tried to clear themselves and their candidate of blame. Yet Eastwood was on the stage primarily because Mitt Romney wanted him there. Romney was deeply impressed by Clint Eastwood's impromptu talk at a fundraising event in Sun Valley, Idaho. "He's just made my day. What a guy!" exclaimed Romney. The Republican candidate then secretly arranged for Eastwood's appearance at the convention.

How could Mitt Romney and his key advisers commit a primetime slot in their carefully scripted program to an un-vetted performance? They had not scheduled a rehearsal. Aides reminded Eastwood of talking points, but they generally allowed him to improvise. Eastwood did, indeed, ad-lib. Just minutes before beginning the routine, he surprised a stagehand by requesting that a chair be placed on the set.

Pundits have rightly characterized Clint Eastwood's sketch as disrespectful to both the President and the Vice-President. Eastwood's theatrical dialogue with the empty chair suggested that Obama told him to "shut up." The actor asked, "What do you want me to tell Romney?" . . . "I can't tell him that, He can't do that to himself." Eastwood then ripped into the Vice President. "Of course, we all know Biden is the intellect of the Democratic Party," he remarked sarcastically. "Just kind of a grin with a body behind it."[39]

Many convention delegates laughed at the one-man, one-prop show, but lots of television viewers and journalists were alarmed.

How low can politics go, they asked? Is this the way to speak publicly about the President and Vice President (or for that matter, any candidate of any party for national office)? The actor did not seem to recognize that his effort to talk trash and draw laughs might upstage and undercut Romney.

Eastwood received the brunt of criticism for this embarrassing episode, but that assignment of blame was not entirely fair. Clint Eastwood was a fine movie director and actor but not a seasoned politician (although he served in the 1980s as mayor of little Carmel-By-the-Sea). Eastwood did not appreciate how much his performance could backfire. Romney's aides, who meticulously planned the convention activities, could have saved him from trouble by scheduling rehearsals and offering guidance.

True responsibility for the unfortunate event was in the hands of the presidential candidate. Mitt Romney wanted to surprise the delegates and television viewers with a presentation by a secret guest. Romney gambled recklessly when he made that decision. He did not perform "due diligence" -- the kind of research and analysis that a smart businessman ought to engage in before investing.

If Romney operated Bain Capital in the manner that he handled preparations for one of the most important nights in his political life, critics might judge him a poor executive.

Why Barack Obama Lost the First Debate in 2012

Barack Obama has an impressive reputation as a skilled communicator. Often forgotten, though, is the poor performance in his first televised encounter in 2012 with the GOP's presidential candidate, Mitt Romney. Obama was not well-prepared for that engagement. Obama's principal weakness in that event was that he did not recognize there is a significant difference between a stump speech and a televised debate. If Obama had looked back at history, he would have seen that presidential candidates often performed well when they understood that televised debates are forms of political theater.[40]

During the confrontation with Mitt Romney, Obama spent very little time looking directly into the camera – that is, into the eyes of the American people. Over much of the 90-minute event, Obama spoke to the moderator, Jim Lehrer. Richard Nixon made a similar mistake in his debate with John F. Kennedy in 1960. Nixon, a former college debater, spoke to his opponent, while Kennedy frequently looked directly at the audience.

Nixon also appeared tired and drawn in the 1960 confrontation, while Kennedy, acting somewhat like Mitt Romney, seemed well-prepared to exploit television's potential for communicating messages to a large audience. With 67 million people watching in 2012, including many undecided voters, the October 3 event called for careful preparation.

Evidently Obama and advisers who trained him for the face-off did not treat this television program as a distinctive challenge. They acted as if Obama's experiences delivering numerous stump speeches would adequately fortify him.

The two candidates approached the big day in strikingly different ways. Obama continued to give speeches to cheering crowds until shortly before the night of the debate. Romney took nearly a week off before the event, disappearing at length to practice. Mitt Romney arrived early at the debate site, spending days in Denver. He hoped to feel comfortable in the high-altitude environment of the "mile-high city," where many people experience nausea or headaches upon arriving at 5280 feet (there is 17% less oxygen in Denver than at sea level). Obama flew into Denver the day of the debate, arriving at 2 PM. The President's automobile pulled into the University of Denver's auditorium minutes before the event began. Romney was already present in the auditorium, getting acclimated in the manner of a seasoned actor.

If Obama and his advisers had looked carefully at Mitt Romney's record in the Republican primaries in 2012, they would have noticed that the GOP candidate performed rather poorly in the early debates, but eventually Mitt Romney recognized the theatrical nature of the problem. At one point in the primaries, Newt Gingrich was surging. Romney seemed halting, awkward, and indecisive in his arguments with Gingrich and other candidates.

Aides who were desperate to improve Mitt Romney's skills in the televised format turned to Brett O'Donnell, a successful coach who made the debate team at an evangelical institution, Liberty University, a major contender in college competition (O'Donnell had also coached several GOP presidential candidates).[41] Shortly after O'Donnell schooled Romney in the theatrics of debate, the candidate dispatched Gingrich and went on to secure the Republican nomination. Pundits observed that Romney had suddenly turned aggressive, decisive, and dominant, skills that O'Donnell fostered.

In some ways Obama's performance resembled Jimmy Carter's last televised debate with Ronald Reagan in 1980, the event that helped make Reagan a strong favorite. President Carter, like Obama, did not vet his strategy with professionals skilled in the art of presidential debating. Occasionally Carter made statements that experienced advisers would have nixed, as when Carter said he asked his daughter, age 12, what was the most important issue of the campaign, and she identified nuclear weapons. Carter's comment became the target of many jokes on late-night television.[42] Obama, too, gave television audiences a memorable statement. Rather than hammer his opponent at a crucial moment in the exchanges, Obama confessed that he was not a perfect president.

Small gestures often become memorable in presidential debates. George H.W. Bush lost favor with voters when he looked at his watch during a 1992 exchange with Bill Clinton and Ross Perot. Bush seemed to want a fast conclusion to the ordeal. Al Gore sighed a lot when listening to George W. Bush in the first 1980 debate, behavior that many viewers considered disrespectful. Barack Obama surprisingly nodded in agreement when Romney delivered key arguments. Occasionally, the President smirked. Much of the time Obama kept his head down as he took copious notes. Memory of those gestures probably lingered in the minds of viewers long after they forgot the candidates' specific talking points.

Barack Obama could have learned from Ronald Reagan, who had a frustrating experience against Democrat Walter Mondale in the first presidential debate of 1984. Mondale was well prepared for that event. His zingers threw the President off-stride. After the debate, pundits speculated that Reagan might be too old to handle the mental challenges of an exchange about policy. Ronald Reagan, of course, had a good sense of theatrics from his years as a Hollywood actor. He knew how to improve public performance. Reagan practiced his lines carefully and made a stunning comeback in the next event. One of the most memorable statements was Reagan's promise that he would not hold "youth and inexperience" against Walter Mondale.

Preparing for a televised debate is a unique challenge. Familiarity with performance in stump speeches or press conferences cannot adequately train an individual for the event. A candidate must be aware of the distinctive theatrical qualities of a televised confrontation. President Barack Obama did not appreciate that uniqueness when approaching his first meeting with Mitt Romney. But Obama, like Reagan, recovered. In the second debate and in later campaigning, Obama planned effectively. If he had not made those adjustments, Mitt Romney might have been inaugurated President of the United States in January 2013.

What Sunk Mitt: GOP Extremism

When analyzing the 2012 election results, pundits often focused on Democratic and Republican strategies. They noted that Barack Obama's organization effectively defined Mitt Romney early in the campaign by characterizing the Republican as a heartless business investor. Pundits noted, too, that Obama more effectively won the public's confidence, convincing voters that he cared sincerely about their problems. Also important, the Democrats ground game operated like a well-oiled machine. Armies of volunteers ensured that pro-Obama voters turned up at the polls on November 6.

The Democrats and Barack Obama created a more successful campaign operation, but that is not the only explanation for their electoral victory. The 2012 contest revealed that ideas are important, too. Democrats more effectively associated the campaign with centrist ideas. Republicans eagerly embraced ideas of the far-right.

The GOP vigorously attempted to portray Barack Obama as an extreme leftist, but the identification never stuck. President Obama promoted himself as a moderately progressive leader who sought a balanced approach to the nation's problems. Obama spoke favorably about private enterprise and entrepreneurial innovation, but he asked the nation's wealthy citizens to "pay a little more" in taxes. Regarding foreign affairs, Obama presented himself as a tough defender of the nation's interests. He talked about coordinating international sanctions against Iran, but he resisted pressure to rush into military action.

Obama came across as a man-in-the-middle to many voters, but Mitt Romney closely identified with radical positions of the GOP.

Perhaps Romney could not avoid taking extreme stands on major issues. Participation in the Republican primaries had been a high-pressure experience. GOP candidates pushed each other to the right as they tried to present themselves to states' voters as authentic and committed conservatives. Romney joined this effort, describing himself as a committed conservative.

Pundits disputed whether Romney truly accepted the radical right's perspective or whether he *acted* like a strong right-winger to satisfy the GOP's base. Whatever the case, Romney's move to the margins on key issues created serious vulnerabilities. He strayed far from the American mainstream.

In 2012 many Americans believed Washington had grown too large and too expensive, but they rejected Mitt Romney's strategy of bad-mouthing the federal government. When Romney faced a question in the primaries about FEMA, the agency responsible for dealing with emergencies such as Hurricane Sandy, he said such relief efforts could be handled better by the states or by private enterprise. That response resonated with the conservatives. It did not appeal to independents that learned about it during the general election.

Lots of Americans felt uncertain about the Affordable Care Act, but they were not comfortable with Romney's broad rejection of legislation that resembled his own efforts to improve health care when he served as governor of Massachusetts. By announcing that he would attempt to eliminate "Obamacare" on his first day in the White House, Romney pleased the right-wing of his party. Millions of Americans liked specific provisions in Obamacare. Romney's remarks left them feeling uncomfortable. Voters worried that Medicare might not be solvent when they retire, but they were not satisfied with Romney's and Paul Ryan's talk about turning Medicare into a voucher program for Americans under the age of 55. Romney and Ryan later tried to soften that language, but their initial remarks aroused concern.

The message that Ronald Reagan recited numerous times in the 1980s – that government is not the solution to our problems; it *is* our problem – no longer resonated in the same way. Even though many voters were not as confident as Democrats about Washington's potential for jump-starting the economy, rebuilding the nation's infrastructure, or promoting equality, they did not accept the judgments of militant conservatives either. Voters were suspicious of the GOP's vigorous rejection of the federal government's role in economic affairs. Some were alarmed by Mitt Romney's 2008 op-ed article, "Let Detroit Go Bankrupt."[43] They appreciated efforts by Presidents George W. Bush and Barack Obama to rescue General Motors and Chrysler.

Mitt Romney also allowed his campaign to be associated with far-right positions on social issues. Romney's stand on abortion troubled many women. It left an impression that, as President, Romney might appoint individuals to the Supreme Court who would attempt to overturn *Roe v. Wade*. Mitt Romney's insistence that marriage should be restricted to unions involving a man and a woman, also troubled some voters. Attitudes toward same-sex marriage had been shifting quickly in the direction of greater toleration, especially among young adults. On immigration, as well, Romney embraced radical positions. He talked about "self-deportation" by illegals and applauded Arizona's harsh immigration law. Hispanics were alarmed. They flocked to the Democrats.[44]

During the final weeks of the campaign, Mitt Romney attempted to pivot. He tried to appear more moderate. In the first debate he said a few nice things about governmental regulation of business affairs, and in the third debate he spoke about international affairs without employing the bellicose language of his earlier speeches. But that strategy made him look like a flip-flopper. He had already staked out extreme positions on controversial issues. Barack Obama effectively reminded viewers of Romney's earlier comments in the second and third presidential debates.

In 2012 radical *i*deas undermined Romney's presidential campaign.

Mitt Romney appeared to stand outside the political mainstream. Strongly conservative rhetoric helped him secure the GOP's presidential nomination, but that speechifying undermined his appeal in the general election.

Trump's Ascendancy Was Not Surprising: Republicans Often Favored Colorful Candidates that Lacked Skill in Governing

How did the Grand Old Party select a real estate mogul and reality TV show host as its candidate for President of the United States? There are many explanations for Trump's success in winning the Republican nomination, but one that is often overlooked relates to history. 2016 was not the first time that an individual lacking experience and skill in governance became a Republican contender for national leadership. Since 1988, several GOP candidates for president and vice president lacked impressive qualifications for national leadership.

Candidates' shortcomings became evident in nominations for Vice President. In 1988 George H. W. Bush chose as his running mate Indiana senator Dan Quayle. Party strategists recommended Quayle, believing his youth and good looks could help the ticket. But Dan Quayle's statements soon raised doubts. Quayle said, "I love California. I practically grew up in Phoenix." On another occasion he announced, "I have made good judgments in the past. I have made good judgments in the future." During a televised debate, a moderator repeatedly asked Quayle what he would first do if the president died or became incapacitated. Quayle stumbled, seeming unable to identify how he would deal with such an emergency.

Twenty years later the party's choice for vice president provoked greater alarm. During the 2008 presidential campaign, GOP presidential candidate John McCain selected Alaska governor Sarah Palin as his running mate. Conservative pundits had been recommending her for the vice presidency, especially William Kristol, who met her during a visit to Alaska. With only days before the national convention, John McCain realized that his preferred choice, Joe Lieberman, who ran for Vice president as a Democrat in 2000, was unacceptable to many Republicans. After a frantic search that relied heavily on the internet, advisers focused on Palin. She could help the campaign, strategists believed, because she was a woman, strikingly beautiful, and had the reputation of a maverick – an image McCain wanted to convey. With very little vetting, McCain chose her. Republican leaders later discovered that Sarah Palin was poorly informed about national and international affairs and grossly unprepared for top leadership.[45]

Democrats are not consistent exemplars of talent selection, of course, but in recent decades they have produced stronger candidates for vice president. Since 1988, the Democrats' choices included U.S. senators with considerable political experience: Lloyd Bentsen, Al Gore, Joe Lieberman, Joe Biden, and Kamala Harris. Only one selection since 1988 was seriously flawed: the choice of John Edwards, the Democrats' nominee for Vice President in 2004. But scandals that wrecked Edwards's political career came to light *after* the 2004 presidential election.

Since 1988, several candidates in the GOP's presidential races lacked readiness for national leadership. In 2000 party leaders advanced the candidacy of George W. Bush, even though the Texas governor lacked a strong grasp of national and international issues. When Bush became president and dealt with the 9/11 tragedy, Iraq, Hurricane Katrina and other challenges, his shortcomings were abundantly evident. Sometimes Vice President Dick

Cheney appeared to have greater influence over decision-making at the White House.

During the 2012 primary contests, several weak candidates in the Republican field received enthusiastic backing from wealthy supporters and grassroots partisans. They briefly rose in popularity and then slipped. Texas governor Rick Perry attracted interest (and money) but stumbled when speaking in public. Congresswoman Michele Bachmann, businessman Herman Cain, and former congressman Newt Gingrich looked like major contenders for a short time but quickly lost favor after receiving scrutiny in the news media. Other candidates appealed to specific constituencies. Rick Santorum, for instance, received support from evangelicals but failed to attract broader support.

A related pattern appeared during the 2016 primaries. Candidates that lacked experience in government enjoyed brief moments of popularity. Dr. Ben Carson's fortunes surged. He burned out after his lack of political knowledge became evident. Carly Fiorina, a tough-talking former CEO at Hewlett Packard, also attracted interest. She, too, quickly wilted. And, of course, many Republican voters favored Donald Trump, despite his frequent plunges into controversy.

Republican leaders should have recognized that their party's dalliances with candidates that lacked experience and skill in governance could become problematic. When a political party denounces the government repeatedly and characterizes entrepreneurs as heroes while denigrating "bureaucrats" in Washington, partisans believe anyone can handle the president's job, even a real estate mogul and reality game show host. When a party allows conservative radicals to impose restrictive tests of ideological purity on presidential hopefuls, talented individuals who are experienced in negotiation and compromise recognize they cannot compete in the primaries (or, like Jon Huntsman in 2012 and John Kasich in 2016, they do compete but fail to attract much GOP support). When strident commentators on radio, television, and the internet wield extraordinary influence in a party's affairs, a candidate that skillfully employs a showman's techniques can emerge as the presumptive nominee.

Reporting on the Republicans' race for the White House concentrated heavily on the bombast of Donald Trump. That emphasis suggested Trump revolutionized GOP politics through the force of his personality. A broader view of Republican practices since 1988 reveals that Donald Trump did not single-handedly create his opportunities. In prior years the Republican Party provided a megaphone for individuals that were colorful but poorly prepared for national leadership. The party's tolerance for resume-challenged candidates cleared a path for Donald Trump's victory in the GOP's primaries.

Donald Trump Owed His Presidential Election in 2016 to Five Men

During the 2016 presidential election, Democratic candidate Hillary Clinton led much of the time in public opinion polls, yet Donald Trump managed to pull off a surprising victory. Trump was effective in stoking resentments. He exploited tensions associated with race, ethnicity, gender, and religion. Trump also excited voters with promises to revitalize manufacturing, create new jobs, and "Make America Great Again." There is another important factor, however, that receives much less attention by the commentariat.

Donald Trump was victorious in large part because he and his party were more effective in stoking fear and hatred of Hillary Clinton than the Democrats were in stirring fear and hatred of Trump. Political scientists refer to this phenomenon as "Negative Partisanship." It is a tendency of voters to despise one candidate and party more than the other. In 2016 negative attitudes toward the "other" candidate were intense in both camps, but Trump and the Republicans excelled in arousing negative feelings toward Clinton. They received valuable help in stoking that partisanship from five influential men. Intervention by those individuals helped push Donald Trump, a deeply flawed presidential candidate, over the top.

It may seem strange that a few people could affect the outcome of a presidential election, but it is, indeed, possible. It would not have taken much in 2016 to swing a few key states in a different direction. Trump won by squeaking past Clinton in three states, Pennsylvania, Michigan, and Wisconsin. His *combined* advantage over Clinton in the three states was 79,646. A mere 40,000 votes for Hillary Clinton, distributed to her benefit among the three, would have given her the presidency. Either number, 40,000 or 79,646 is miniscule in comparison to all the votes cast for president in those three states: well over thirteen *million* (specifically, 13,791,377).

The five men under consideration here did quite a lot to give Trump the victory. In fact, actions by *any one of them* could delivered the White House to Donald Trump. When the involvement of all five is considered together, their potential to influence the outcome is substantial. Absent their participation, Clinton's win would have been huge.

The five men that made a significant impact are Rupert Murdoch, David Pecker, Michael Cohen, Vladimir Putin, and James Comey. Murdoch and Pecker were influential opinion makers in the mass media. Michael Cohen was Donald Trump's personal lawyer. Vladimir Putin was, of course, the President of Russia, and James Comey was director of the FBI.

RUPERT MURDOCH

Murdoch, leader of a huge media empire that promoted conservative politicians and causes, affected American politics in 2016 through his media platforms' pro-Trump coverage and critical treatment of Hillary Clinton. This partisanship was evident in diverse Murdoch enterprises but especially on Fox News.

Editorial opinion published in Murdoch's companies typically reflected the mogul's sentiments. In February 2003, *The Guardian*'s Roy Greenslade provided an impressive example of Rupert Murdoch's influence over media operations. Greenslade's broad survey of Murdoch-owned newspapers, including titles in Britain, Australia, and New Zealand, revealed Murdoch's "unerring ability to choose editors across the world who think just like him." Those editors all sang "from the same hymn sheet."[46]

Fox News operated in a related manner. The network leaned sharply in favor of Republicans. In 2016 Rupert Murdoch took time before settling on Trump. But once he made the decision, his television network and newspapers jumped on the Trump bandwagon.

Trump and Murdoch had a long-term relationship.[47] For years Donald Trump's daughter, Ivanka, served as trustee for two Murdoch daughters. Rupert Murdoch mentored Ivanka's husband, Jared Kushner, in business affairs. Murdoch's relationship with Donald Trump went through some rough patches before Trump became the presumptive Republican nominee. Then Murdoch visited Trump at his International Golf Links in Scotland. The two men embraced, renewing their friendship.

From that point on, the vast media outlets in Murdoch's domain portrayed Donald Trump enthusiastically. Some Fox News stars, such as Sean Hannity, praised Trump in such effusive language that they sounded like campaign managers. Fox's treatment was much more negative regarding Democrat Hillary Clinton.

In December 2017, Harvard's Shorenstein Center on the Media, Politics, and Public Policy published a study that analyzed news coverage during the 2016 campaign by the nation's major television networks and newspapers. Among all these sources, Fox News had, by far, the highest percentage of positive treatments of Trump and the highest percentage of negative treatments of Clinton.

During the 2016 election, Fox's popular prime-time hosts, such as Bill O'Reilly and Sean Hannity, provoked controversy because of their judgments that favored Republicans and denigrated Democrats. Behind the scenes, much less in the public light, was the powerful and opinionated leader of the corporation. Rupert Murdoch cast a large shadow over opinion-making at Fox News.

DAVID PECKER AND MICHAEL COHEN

These two played important roles in the concealment of Trump's alleged sexual relations with a porn film star and a Playboy model. Court documents revealed that David Pecker, CEO of American Media, Inc. and Michael Cohen, Trump's personal lawyer, kept information about the relationships from the public by providing payments of $130,000 to the adult film star and $150,000 to the Playboy model. Pecker received immunity from federal prosecution for providing details. Michael Cohen pleaded guilty to eight criminal charges, including campaign finance violations associated with payments to the women. Eventually, Cohen testified against Trump and criticized him strongly in numerous appearances in the national media and in the "hush money" trial in New York in 2024.[48]

Some analysts say it would have made little difference if claims about Trump's sexual encounters had become public before the election. They note that the "Access Hollywood" recording hit the news in October 2016 and showed Trump talking about grabbing women's private parts. Yet the information didn't significantly harm Trump's campaign.

The Access Hollywood recording did not have a powerful impact on Trump's candidacy in large part because of election mischief promoted by the fourth individual on the list.

VLADIMIR PUTIN

Friday, October 7 should have been a disastrous day for candidate Trump. At 12:40 PM the Obama administration released intelligence agency reports that accused the Russians of election interference to benefit Trump. At 4:03 PM, the *Washington Post* broke the story about Access Hollywood tapes. If American voters had time to digest these two extraordinary news reports, Trump's campaign would have been in serious jeopardy.

But just a half-hour later, thanks to Russia's involvement, WikiLeaks released a vast tranche of emails stolen from the accounts of a Democratic leader, John Podesta. Among the communications were details about Hillary Clinton's unpublished speeches to banks and information about her campaign strategies. This information quickly changed the news focus to Clinton's emails. Hillary Clinton's lead began to dissipate.[49]

Stolen emails represented just one of numerous actions that involved infiltration of social media sites by Russian trolls and technical specialists at the G.R.U., Russia's military intelligence agency. The Russians penetrated American internet sites. They achieved a strong presence on Facebook, Instagram, and Twitter. In 2016 millions of Americans had no idea they were looking at messages crafted by agents of a foreign power. In October 2017, Facebook executives acknowledged that the Russians succeeded in reaching 126 million users. Subsequent reports indicated that Russian agents managed to circulate 131,000 messages to Americans on Twitter and posted more than 1000 videos on YouTube. In April 2020 the Senate Intelligence Committee concluded that "Russia sought to shake faith in American democracy, denigrate then-candidate Hillary Clinton and boost her rival Donald Trump."

JAMES COMEY

Murdoch, Pecker, Cohen, Putin – all were motivated to boost Trump's election changes. The fifth man on the list did not intend to tip the scales in Donald Trump's favor, but his inept handling of intelligence nevertheless undermined Hillary Clinton's candidacy. FBI director James Comey made three extraordinary statements to the American public in 2016, one in July and two in October. Comey's remarks ensured that the confusing and troublesome topic of Hillary Clinton's emails remained front and center during the final days of the election campaign.

Ordinarily, FBI directors do not speak to the public about investigations in progress, especially one that is underway concerning a presidential candidate a short time before the date of the election. But James Comey felt compelled to speak.[50] His first intervention occurred on July 5, 2016. Comey said he would not pursue legal action, but he used harsh words, reprimanding Hillary Clinton for being "extremely careless" with emails when she was Secretary of State. His unusual public criticism soiled Clinton's image. In October, just ten days before the election, James Comey was on television, reporting that the F.B.I.'s investigation would be re-opened because additional emails had been discovered. Seven days later, Comey appeared on television again and put Clinton in the clear. Nate Silver, one of the top voter analysts, concluded that Comey's three surprising announcements may have pushed voters to Trump's camp in Pennsylvania, Michigan, Wisconsin, and Florida and perhaps in Arizona and North Carolina as well. Silver estimated that Comey's intervention probably sliced four percentage points off Clinton's support.

Comey's actions crushed Hillary Clinton's lead.

CONCLUSIONS

These details suggest that Trump was not as broadly popular in 2016 as many believed at the time. Intervention in election affairs by five men made a significant impact on the outcome. The men's activities helped shape America's and the world's troubled history in the years of Donald Trump's reckless leadership.

Was Hillary the Wrong Candidate Given Her High Unfavorable Numbers? No. Any Democrat Would Have Been Slimed

Some Democrats felt buyer's remorse after seeing Hillary Clinton face withering attacks. They wondered if a more popular Democrat could have discovered an easier path to victory against a deeply flawed candidate like Donald Trump. But in view of Hillary Clinton's shifting fortunes over several decades, it seems unlikely that some other Democrat could have finished the presidential campaign with a squeaky-clean image. Hillary Clinton was generally popular until she announced her intention to compete in the 2016 presidential race. During two decades of public life up until the time she left the office of Secretary of State in early 2013, Hillary Clinton frequently ranked in national surveys as America's most admired woman. Her strong disapproval ratings in 2016 demonstrate, to a large degree, the potential of partisan image-making to arouse doubts in the minds of voters.

A broad historical view of Hillary Clinton's climbs and falls in opinion polls suggests that much, but certainly not all, of her difficulties during the presidential campaign were shaped by the GOP's intense negative messaging. Hillary Clinton lost ground when news came to light about emails and questions arose about practices at the Clinton Foundation. Political assaults played a role in moving voters' perceptions to the downside.

From 1993 until the end of 2015, Hillary Clinton often ranked first in the Gallup organization's annual survey concerning admired woman.[51]

Gallup asked, "What woman that you have heard or read about, living today in any part of the world do you admire most?" Hillary Clinton placed first in 1993 and she appeared first several times over the next decade, surrendering the top spot a few times to Mother Teresa and Laura Bush. Between 2002 and 2015, Hillary Clinton came in first every year.

Evidence of Mrs. Clinton's earlier popularity appeared in an *ABC News/ Washington Post* poll. The survey asked respondents if they had a favorable or unfavorable impression of Hillary Clinton. In 2013 Mrs. Clinton enjoyed a high approval rating of 67%. She had not announced her candidacy for president at that time. Secretary Clinton's approval ratings began to drop significantly after she announced in April 2015 that she intended to run for president. At that point she became a primary target for the GOP's messaging machine.

On August 31, 2016, the *Washington Post*'s headline identified the severity of her slide in the polls, reporting, "A Record Number of Americans Now Dislike Hillary Clinton."[52] Among registered voters, Hillary Clinton's disapproval score was almost equal to Donald Trump's disapproval numbers. In late August 2016 Clinton had a 59% unfavorable rating. Trump's unfavorable rating was only a point higher at 60%.

Of course, Hillary Clinton stumbled at times during her presidential campaign. She had difficulty answering questions about her private email server, and her statement at a fundraiser in which she characterized half of Donald Trump's supporters as a "basket of deplorables" provided ammunition for her critics.

But Hillary Clinton's slips during the campaign were not severe. Much of the evidence presented against her that supposedly demonstrated untrustworthiness lacked substance. Republicans often invoked old charges that did not hold up under scrutiny, such as complaints about Clinton's handling of the Benghazi tragedy in Libya. Filmmaker Michael Moore communicated disdain for those bogus accusations in an appearance on Bill Maher's television show. When Rick Lazio, Hillary Clinton's opponent in the New York senate race of 2000, referred to Clinton as "a scandal factory" and complained that Mrs. Clinton had been involved in "cattle futures," Moore responded sarcastically, "I withdraw my support of Hillary Clinton. I forgot about the cattle futures."

To some degree, President Barack Obama became a beneficiary of Hillary Clinton's difficulties. Until 2016, Obama suffered from generally disappointing presidential job approval ratings. On numerous occasions during his first seven years in the White House Obama's approval score fell to the low 40% level. One of the President's steepest drops (to 40%) occurred in early November 2014. Obama did not enjoy a sustained climb out of his poor standing until February 2016 and beginning in the summer of 2016 his approval consistently scored above 50%. Obama's improved position seems attributable, in part, to a decline in criticism aimed specifically at him. In 2016 the GOP directed its invective at Hillary Clinton.

A well-coordinated campaign to slime Hillary Clinton changed her image quickly from an admirable national leader to a deeply flawed one.

FOUR

BOOMING AND CRASHING ECONOMIES

During the 1992 presidential election, Democratic election strategist James Carville famously observed that Americans had their minds on "the economy, stupid." Carville's point remains relevant. Impressions about economic conditions frequently influence voters' decisions about the candidates.

The first analysis points to the value of this judgment when interpreting outcomes in the 1980 and 1984 presidential elections.

The second asks if there is a salient factor in the nation's long history of recessions and depressions. Those numerous meltdowns had diverse causes. Nevertheless, this analysis identifies a key factor. Extreme commitments to laissez-faire led to lax financial deregulation. Financial meltdowns followed. Republicans and Democrats responded differently to proposals for dealing with the problem. An examination of causes and reactions to the Great Recession of 2007-2009 illustrates the point.

Unfortunate Jimmy Carter; Lucky Ronald Reagan

Jimmy Carter's years in the White House are remembered especially in connection with troubled economic times, while the president who followed him, Ronald Reagan, is often associated with a booming economy. Histor-

ical situations in the 1970s and 1980s were more complex than this invidi-
ous comparison suggests, however. Jimmy Carter did not deserve the harsh
criticism on economics that was commonly directed at him. His leadership
was not the primary cause of hard times in the late Seventies, and one of his
most important presidential decisions put the United States on the road to
economic recovery.

Surging petroleum prices were an especially significant factor in the
nation's economic slump in the Seventies. In October 1973 a decision by
leaders of the Organization of Petroleum Exporting Countries (OPEC)
made inflation soar. OPEC boosted the price of a barrel of oil by more than
300%. Later in the decade, OPEC struck again. In 1979 the cartel backed a
new series of hikes that nearly doubled the price of a barrel of oil. Overall,
petroleum prices climbed from $3 a barrel to $34 a barrel between the end
of 1973 and the summer of 1979. These actions led to spikes in the cost of
food, goods, and services. Soaring energy prices were at the foundation of
inflation and economic stagnation.

No President of the United States came up with a remedy in the Seventies that quickly overcame the difficulties. President Richard Nixon could
not deal aggressively with the challenge of growing inflation. Gerald Ford,
the Vice President who replaced Nixon, also tried to check inflation. Ford
announced a WIN program in the fall of 1974 (the acronym stood for "Whip
Inflation Now"). Yet the problem continued. WIN buttons soon became an
object of ridicule. Some Americans wore them upside down. "NIM," they
said, meant "No Immediate Miracles."

Jimmy Carter assumed the presidency in early 1977 and served during
some of the worst economic conditions of the decade. In 1979, annual inflation in the United States reached 11.3%, and it climbed to 13.6% in 1980.
Carter talked about creating a long-term energy policy that would reduce the
American people's heavy dependence on fossil fuels, and for the short term
he recommended personal cutbacks in energy consumption. Many Americans criticized these proposals.

In August 1979 Jimmy Carter made an appointment that proved
wise for the U.S. economy in the long run but weakened Carter's strug-

gle to hold on to the presidency. Carter selected Paul Volcker to chair the Federal Reserve. Volcker took quick action to deal with the vexing problem of inflation. Under his leadership, the federal funds rate climbed to 19.1% in 1981. The prime rate briefly hit 21 ½% in December 1981.Volcker's Fed also reduced the money supply. These bold actions eventually pressed the brakes on inflation. But the remedies were painful. The Federal Reserve's policies slowed the entire U.S. economy. Building projects came to a halt. Farmers that relied on heavy borrowing and mortgaged property felt like they were in a full-blown depression. Ultimately, though, the Fed's strategy worked. By late 1982 and early 1983, the inflation rate was falling. In subsequent years business and employment improved.[53]

During the Volcker-led squeeze, G. William Miller, Jimmy Carter's Secretary of the Treasury and Charles Schultze, chairman of the Council of Economic advisers, worried that the Fed's actions could spike unemployment, deepen the recession, and sink the Democratic president's reelection chances. They questioned aspects of Volcker's plan. Despite criticism from those members of the administration and others, President Carter supported Volcker in public statements.

Admirers of Ronald Reagan boasted that his economic policies brought victory in America's long-term battle with stagflation. Economic progress returned in the 1980s, they noted. It was, as Reagan's reelection campaign announced in 1984, "morning again in America." Reagan succeeded while Jimmy Carter failed, they argued.

That story is much too simple. Reagan's leadership played a role in the recovery, but the Republican president was lucky, too. He reaped the benefits of Jimmy Carter's decision to appoint Paul Volcker.

Reagan was fortunate in another respect. The expansion of global oil production in the Eighties loosened OPEC's stranglehold on the U.S. and global economies. Some of the major producing countries, including the largest at the time, Saudi Arabia, released more oil to the international market. New wells in the North Sea, Mexico, Alaska, and other regions added to global supplies. By 1986 oil prices were only a fraction of the elevated levels they had reached late in Jimmy Carter's administration. As energy costs declined, corporations paid less to manufacture and transport goods than in the late 1970s. American workers no longer had to surrender large portions of their earnings to fill their cars with gasoline or heat their homes. After energy costs plummeted, the U.S. economy turned healthy.

When journalists assess Jimmy Carter's place in history, they should recognize that Carter's policies were not the principal cause of difficult economic times in the Seventies. No leader could quickly overcome the challenges. At least Carter tried to deal with the crisis, most notably when he named Paul Volcker as Fed chairman. That decision contributed to his defeat in the 1980 presidential election, but it led ultimately to America's victory over inflation.

The Perils of Deregulation: 1929 to 2008

In 2008 stock markets plummeted, major investment banks collapsed, and the federal government rescued faltering behemoths like Fannie Mae, Freddie Mac, and AIG. At the time, some Americans looked back to the history of the 1930s as they sought insights on the causes of financial meltdowns and remedies for overcoming them. Unfortunately, answers could not be identified with confidence. Historians and economists disagreed sharply about principal factors that produced an economic collapse in the Thirties. The key factors listed in monographs and textbooks that explained sources of the crash were numerous. Nevertheless, a comparative examination of the Great Depression and the Great Recession yields some insights regarding the causes of economic collapses and remedies for dealing with them.

Interpreters usually mention stock market speculation as a catalyst for the meltdown on Wall Street in late 1929, but they suggest the stock market crash represented only an early indication of deeper problems. The Great Depression lasted for a decade, they point out, because more profound economic weaknesses were at play. Trouble resulted from maldistribution of wealth, trade protectionism, international debts from the First World War, currency contraction, failed leadership at the Federal Reserve, overdependence on the gold standard, poor banking practices, a flawed credit structure, and other problems. Historian Alan Brinkley reported that economists, historians, and others have argued for decades about the causes of the Great Depression without reaching any consensus.[54]

One element in that history, however, appears relevant for comparative analysis. In both 1929 and 2008 there was an absence of effective regulation of business practices. Reckless speculation got dangerously out of hand. Financiers were able to market risky investment products without public oversight. Those loose practices contributed to a meltdown of the national and international financial systems. Shortcomings in regulation also brought America's finances to the brink of catastrophe during the Great Recession of 2008-2009. Fortunately, decisive action by leaders from the Federal Reserve, the Treasury Department, and Congress saved the United States and the world from the kind of disintegration that wrecked markets in the 1930s. Leaders in Washington learned valuable lessons from the history of the Great Depression.

Some absorbed lessons from history, but not all.

Democrats were the primary champions of acting on history's lessons. They did not promote oversight by governmental agencies in response to the Great Recession simply because they were enamored of "Big Government." Democrats favored regulations largely because they were cognizant of America's troubled record of financial crashes. Wild swings in the business cycle had occurred throughout U.S. history. The American people experienced difficult times after major recessions and depressions in 1819, 1837, 1857, 1873, 1893, and 1907, to name a few among several large declines in the business cycle. The monster depression of the 1930s was the most devastating of these crashes. It lasted more than a decade.

This history of financial instability did not substantially affect the outlook of many Republicans. Shortly after the Great Recession of 2007-2009, many of them vehemently opposed regulatory reforms proposed by Democrats, especially the Dodd-Frank Wall Street Reform and Consumer Protection Act. Years later, Republicans cheered presidential candidate Donald Trump when he advocated widespread deregulation of the U.S. economy. Many Republicans favored applications of laissez faire, a conviction that government's role in economic affairs should be strictly limited so that "free markets" could work their productive magic.

A laissez-faire approach to economic matters had been applied vigorously during the 1920s. The Treasury Secretary in Republican administrations during much of the decade, Andrew Mellon, called for downsizing the government's role in economic affairs and governmental deregulation. In the years of a surging stock market, Mellon received considerable praise as key architect of a strategy that appeared to deliver long-lasting prosperity. But when markets began to decline, Mellon rejected calls for governmental action. The slide would "purge the rottenness out of the system," he judged. "Values will be adjusted, and enterprising people will pick up the wrecks from less competent people." Mellon's harsh leave-it-alone advice appeared in his recommendation to "liquidate labor, liquidate stocks, liquidate farmers, liquidate real estate."[55] Mellon, admired as a brilliant economic leader in the Twenties, looked like a villain to many Americans when hard times came in the early Thirties. During the financial crisis, Republican president Herbert Hoover relieved Mellon of his responsibilities at the Treasury Department.

Many financial experts did not recognize a crash was coming in the 1920s. During flush times, market watchers often expressed supreme confidence about business conditions. The *Wall Street Journal* announced at the beginning of 1929, "One cannot recall when a new year was ushered in with business conditions sounder than they are today." Economics professor Irving Fisher of Yale observed in the autumn of 1929 that, "Stocks have reached what looks like a permanently high plateau."

The situation was not as sanguine as many imagined, because financial institutions were marketing highly speculative and risky products to a gullible public. In the stock market, brokers got attractive commissions for selling securities with money borrowed from banks. Then they lent cash to customers at a higher rate of interest than they paid the banks and pocketed handsome profits. Lots of investors bought stocks on "margin," providing only a fraction of the cost as a down-payment. Their risk assessment seemed wise because the value of securities appeared to be surging permanently.

When the crash came, many investors who took those risks could not meet their debt obligations.

Also troubling were "investment trusts" which pooled money to speculate in diverse securities. The managers of these instruments refused to disclose their stock holdings. Sometimes they invested in other investment trusts. With relatively small amounts of capital, they leveraged funds extensively. The practice delivered attractive earnings in flush times, but several investment trusts collapsed like a house of cards after 1929.

The crisis of the 1930s might have been averted if there had been more transparency so that investors had access to useful information. It could have been less dangerous if financial regulation of investments promoted responsible business practices. Those protections were lacking in the 1920s.

In 1933 and beyond, President Franklin D. Roosevelt's administration promoted governmental regulation. FDR and Democrats in Congress created a burst of new legislation that supported oversight in financial affairs. The New Deal created the Securities and Exchange Commission to monitor the stock market, required the separation of commercial and investment banks, insured bank deposits, and established rules designed to make business practices more transparent. These reforms promoted stability in banking and other financial activities for several decades. Lessons from this history were lost on leaders in the 1980s. President Ronald Reagan's administration championed "deregulation," an initiative that contributed to the Savings and Loan crisis.[56] In the early Eighties several rules for the operation of S & Ls disappeared. Some S & L executives then engaged in highly speculative investments. When their institutions got into trouble in 1985, the executives tried to conceal embarrassing information from the public. Eventually, many S & Ls went under. Congress had to step in to clean up the mess. Rescue efforts cost $125 billion. American society paid dearly for radical deregulation of savings and loan institutions.

Lack of regulation was a factor in the Great Recession, as well.[57] The problems began to appear in 2007 and turned into a full-blown crisis in late

2008 and early 2009. Much of the trouble related to subprime mortgages, which became popular in the early 2000s. Banks and mortgage companies provided loans to many people that could not afford to maintain them. When home prices soared, buyers with limited resources thought they could take on heavy debt and quicky enjoy large gains. Financial companies combined the "subprime" mortgages of highly leveraged homebuyers, selling them in bundles to investors. When the housing market collapsed, these "collateralized debt obligations" quickly lost value. Eventually, many huge financial institutions were in danger of collapse. Federal authorities worked diligently to rescue Bear Stearns and Lehman Brothers, huge investment banks, AIG, a major insurance company, and other large financial institutions.

During that emergency, George W. Bush's Treasury Secretary Henry Paulson, Jr. and Barack Obama's Treasury Secretary, Timothy Geithner, found ways to pump money into troubled firms. Their recommendations sparked angry Republican criticism of "bailouts." But legislators, especially Democrats, ultimately backed the recommendations. Ben Bernanke and the Federal Reserve aided those efforts by creating liquidity in the financial system.

The final report of the *National Commission on the Causes of the Financial and Economic Crisis in the United States* identified the fundamental cause of meltdowns during the Great Recession. It said America's financial system had operated like "a highway where there were neither speed limits nor neatly painted lines." When the financial crash occurred, "sentries were not at their posts, in no small part due to the widely accepted faith in the self-correcting nature of the markets and the ability of financial institutions to police themselves." The Commission drew attention to more than 30 years of deregulation that had preceded the Great Recession. It blamed leaders in Washington, including officials at the Federal Reserve, the White House, and legislators in Congress that "stripped away key safeguards, which could have helped avoid catastrophe."[58]

There were many causes of depressions and recessions over the course of American history. One factor, however – lax regulation of financial markets

– was a notable feature in those painful economic downturns. In modern times Democrats generally recognized that lax regulation was an important source of the difficulties. Republicans tended to ignore that explanation. They often treated government involvement in financial affairs as a problem, not a solution.

FIVE

MOVIES AND POLITICS

Can insights be obtained about the growing problem of Republican extremism in modern U.S. history by citing lessons from popular films? Many are doubtful. They complain that Hollywood's productions often distort the historical record to attract audiences and earn profits. They criticize the creators of these films for inventing characters and scenes and simplifying history to make their stories understandable and appealing for diverse audiences.

These articles challenge the familiar negative assessments. The interpretations maintain that well-crafted movies can stir the public's thinking about lessons from history. In some cases, popular films threw light on the growing problem of Republican extremism in American politics. The movies under consideration here relate to the leadership of Richard Nixon, Ronald Reagan, George W. Bush, and Donald Trump.

One of the essays draws attention to Republican resistance to television productions that depicted the leadership of Hillary Clinton. The GOP's objections posed challenges to cherished traditions regarding freedom of speech.

Nixon, by Oliver Stone: A Revealing Psychohistory

When a Hollywood filmmaker portrays a famous figure from the past, critics often express outrage over the portrayal. They denounce the filmmaker for taking too many artistic liberties and distorting the historical record. Oliver Stone came under that kind of attack in 1995 when he released *Nixon,* a dark and disturbing portrayal featuring actor Anthony Hopkins as President Richard M. Nixon.

Years after the movie's release, that critical reaction appeared less valid. New evidence came to light that suggested Oliver Stone delivered several insights. Documents, tape recordings, interviews and testimonials revealed that Richard Nixon was somewhat like the maladjusted and sinister individual depicted in Stone's movie. Those revelations confirmed that Nixon had been troubled by deep insecurities. He frequently lied to the public, broke laws, pursued imagined enemies, and abused power. Oliver Stone's psychohistory of the flawed leader was not perfect. It contained some questionable depictions. Like many Hollywood productions about famous people, the filmmaker simplified, compressed, and invented to design a coherent and compelling story. In view of new information that revealed White House shenanigans, Stone's *Nixon* contributed to the public's thinking about history and its lessons.

When Oliver Stone promoted his movie back in 1995, he claimed the production offered a sympathetic but also critical portrait. Richard Nixon was a tragic figure, Stone emphasized. Emerging from a humble background, the future president climbed quickly in post-World War II American politics. Nixon "rose to the top then collapsed in a heap of hubris," said Stone. The movie probed the origins of Nixon's self-destructive personality by drawing attention to his childhood in poverty, his stern parents, and resentment toward privileged Americans associated with the Eastern Establishment. Nixon's jealousy and hostility aimed especially at the Kennedys.

Oliver Stone's movie resembled Orson Welles's *Citizen Kane* (1941). Welles's acclaimed film presented clues for understanding the motivation of a character that resembled William Randolph Hearst, a powerful newspaper publisher and politician. Stone looked to Nixon's experiences in youth and as a young man for insights into his later behavior, especially actions that led to the Watergate scandal. Oliver Stone tried to make sense of a memorable speech Nixon gave to staffers when the disgraced President was about to leave the White House. That talk, which invoked personal memories from Nixon's younger days, sounded disjointed. Stone's drama treated Nixon's references as important hints about his personality formation.

Oliver Stone's movie appeared in late 1995, a year and a half after Nixon died and at a time when Nixon seemed less sinister than during the time of the Watergates hearings. Richard Nixon had worked assiduously after leaving the White House to improve his public image. To a considerable degree, he succeeded in shaping a revised perspective on his place in history. By 1995, many Americans remembered Richard Nixon as the architect of bold foreign policies and as a surprisingly liberal leader in domestic affairs, exemplified by his support of environmental reforms. In view of the late President's improved standing since his embarrassing resignation, Oliver Stone's movie struck many viewers as heavy-handed and disrespectful.

Several critics savaged the film. They were unhappy with Stone's portrayal of a paranoid, immoral, hard-drinking, unstable, and power-hungry tyrant. Stone's depiction "is not Nixon," protested the President's longtime friend, Ray Price. Historian Stephen E. Ambrose, who published a three-volume biography of Nixon, complained of inaccurate details.[59] "If [Stone] wants to get deep into Nixon's character, he's got to get those drinks out of [Nixon's] hands," complained Ambrose, referring to the movie's depictions of alcoholic consumption. Stone's "got to clean up [Nixon's] language, too," insisted Ambrose. One of the most damning objections came from Diane Disney Miller, daughter of Walt Disney. She apologized publicly to Nixon's two daughters. Miller expressed shame that her father's company distributed a film that "did a disservice to your family, to the presidency, and to U.S. history." President Nixon's legacy would endure, asserted Miller, because "he left the world a better and safer place for millions of people . . ."

So much information appeared after 1995 about Richard Nixon's responsibility for criminal conspiracies, expanding death and destruction unnecessarily in the Vietnam War, and more, that Rutgers historian David

Greenberg concluded the new evidence rendered "the pro-Nixon hagiography of yesteryear a musty artifact." Breakthroughs began to appear a year after the release of Stone's movie. Historian Stanley Kutler and the liberal advocacy group, Public Citizen, filed a lawsuit against the National Archives and Records Administration that eventually won release of more than 3000 hours of White House recordings (previously only 63 hours had been made public). The final 340 hours of recordings became available for study in 2013.

Several important books followed, analyses that described a duplicitous politician. Kenneth Hughes's *Chasing Shadows* described Nixon's interference in President Lyndon Johnson's negotiations with North Vietnam shortly before the 1968 presidential election. *The Nixon Tapes*, edited and discussed by Douglas Brinkley (Rice University) and Luke A. Nichter (Texas A & M University – Central Texas) showed diverse examples of mischief at the White House, and *One Man Against the World* by Pulitzer Prize-winning journalist Tim Weiner connected much of the President's lying and criminal behavior to his decision-making regarding the Vietnam War.

Some of the most intriguing evidence about Richard Nixon that fortified Oliver Stone's portrayal appeared in Bob Woodward's book, *The Last of the President's Men,* published in 2015. Woodward drew insights from lengthy interviews with Alexander Butterfield, a Nixon aide who told the Watergate committee about the existence of secret recordings. Butterfield characterized the Nixon White House as "a cesspool." He reported that the President encouraged sycophants to attack "enemies" (politicians, print and television journalists, and antiwar protesters, among others). Alexander Butterfield described Nixon's efforts to remove the "infestation" of portraits of John F. Kennedy in the staff's offices (which backs up Stone's speculation about the President's obsession with the Kennedys). As for drinking and swearing, evidence from Butterfield and other sources showed the president was much more engaged in these excesses than biographer Stephen Ambrose recognized.

Journalist Bob Woodward summed up an impression that emerged from examining the tapes. Woodward said the recordings "depict a White House full of lies, chaos, distrust, speculation, self-protection, maneuver, and counter-maneuver, with a crookedness that makes Netflix's 'House of Cards' look unsophisticated."

Evidence in tapes, documents, interviews, and other sources suggests that Oliver Stone delivered thoughtful judgments when he offered a film-based portrait of the controversial President. It is now clear that the real Nixon was an even darker figure than the disturbing, unbalanced character Anthony Hopkins played in Stone's 1995 movie. Like many other examples of history from Hollywood, *Nixon* contained artistic flourishes that mixed fact with fiction. Nevertheless, the movie contained relevant clues that showed how Richard Nixon, an impressive achiever, ultimately became a tragic figure. Stone's portrait resembles the true Richard Nixon more than outraged critics recognized in 1995.

Nixon Acted Like Hollywood's Patton. It Got Him in Trouble

In the 1970 movie *Patton* actor George C. Scott portrays George S. Patton, a U.S. officer in World War II. General Patton received considerable criticism for his tough, uncompromising, behavior, but he won acclaim for impressive victories. The Oscar-winning film about this feisty warrior was hugely popular. It is best remembered for the opening scene showing Patton appearing to address a large group of unseen soldiers. The highly decorated general announces, "Americans love a winner and will not tolerate a loser. That's why America has never lost and will never lose a war. Because the very thought of losing is hateful to Americans."

Millions of American viewers found those words inspiring. One of the film's many fans, Richard Nixon, President of the United States, acted on that inspiration. By modeling himself on the image of General Patton, Nixon eventually got into a heap of trouble.[60]

The movie about Patton helped President Nixon muster the courage to make a controversial decision. In spring 1970 Nixon was trying to decide whether to sanction an invasion. He had supported secret bombings of Cambodia, the country adjacent to Vietnam, to stop North Vietnam from supplying communist insurgents in South Vietnam, but the infiltration continued. The president thought about authorizing military operations in Cambodia but recognized the actions would be highly controversial. It would appear to be an expansion of America's already troublesome military involvement in Vietnam.

Nixon watched *Patton* with his family on April 4, 1970, and then watched it again on April 23, A few days after his second viewing, Nixon ordered U.S. and South Vietnamese troops into Cambodia. In tough language that resembled George C. Scott's monologue in the movie, the president told a television audience, "we will not be humiliated, we will not be defeated," When the chips are down, "the world's most powerful nation" should not "act like a pitiful helpless giant." Nixon said he would rather be a one-term president than have two terms "at the cost of seeing America become a second-rate power and see this nation accept the first defeat in its proud 190-year history."[61]

The college students' reaction to the president's decision was extraordinary. Many students thought the invasion of Cambodia suggested the United States was increasing its military commitments in Southeast Asia rather than reducing them. On many campuses, students held emergency meetings, planned rallies, participated in demonstrations, and demanded cancelation of classes. Strikes broke out on more than 450 campuses. At Kent State, a university in Ohio, national guardsmen on the university grounds fired into a crowd, killing four students.

Despite the upheaval and tragedy, Nixon continued to manifest his enthusiasm for *Patton*. Discussion of the movie came up when the president brought forty-five business and financial leaders to a meeting at the White House. Nixon asked the visitors if they had seen *Patton*. After watching several hands go up in the crowd, he reminded the visitors of General Patton's boldness in the Battle of the Bulge. Nixon noted that various generals thought Patton's plan could not work, but the general completed "perhaps the greatest movement of forces in the whole history of warfare in a short time." Richard Nixon drew a lesson from the movie. He said, "You have to have the will and determination to go out and do what is right for America." Guests at the event responded with a burst of applause.

A short time later Nixon flew to his estate at San Clemente and brought along a copy of *Patton*. He showed the film to educate his staff. Presidential assistant Bob Haldeman urged members of the White House team to watch the movie to better understand Nixon's behavior during a critical time in his leadership. One of these individuals, Secretary of State William Rogers later told Twentieth Century Fox chairman Darryl Zanuck that the president was a walking ad for the film. *Patton* "comes up in every conversation," reported Rogers. He recalled that aides frequently discussed the movie in the back corridors of the White House.[62]

Despite Nixon's great admiration for General Patton, he was unable to show nerves of steel when facing a national uproar over his decision to invade Cambodia. The president began to back off from a vigorous defense of his actions. But privately he continued to imitate the toughness of General Patton.

Nixon demanded a much more aggressive posture in the government's dealing with antiwar groups. He called in his staff and encouraged them to stand up against critics of his policies in Congress and in the streets. The president also called in leaders from the CIA, the FBI, and the Defense Intelligence Agency. Nixon wanted these officials to take bolder action against opponents of his policies. He told aides he was disappointed that the FBI and CIA failed to quell the uproar during the period of anti-war demonstrations. Nixon expressed interest in unorthodox measures to deal with the challenges. The president's words encouraged a member of his administration, Tom Huston, to make a proposal that involved spying on private individuals, interception of the mail, and burglarizing homes. Nixon supported this extraordinary recommendation, but FBI director J. Edgar Hoover and Attorney General John Mitchell objected to it. They convinced the president to put aside Huston's plan.

According to the president's top assistant, Bob Haldeman, May 1970 "marked a turning point for Nixon." In that month Nixon began to encourage secret activities, including a program of domestic surveillance. The "turning point" occurred just days after Nixon found inspiration in George C. Scott's portrayal. With new determination, the president called for hardball tactics against perceived enemies. That shift put Nixon and his men directly on the path to a break-in at the Democrats' headquarters in an office building, televised investigations of scandals, and the president's resignation in 1974.

Explanations about Richard Nixon's fall from grace are necessarily complex. The president's infatuation with a movie about a tough general provides only a few clues for understanding his self-destructive behavior. Yet the timing of President Nixon's move toward extra-legal tactics relates closely to his excitement about the movie. Richard Nixon's enthusiasm for *Patton* appears relevant to the broader history. Evidently, the movie was a significant factor in exciting the president's engagement in extremist activities that violated America's democratic traditions. This may be a case in which art not only imitated life, but life imitated art.

A Movie that Identified the Dangerous Implications of the Watergate Scandal

When the movie *Spotlight* dramatized investigative journalism and won the Oscar for best picture, commentators in the media noted that the movie's creators were inspired by story-telling techniques and cinematography applied in *All the President's Men*. That 1976 production effectively portrayed the tedious work of journalists at the *Washington Post* who investigated the Watergate break-in. *All the President's Men* received accolades as a brilliant artistic achievement, but it also deserved recognition as a significant commentary on history. The film showed the Watergate scandal was not a minor event. It showed the Nixon Administration's involvement in surreptitious plotting constituted a serious threat to American democracy.

All the President's Men begins by showing a security guard calling the police after he notices tape on a door at the Watergate complex in Washington, D.C. When five men are arrested in association with a break-in, two young reporters at the *Washington Post*, Bob Woodward, and Carl Bernstein (played by Robert Redford and Dustin Hoffman), doggedly seek information about the incident. Sometimes their investigative efforts reach dead ends. They discover fragmentary evidence, but the *Post*'s tough editor requires additional sources. Fortunately for the reporters, a secret contact from inside the government offers valuable clues. Eventually Woodward's and Bernstein's articles produce details about extensive abuses in Richard Nixon's administration. In the movie's final scene, the two journalists type their full story. A montage summarizes Richard Nixon's declining fortunes, his resignation, and Vice President Gerald Ford's ascension to the presidency.

Actor Robert Redford, who provided much of the inspiration for making *All the President's Men*, had been suspicious of Richard Nixon long before news about the Watergate scandal broke. When Redford was thirteen years old, he received an athletic scholarship from then-senator Richard Nixon. Years later, Redford recalled that he "never believed a word [Nixon] said" during the ceremonies. When shaking Nixon's hand, Redford felt "absolutely nothing . . . it was just empty." As an adult Redford wondered why journalists did not recognize Nixon's insincerity.

While on a train to promote his 1972 movie, *The Candidate*, Redford asked journalists why members of their profession were not investigating the Watergate break-in more aggressively. Reporters on the train said Watergate appeared to be business as usual in Washington. They thought Americans would never learn the truth. Redford was appalled by their cynicism. After reading articles by Woodward and Bernstein, Redford contacted the *Post*'s reporters. Robert Redford's advice helped Woodward and Bernstein to improve a book they were writing about their investigation of the Nixon administration's activities. Eventually the journalists and the movie star worked out an agreement for production of a film that carried the same title as the book.

All the President's Men (the movie) identified the enormity of Watergate crimes. That message is especially clear in two scenes that show Woodward meeting a secret contact in a Washington garage. Decades later the public learned this informant's name. Mark Felt was a special agent at the FBI. Felt (played by Hal Holbrook) berates Woodward for getting bogged down in small details and missing the bigger picture. He says people associated with the White House were involved in bugged conversations, phony press releases, and faked letters. The conspirators canceled Democratic Party rallies, investigated the private lives of politicians, planted spies, and stole documents. The informant urges Woodward to look for culprits in high places. The crimes involve "the entire intelligence community" including "The FBI, CIA, Justice – it's incredible." He says "the cover-up had little to do with it. It was mainly to protect the covert operations." In other words, the break-in at the Watergate office complex represented just the surface of a much larger problem.

Americans needed to hear that message in 1976. Information conveyed by the movie's secret contact challenged a claim that Nixon's apologists promoted. While acknowledging that news about the Watergate scandal was disturbing, some of Nixon's defenders tried to put his troublesome record in perspective. They maintained that other presidents committed errors that were as bad or worse. This viewpoint gained traction in later years. More than 4 in 10 Americans in Gallup and AP polls said in the 1980s that Watergate was "just politics, the sort of thing that both parties do." Some apologists tried to balance negative information about Nixon and Watergate with a positive view of the President's achievements in foreign policy. They emphasized the Nixon Administration's successes in improving relations with China and the Soviet Union. *All the President's Men* questioned these charitable assessments of Richard Nixon's leadership.

The appearance of *All the President's Men* in the spring of 1976 came at an unfortunate time for Gerald Ford. Richard Nixon had appointed him as Vice President after Spiro Agnew stepped away from the vice presidency in disgrace. After Nixon resigned and Gerald Ford became the nation's chief executive, Ford pardoned Nixon unconditionally. Gerald Ford hoped to keep reminders of Watergate at a minimum when he sought a new term in the White House during the 1976 campaign. But the arrival of *All the President's Men* in theaters across America made his task difficult.

Democrats could hardly believe their good fortune when they saw advertisements for *All the President's Men* in the spring of an election year. Basil Patterson, Vice Chair of the Democratic National Committee, said there had been a national effort "to exclude from our consciousness the painful, unpleasant, unacceptable memories of the Watergate debacle." He noted that *All the President's Men* "revives all the recollections and the emotions." William Vander Heuvel, New York co-chair of Jimmy Carter's presidential campaign, believed "the movie will have a major impact on the 1976 campaign" because "it takes a subliminal issue and puts it back in the front ranks of people's minds."

The presidential race was close, and the film may have been a factor in the election outcome. In the first months after *All the President's Men*'s appearance Democrat Jimmy Carter, a little-known governor from Georgia, suddenly emerged as a popular contender. Carter presented himself in the primaries and in the general election as the right person to cleanse American politics after Watergate. "I will not lie to you," promised the Washington outsider. By the fall of 1976, however, Carter was stumbling. His 30-point lead had disappeared. The race was so tight that Jimmy Carter did not know he had been elected President until 3:30 AM on the day after polls closed. Carter won the popular vote by only 50.8% to 48.2%, and he took the electoral vote by just 297 to 240.

In such a tight contest, the film may have influenced voters' thinking, but the movie was only one among numerous factors that could have affected judgments. Other difficulties that Gerald Ford encountered during the 1976 campaign probably also made an impact on voter sentiment. The Republican Party had been weakened during a bitter primary fight in which Gerald Ford had to fend off harsh criticism from candidate Ronald Reagan. By September 1976 reports showed that business growth had stalled, and unemployment and inflation were rising. During a televised debate in October, Ford mistakenly claimed "there is no Soviet domination in Eastern Europe, and there never will be under a Ford administration." His statement contrasted sharply with the facts. And, of course, Gerald Ford's pardon of Richard Nixon upset many Americans. After President Ford announced that he would absolve Nixon in 1974, 53% of Americans surveyed opposed the decision. Only 38% agreed with it.

The movie, *All the President's Men,* was one among many elements that may have contributed to Gerald Ford's loss in 1976. Judgments about the movie's impact must remain speculative.

With more confidence, however, we can conclude that *All the President's Men* was more than just a fine work of cinema that featured strong storytelling, good acting, fine direction, and impressive cinematography. The movie delivered hard-hitting political commentary. It boldly addressed controversial issues. With greater courage than many other filmmakers of the Seventies, Robert Redford and the movie's production team challenged audiences to recall serious threats to American democracy posed by the Watergate scandal. Their movie revealed how extremist behavior by a corrupt president made a nefarious impact on American politics.

Movie Power: The Influence of Michael Moore's *Fahrenheit 9/11*

When filmmaker Michael Moore released his controversial movie, *Fahrenheit 9/11* in 2004 debates raged about the film's partisanship, its truthfulness, and its potential to influence the outcome of a presidential election. Now, decades later, it is evident that Moore's film, Hollywood's largest-grossing documentary film at the time, was spot-on in its depiction of Republican politics. It showed how flawed thinking of GOP leaders, especially that of President George W. Bush, put the nation on a disastrous course.

When Michael Moore presented hard-hitting attacks on President George W. Bush's policy of invasion, war-making, and military occupation in Iraq, many critics denounced the movie as over-the-top propaganda. Since 2004, however, just about all major points that Moore stressed in his movie have been widely reported and discussed in the national media. With the benefit of time, it is evident that Moore's film offered perceptive observations about President George W. Bush's vulnerabilities and errors.

Fahrenheit 9/11 criticized President George W. Bush's call for the bombing and invasion of Iraq in the spring of 2003. The film questioned the Bush Administration's suggestions that Iraqi leader Saddam Hussein had close ties to al Qaeda and that Iraq played a significant role in the 9/11 tragedy. *Fahrenheit 9/11* also challenged the Administration's warnings that Saddam Hussein aimed to build an arsenal of nuclear weapons. [63] These claims aroused substantial controversy at the time. But by 2008, when Barack

Obama won the Democratic Party's nomination for President of the United States, his reputation as an outspoken critic of warmaking in 2003 helped propel him to victory. By that time, many Americans were sharply critical of the Bush administration's decision-making.

Michael Moore's film made several other points that later became well-recognized. *Fahrenheit 9/11* drew attention to the Bush family's close ties to the Saudi royal family. The movie showed abuses against Iraqi prisoners by American guards. It revealed the devastation American-led war-making brought to Iraqi society. Moore's film noted that the U.S. Congress quickly endorsed the Patriot Act after the shock of 9/11. The filmmaker showed legislators did not adequately consider the measure's potential to undercut civil liberties in the name of national security. *Fahrenheit 9/11* also revealed that prominent individuals in America's news media did not exercise much critical judgment when they reported the Bush Administration's claims about Iraq during the lead-up to war.

Most Republicans did not react well to Moore's film when it was released in 2004. They sensed the movie could influence public opinion and undermine President George W. Bush's campaign for re-election. The conservative pollster Frank Luntz's survey, conducted in August 2004, revealed that potential. Luntz discovered that 37% of Republicans who watched a screening of *Fahrenheit 9/11* were unlikely to vote for Bush after watching the film. Defenders of the Bush Administration responded to this survey and other evidence of the movie's persuasive power with a vigorous counter-offensive. In numerous appearances on radio and television, Republican politicians denounced *Fahrenheit 9/11* and its creator.

Michael Moore hoped his movie would affect the outcome of the 2004 presidential election, saying, "I believe the film is going to bring hundreds of thousands of people to the polls who otherwise were not going to vote." But President George W. Bush won re-election in a close race. The efforts to create doubts about the movie evidently affected public opinion. It is difficult, however, to measure the film's overall impact. Perhaps *Fahrenheit 9/11*'s appearance in 2004 made the election closer than it would have been otherwise.

Michael Moore's effort to address serious issues in a partisan but humorous way had excited strong criticism when he released his first documentary film in 1989, *Roger & Me*, and these complaints appeared as well in 2004. Yet Moore's approach was later recognized as a successful technique for arousing the public's curiosity about the news, especially the interest of young Americans. Left-oriented comedians Jon Stewart and Stephen Colbert employed related strategies in their popular television shows. Also, in documentary feature films such as Morgan Spurlock's *Supersize Me* (2004) and Bill Maher's *Religulous* (2008) Moore's strategy of flavoring political commentary with humor was abundantly evident.

Michael Moore's influence extended, as well, to the conservatives' political camp. Figures on the right who were aware that *Fahrenheit 9/11* had the potential to wreck President George W. Bush's 2004 campaign used cinema to attack the leading Democratic presidential candidate in early 2008, Hillary Clinton. A conservative organization, Citizens United, planned to release a hard-hitting documentary, *Hillary: The Movie*, shortly before the Democrats' presidential primaries. The Federal Elections Commission ruled that broadcast of *Hillary: The Movie* on cable TV close to the time of primary elections violated terms of the McCain-Feingold Act. Citizens United appealed that judgment all the way to the U.S. Supreme Court and won in 2010. The Court's decision allowed generous contributions to political action committees. The ruling gave Michael Moore and other filmmakers on the left expanded possibilities for influencing elections with politically charged films. But the Supreme Court's decision also established opportunities for wealthy adversaries of progressive politics to fund movies with a political punch.

The controversies that swirled around *Fahrenheit 9/11* in 2004 revealed an important development in American cinema. They showed that a highly entertaining and agenda-driven documentary film could ignite public debates about major issues of the day. Since 2004, other strongly opinionated filmmakers, such as the directors of *Inside Job* (2010) and *Waiting for Superman* (2010) have aroused heated discussions. Michael Moore cleared a path for politically motivated artists by crafting provocative films about controversial topics such as *Roger & Me*, *Bowling for Columbine*, *Sicko*, and *Capitalism: A Love Story*. The most notable example of Moore's efforts to affect change through the persuasive power of cinema is *Fahrenheit 9/11*. That film showed how extremist Republican politics led the United States into a disastrous invasion and occupation of Iraq.

The Politics of *The Reagans* Movie

Relatively few Americans saw the CBS Television mini-series, *The Reagans*, when it was released in 2003 [a different, 2020 miniseries on television carried the same name]. A barrage of protests from Republicans and conservative groups evidently convinced CBS executives that the controversial series was more appropriate for a small, Showtime audience than a network broadcast.

Reagan supporters warned leading advertisers about *The Reagans* by dropping hints about a possible conservative boycott of CBS programming. Their success in frightening executives at CBS revealed that intimidation worked in the entertainment industry. Political partisans managed to block a dramatic presentation of history they did not like. These actions served the cause of censorship. Of course, critics of the television series did not acknowledge that their actions represented an assault on freedom of speech. Instead, they claimed to be champions of "accurate" and "balanced" depiction of history.

Ed Gillespie, chairman of the Republican National Committee, complained *The Reagans* contained language that Ronald Reagan never actually used, and they objected to the film's critical portrayal of the former president.[64] Gillespie asked CBS to allow Reagan's associates to examine the film for historical accuracy before broadcast. Otherwise, said Gillespie, the network should place a disclaimer on the screen every ten minutes advising viewers that the drama contained fictional material.

If filmmakers were to follow Gillespie's recommendations, just about every historical drama would be off-limits for Hollywood and network television. "Docudrama" is, by its very nature, interpretive. Dramatic representations of the past *always* contain inventions because the creators of these films must imagine conversations and actions that have not been recorded. Also, the films are unbalanced because artists can never represent an entire life in their portrayals. They must select examples, and those choices reflect judgments.

Since the time of Shakespeare's historical plays, virtually all docudramas have offered hard-hitting, opinionated viewpoints. Most films and television dramas that excited public interest in history delivered partisan portrayals of events and people. They were all "controversial" in some way. "Roots," the influential television series that aroused the American public's interest in the history of slavery, portrayed most blacks as noble and depicted most white characters in the story as exploitative.

The Reagans contained information that could please both enthusiasts and detractors. A reporter who saw the script indicated that it showed the president's political skills and commitment to his beliefs and gave him credit for ending the Cold War. On the other hand, it highlighted his forgetfulness and inadequate management of his staff, and it portrayed his wife, Nancy, as an influential First Lady who sought advice on policy matters from astrologers. Since 2003, several books about Reagan's presidency described these characteristics.

Republicans were particularly angry about a line in the script that suggested Ronald Reagan was not motivated to act aggressively when the AIDS crisis appeared. In the miniseries the president says, "They that live in sin shall die in sin." After much protest, CBS agreed to remove the offending statement, but the comment was not completely out of character. Edmund Morris, a Reagan biographer who shadowed the president at the White House, reported Reagan said, "Maybe the Lord brought down this plague" because "illicit sex is against the Ten Commandments."

Did critics of the CBS mini-series feel that the only truthful portrait of Reagan was a saintly and heroic one? Must all dramas about Thomas Jefferson, author of the Declaration of Independence, overlook his ownership of slaves? Should filmmakers crafting films about FDR or JFK avoid reference to their dalliances with women? Should historical novels present only inspiring depictions of national figures? The emphasis on positive portrayals suggested by Gillespie and his colleagues could produce a sterile and limited understanding of history.

Some critics insisted docudramas should concentrate on stories about the deceased, not living figures such as Ronald and Nancy Reagan. If that requirement applied, we would need to wait decades before seeing dramas about prominent people in modern life. The complaints leveled by Gillespie and others did not constitute noble efforts to ensure fair treatment of historical subjects. They represented a form of intimidation. The protesters did not agree with the point of view offered by CBS Television's docudrama, and they wished to prevent broadcast of the mini-series. Censorship was not sanctioned in television broadcasting in 2003, but the actions of Gillespie and others came close to suppressing communication of historical interpretation. Gillespie and other GOP leaders took an extremist position against artistic expression.

Attacks on Films About Hillary Clinton: Threats to Free Expression

Reince Priebus, Chairman of the Republican National Committee, told NBC and CNN television executives that he would request that his party shut the two networks out of the GOP's presidential debates during the 2016 primary race. Priebus issued the threat because NBC had a drama in production about Hillary Clinton and CNN planned to release a documentary film about her. The GOP chairman pointed out that Mrs. Clinton was the Democrats' likely candidate for president in 2016. By depicting her life and activities, these movies might bolster Mrs. Clinton's fortunes in the next presidential race. Others, including several GOP state party chairmen, warned that the two film productions could influence voters. They stressed that television networks with reputations for objectivity should not sponsor films that masqueraded as unbiased productions. [65]

These critics of NBC and CNN spoke about film as if it is fundamentally different from print journalism. But in 1952, a unanimous decision of the U.S. Supreme Court in the "Miracle" case gave filmmakers rights like those enjoyed by writers. The Court placed filmmaking under the protective umbrella of the First Amendment. In subsequent decisions the Court expanded that understanding. Justices treated filmmaking as a form of speech. They maintained that filmmakers deserve rights of free expression as do authors of books and articles.

Moviemakers are no longer encumbered by the kind of censorship that was in place until the 1950s, yet they sometimes encounter informal types of speech suppression. Warnings issued by Reince Priebus and other critics reflected that different, more subtle kind of pressure.

Individual films released by the television networks do not constitute official or corporate endorsements of candidates or famous persons. Instead, they are the interpretations by specific artists who operate as subcontractors. Those movies, when they deal with history or politics, deliver cinematic op-eds. In the case of CNN's documentary film about Hillary Clinton, the network assigned director Charles Ferguson to operate as the film's principal "author." Ferguson was well-known for a hard-hitting documentary film about the 2008 financial crisis, *Inside Job* (2010). That production criticized *both* Presidents George W. Bush and Barack Obama for failing to challenge powerful financial interests. Charles Ferguson's filmic op-ed about Mrs. Clinton had the potential to be critical of its subject as well as supportive.

Maureen Dowd of the *New York Times* discussed issues raised by Priebus. Dowd pointed to the unusual power of movies to influence viewers. "Films can dramatically alter the way famous people are viewed," she observed. Movies make their subjects quite glamorous and sympathetic (or quite unsympathetic). "Clever filmmakers can offer up delicious soufflés of propaganda and storytelling, putting a new imprint on the historical record."[66] True. But if movies, documentary films, and op-eds in newspapers are forms of speech, what is the problem? Don't journalists, too (like Dowd, an influential columnist) "alter the way famous people are viewed" and present "delicious soufflés of propaganda and storytelling"? Surely some of Dowd's columns "put a new imprint on the historical record."

Priebus and other critics of NBC's and CNN's filmmaking plans characterized moviemakers as significantly more influential than speakers on television and radio and print journalists. Mika Brzezinski communicated that impression when speaking about the controversy on television's *Morn-*

ing Joe. She suspected NBC's movie about Hillary Clinton could impact the 2016 election.[67]

It could. But news stories, op-eds, radio broadcasts, and numerous other statements about politics can also make an impact on elections. Filmmakers do not have the last word or necessarily the most influential word about politics. Each cinematic artist contributes one among many voices in the nation's ongoing political conversations.

Why did Reince Priebus apply pressure against the NBC and CNN productions?

Perhaps his efforts aimed to excite the conservative base's agitation over supposed liberal bias in the mainstream media. Perhaps his protest aimed to discredit Hillary Clinton, as Republicans did in 2012 through accentuated criticism of the State Department's handling of the tragic incident in Benghazi, Libya. Or, perhaps, he aimed to influence the movies' interpretation. An outpouring of protest could leave executives at NBC and CNN eager to head off criticism by encouraging more negative assessments of Hillary Clinton. A manufactured controversy might serve, as well, to leave television viewers with an impression that the NBC and CNN films were grossly biased.

Whatever the RNC Chairman's purpose, his pressure tactics were troubling. Movies, too, are essential contributors to the public's thinking about American democracy. They play an important role in the "marketplace of ideas."

The Caine Mutiny: A Movie GOP Leaders Should Have Watched in 2016

When Republican leaders worried that Donald Trump, a reckless candidate, was emerging as the GOP's front-runner in the GOP's 2016 primaries, they found themselves in a dilemma much like U.S. Navy officers faced in an old Hollywood movie, *The Caine Mutiny*. Numerous Republican leaders wanted to replace their flawed and troublesome candidate with a more respectable, mainstream politician. If they called for that controversial action, however, they would face extraordinary backlash.

The story in *The Caine Mutiny* (1954) was relevant to problems faced by establishment Republicans in 2016. The movie features Humphrey Bogart as the skipper of an American ship during World War II. Lieutenant Commander Queeg appears rigidly authoritarian and emotionally unbalanced. During a storm at sea, officers conclude Queeg's faulty leadership puts the ship and crew at risk. They relieve him of command. During a court martial, Queeg's nervous testimony leaves an impression that the officers' rebellious action was appropriate. But later, in a riveting scene, a lawyer that successfully defended the mutineers confesses to a guilty conscience. He blames the officers for turning on Queeg rather than helping him. They took advantage of Queeg, he charges, and had a role in his downfall.

Much like the officers who wrestled with the idea of removing Queeg from command, many leaders in the Republican Party wanted to remove Trump in 2016. In view of Trump's behavior during the primary races, his critics in the GOP had a stronger case for removal than Navy officers in *The Caine Mutiny*. Humphrey Bogart's movie character has some redeeming qualities, including long-term experience in naval operations. Donald Trump did not have experience in governance when he campaigned in 2016. Trump lacked the temperament and emotional stability to serve as president and commander in chief of the armed forces.

The reasons for growing disaffection with Trump inside the GOP were clear in 2016. Donald Trump's comments alienated women, Hispanics, blacks, and Muslims. He had been vindictive when dealing with prominent individuals that criticized or displeased him. Especially troubling, Trump engaged in a nasty public feud over remarks made by the father of a fallen Muslim American soldier. Trump's organization refused to admit journalists to campaign rallies because they had written critical articles about that situation. Trump also alarmed GOP officials by criticizing two prominent Republicans, Senator John McCain and Speaker of the House, Paul Ryan.

Donald Trump's controversial statements about domestic matters were troubling enough, but his comments on foreign policy intensified feelings of alarm. Trump raised questions about US support for NATO, seemed unaware of Russian aggression in Ukraine, and appeared to justify Russia's takeover of Crimea.

Worries about Trump's capacity to serve as commander in chief related especially to his comments about nuclear weapons and nuclear warfare. Trump asked a military adviser, "If we have [nuclear weapons}, why can't we use them?" Trump said he would not rule out nuclear strikes in Europe or the Middle East, and he wanted Japan and other nations to possess nukes. Tony Schwartz, ghostwriter for Trump's book, *The Art of the Deal*, offered a shocking assessment based on a lengthy business relationship with Donald Trump. "I genuinely believe," said Schwartz, "that if Trump is to get the nuclear codes, there is an excellent possibility it will lead to the end of civilization."

At the foundation of these criticisms was speculation that Trump was emotionally unstable. Pundits conjectured about a "narcissistic" or "paranoid" personality. Some prominent figures, including President Barack Obama, took the unusual step of calling Trump "unfit" for the job. Liberal columnist Eugene Robinson said he used to think Trump was "being crazy like a fox," but became "increasingly convinced that he's just plain crazy."

Commentators associated with right-oriented politics sounded warning bells as well. Like Navy officers in *The Caine Mutiny*, they claimed the Queeg-like candidate should not have his hands on the Ship of State's steering wheel. Conservative pundit Charles Krauthammer said Trump exhibited "an infantile hunger for approval and praise, a craving that never can be satisfied." Krauthammer noted that prominent figures questioned the candidate's "psychological stability, indeed sanity . . ." Robert Kagan, a foreign policy analyst who advised Republicans, characterized Trump as "dangerously unstable." If Trump became president, Kagan warned, his "self-destructive tendencies would play out on the biggest stage in the world, with consequences at home and abroad that one can hardly begin to imagine." Fifty senior Republican national security officials signed a letter that warned Trump "would be the most reckless president in American history."

Like officers in *The Caine Mutiny*, discontented Republicans faced huge challenges. If they backed a rebellion, there would be severe blowback. Donald Trump received enthusiastic support from millions of voters in the primaries. If GOP leaders tried to remove him, angry partisans would say party elites rejected their votes. Trump might react by supporting claims about a conspiracy to deny him a victory. The resulting dispute could tear the Republican Party to pieces.

Does the movie's final message about broader responsibility for a leader's behavior have any relevance to the GOP's situation during the 2016 primary races? In *The Caine Mutiny* Commander Queeg is not the sole threat to the ship's security. The story suggests top officers on the Caine also are to blame for the crisis in leadership.

In 2016 several pundits charged the GOP's movers and shakers with creating a political environment in which a candidate like Trump could flourish. *Washington Post* columnist E. J. Dionne, Jr. made that case in an op-ed. Trump "is first and foremost the product of a Republican Party that has exploited extremism since President Obama took office," argued Dionne.[68] Many among the GOP's elite failed to denounce Trump's nativism, racism, and sexism, he pointed out. For too many years the party's elite promoted an economic message favorable to big business leaders. They gave inadequate attention to the economic struggles of ordinary Americans. Dionne suggested the GOP's problem was larger than Trump, and it would remain significant long after the 2016 election.

E. J. Dionne's analysis was pertinent. Alarmed establishment Republican leaders had substantive reasons to oppose Trump's ascendancy in their party's race for the presidential nomination. They saw clearly that Trump was likely to shatter political traditions, push the Republican Party in troublesome new directions, and act like an authoritarian. But it was too late to affect the outcome of the party's nomination process. A "mutiny" would not be tolerated by Trump's growing base of supporters. Preventing a rebellious candidate like Trump from hijacking the party would have required development of a different political culture in the GOP long before the shock waves of 2016 occurred.

SIX

CONSERVATISM TURNS RADICAL

An excellent book about problems related to modern conservatism and the modern Republican Party presented its thesis directly in the title: Rule and Ruin: The Downfall of Moderation and the Destruction of the Republican Party. *The book's author, Geoffrey Kabaservice, asked how American politics became "unmoored from what once was called the Vital Center." Moderate Republicanism, he noted, largely disappeared. Radicals transformed the Republican Party into an organ of an extreme conservative ideology. They purged the GOP "of all who resisted the true faith."*[69]

This chapter provides examples of the problem Kabaservice described. The first analysis explores implications of the "true faith." It notes that radical conservatism began to resemble fundamentalist religiosity. The second analysis points to militant Republicans' firm resistance to numerous proposals for reform. The GOP's ideologically driven rejection of governmental action blocked efforts to address major societal problems.

The Right's Political Religion

In 2005 Robert Reich, who had been Secretary of Labor in Bill Clinton 's administration, criticized radical conservatives in a book, *Reason: Why Liberals Will Win the Battle for America*. Reich complained about extreme partisans on the right that talked like they possessed a monopoly on truth.

They express "fervent certainty that they're correct and necessary, and [show] disdain for those who disagree," observed Reich. These political opinions had the "same intoxicating quality" that religion has to a fundamentalist, he noted. Facts are not especially relevant. "Judgments have to be accepted as a matter of faith."[70]

Robert Reich made a relevant point when likening the world view of militant conservativism to religious fundamentalism. Radical rightists often demonstrate a tenacious commitment to preconceived ideas, the teachings of their creed. They point to a respected canon, praising books for key insights and treating them like scriptures. Radical conservatives admire luminaries that identify tenets of their belief system – political wise men and women that serve like priests, pastors, rabbis, or mullahs of a political faith.

A comparison of political fundamentalism with religious fundamentalism does not imply hostility toward religious belief. The point that Reich made and that many other commentators stress is that belief, faith, and certainty are not well-suited for addressing political issues. Evangelicals and other religious groups are not singularly responsible for conservative stands on secular issues. Commentators and politicians on the right frequently express fundamentalist-style viewpoints about free-market economics, stands in the culture wars, and positions on international affairs. Faith is a respected quality regarding personal religious conviction, but faith is problematic when applied to complex political topics.

It is intriguing to examine comments by thoughtful and influential political analysts of modern American conservatism and Republican politics. Some of these observers point to resemblances in the Right's rhetoric to religious faith. Even though these writers do not expressly argue that fervent conservatives act like pious religionists, they invoke related language. The terms they employ suggest that intense belief is a distinctive characteristic of modern conservative thinking, especially in its radical forms. These analysts conclude, as well, that fundamentalism is far more characteristic of attitudes in the Republican Party than in the Democratic Party.[72]

One of the most influential books published early in the twenty-first century that employed religious terms is journalist Thomas Frank's *What's the Matter with Kansas: How Conservatives Won the Heart of America* (2004). Frank wrote about "true believers" who were driven by contempt for supposedly powerful and wicked representatives of liberalism. When these conservatives sought support for their cause, he observed, they proselytize "one convert at a time." Frank pointed out that "Conservatives often speak of a conversion experience, a quasi-religious revelation." Once these individuals become committed, they embrace a worldview that appears to provide all-inclusive answers to life's problems. "Everything fits together, everything has its place . . . in the awesome clarity of the conservative vision." Thomas Frank explained that much like splintering religious sects, advocates of this quasi-religious political outlook frequently engaged in angry grudges about doctrine. They excommunicated individuals in their movement that they judged guilty of "this or that bit of heresy or thought-er[73]"[73]

Fareed Zakaria, an astute observer of national and global affairs, pointed to the danger of treating politics like religious zealots. Describing conditions in the Middle East, Zakaria noted that political opponents of regimes in the region often employed the language of religion, with its claims about fundamental, unquestionable truths. "This combination of religion and politics has proven to be combustible," noted Zakaria. "Religion, at least the religion of the Abrahamic traditions (Judaism, Christianity and Islam), stresses moral absolutes." But politics, wrote Zakaria, "is all about compromise." The consequence of a religion-like approach to debates about governance in the Middle East "has been a ruthless winner-take-all attitude toward political life." . . .[74]

In the 1980s, 1990s and early 2000s, other commentators employed religious analogies when describing right-wing thinking. Michael Lind, who had worked inside the conservative movement before abandoning it, noted that rightists often promoted an extreme philosophy of laissez faire. They treated the concept as a Holy Word passed down from the heavens. "American conservatives have adopted free-market fundamentalism, in its crudest forms, as their political religion," reported Lind.[75] David Brock, who also worked on the right before abandoning the conservative movement and attacking it, noticed conservatives displayed a "religious-like faith and fervor" when criticizing President Bill Clinton.[76] Journalists Daniel J. Balz and

Ronald Brownstein observed that hatred toward federal power had become an "article of faith" for many partisans on the right. A contemptuous attitude toward the state was central to "the new conservative catechism."[77] Sidney Blumental, a journalist, and later adviser to President Clinton, observed that conservatives' battles over political doctrine sounded like disputes between religious factions that splintered over interpretations of their canon. Each group acted like a "sect mobilized around its own internally consistent theoretical system," said Blumenthal.[78]

Fundamentalist-style rhetoric promoted a zero-sum political perspective. By treating political conflict like a religious struggle, many politicians on the right expressed disdain for "liberals" and "progressives." They portrayed struggles with the opposing party as fights-to-the-finish, take-no-prisoners battles against contemptible enemies. Vanquishing Democrats seemed justified in view of the frightening ideas the radical right associated with the despised "left." Religious-like rhetoric contributed to the growth of Republican extremism.

The RepubliCAN'T Party

Republican legislators and their supporters in the national media often refer to the "Democrat Party." If they used proper English, they would speak about the *Democratic* Party. They have a purpose in distorting the name. By abbreviating, they alter the meaning. References to the "Democrat Party" cancel positive images associated with "democratic." *Democrat* Party has a harsh sound. It rhymes with Autocrat (a ruler that exploits absolute power) and Plutocrat (someone whose power and influence derives from extraordinary wealth). Republicans that incorporate references to the Democrat Party knowingly apply poor English to promote negative impressions.

Democrats are generally silent on this matter. They do not challenge the insult. Ignoring it has not brought a reduction in verbal aggression. In fact, Republicans' comments about the "Democrat Party" became *more* common, in recent years, not less.

There is a way for Democrats to deal with the slur. When Republicans employ the term in political discussions, Democrats can react with references to the RepubliCAN'T Party. It is appropriate that Democrats react that way. This is not simply a matter of matching one abuse with another. The two examples of name-manipulation are different. References to the "Democrat Party" *do not imply anything* about the Democrats' positions on substantive issues. References to the RepubliCAN'T Party *are* relevant. They communicate an accurate assessment of GOP stands on important ideas and policies.

The "RepubliCANT Party" often tries to *avoid* governance. It frequently opposes bills that support robust federal action in domestic affairs. Republicans champion spending on the military for national defense, but they often turn their backs on proposals for action in the domestic sphere. Republicans view the private sector, not the public one, as the appropriate venue for achieving progress. They assume American society will improve enormously if the federal government gets out of the way and lets free markets flourish. Ronald Reagan expressed that outlook in his first inaugural address, arguing, "Government is not the solution to our problem; government *is* the problem." Grover Norquist, an influential adviser to Republicans on tax policy made his point with a touch of sadistic humor. He said, "I just want to shrink [government] down to size where we can drown it in the bathtub."

Republicans fight hard to win elections, acting like they are eager to govern. Once in Washington, however, they often rejected calls for legislative action. In many respects, the GOP became the party of NO. Mitch McConnell, longtime Republican leader in the Senate, was a key spokesperson for the strategy. He marshalled almost total party opposition to President Barack Obama's agenda. Later McConnell wanted to stymie President Joe Biden's programs as well. McConnell liked to refer to himself as the Grim Reaper – the one who held the scythe leading to the chamber where the Democrats' proposals from the House of Representatives went to die.

On many issues, Republicans governed like an anti-government party. They did not have a strong domestic program. They favored a negative one that was designed to shrink the government by cutting taxes and eliminating regulations.

At the Republican National Convention in 2020, GOP leaders showed how extensively this approach to governing had become. They refused to honor a longstanding political tradition. Normally, party leaders publish a "platform" that identifies stands on key issues. In 2020, the GOP did not offer one. Journalist Annie Lowery drew attention to the party's lack of issues and programs in *The Atlantic*. The title of her article, "The Party of No Content," identified the problem.[79]

Calling the GOP the RepubliCAN'T Party succinctly communicates the idea that it became a party of no content. The appellation is appropriate because Republicans have long resisted addressing serious problems.

Here are just a few examples. On some of these issues, just a few Republicans registered support. On others 100% of GOP legislators rejected proposals for action to deal with major problems that needed attention.

- When asked to support the Affordable Care Act, which assisted millions of uninsured Americans, Republicans responded No, **can't** do it.

- When asked to put millions of undocumented immigrants on a path to citizenship, including children that grew up in the USA, the GOP"s response was, no, **can't** do it.

- Asked to support the Consumer Financial Protection Bureau after the financial crisis of 2008 revealed numerous abuses, Republicans responded, **can't** do it.

- Asked to support nationwide election reforms to expand and protect citizens' right to vote, Republicans said, **can't** do it.

- When asked to back campaign finance reform to prevent "dark money" from "buying" candidates and elections, Republicans responded, **can't** do it.

- Asked to support environmental measures to protect the planet and its people, Republicans responded, **can't** do it.

- Asked to protect citizens from another Great Recession by supporting the Dodd-Frank Financial reforms, Republicans said, **can't** do it.

- When asked to back the American Recovery and Reinvestment Act (the "stimulus") to help families and businesses recover from the financial crash of 2008, the GOP responded, **can't** do it.

- Asked to back a large infrastructure bill to address long-neglected projects, Republicans responded, **can't** do it.

- When asked to support background checks on gun purchases, Republicans responded, **can't** do that.

- When asked to deal boldly with storms, floods, droughts, and fires that have become more common and intense because of climate change, the GOP's response was, **can't** do it.

- Asked to raise the federal minimum wage above the ridiculously low rate of $7.25 per hour, Republicans said, **can't** do it.

The term RepubliCAN'T Party is more than just an amusing way to counter remarks by politicos that inappropriately talk about the "Democrat Party." RepubliCAN'T is a relevant appellation. On far too many issues Republicans failed to recognize that governing involves more than shouting "No" when bills are introduced to deal with significant societal challenges. The GOP could govern more effectively if it exhibited a positive attitude about leadership in Washington. It could serve the American people better if it recognized that government has the potential to make useful contributions to American society.

The GOP's distorted view has been prominent since the 1980s. President Reagan's message that government "is the problem" and his joke that "The nine most frightening words in the English language are, 'I'm from the government, and I'm here to help'" set the tone. In recent years Republicans have articulated negative views often. They spoke critically and contemptuously about the federal government and promised to diminish its role in U.S. society. They called for shrinking federal agencies, removing "bureaucrats," and abolishing regulations. When campaigning for reelection, they boasted about successes in downsizing government.

Republicans presented a profoundly negative view of governance. They defined progress almost solely in terms of reducing the federal government's role in the lives of the American people. This constricted view of political leadership ignored a more fundamental responsibility of officials serving in Washington. Those leaders needed, of course, to challenge burdensome governmental intrusions into citizen's affairs. But elected officials had responsibilities to the American community as well, not just to individuals.

A key leader in the early Republican Party, Abraham Lincoln, stated this balance memorably. Lincoln said, "The legitimate object of Government is to do for a community of people whatever they need to have done but cannot do at all, or cannot so well do, for themselves in their separate and individual capacities. But in all that people can individually do as well for themselves, Government ought not to interfere." When another great Republican, President Dwight D. Eisenhower, ran for reelection 1956, the GOP called Lincoln's words "the great truth" in the party's "Declaration of Faith."[80]

Today's Republicans would be wise to remember Lincoln and Eisenhower's message. It is not enough to apply the wrecking ball to the government. Leaders in Washington need to put government to work solving problems.

SEVEN

THE PSYCHOLOGY OF TRUMP AND MAGA

Not surprisingly, psychologists, psychiatrists, and other health profes-
sionals had a lot to say about Donald Trump's mind and behavior as well as
the loyalty of his MAGA followers. In The Dangerous Case of Donald Trump,
27 medical professionals concluded that Trump's mental health posed a "clear
and present danger" to the nation.[81] *In* Too Much and Never Enough: How
My Family Created the World's Most Dangerous Man, *Mary Trump, a clin-*
ical psychologist and Trump's niece, called her uncle a textbook narcissist.[82] *In*
numerous articles, journalists have tried to explain why so many Americans
remained loyal to Trump despite his disruptive and flawed leadership.

The following analyses draw upon ideas from psychology to explain the
man and his acolytes. The first points to Trump's intense hostility toward his
predecessor at the White House, Barack Obama. President Trump displayed
such intense determination to overturn accomplishments of the Obama admin-
istration that it is intriguing to inquire about the source of his animus. Study of
Donald Trump's emotional response to an embarrassing moment in his personal
life – a situation involving Obama -- may explain much of that hostility. The
next analyses seek insights on politics from two of the most famous research
investigations in the field of social psychology. These studies from the 1950s

and 1960s may help explain why so many members of the GOP's base adored Trump and believed his lies.

Strange Obsession: Trump's Obama Complex

Journalists were astonished when President Donald Trump took verbal shots at President Obama (without naming him) in a speech intended to de-escalate a conflict with Iran on January 8, 2020. In that kind of international crisis, U.S. presidents ordinarily encourage a united American front. Yet Trump's remarks had a *disuniting* effect. President Trump presented a sharply negative judgment about Obama's leadership. He criticized Obama's "very defective" and "foolish Iran nuclear deal." Trump claimed missiles fired by Iran at bases housing U.S. troops were financed "with funds made available by the last administration." That statement suggested blood would be on Obama's hands if Americans died in the bombings. Journalists said it was unusual for a president to lash out at his predecessor when delivering an important foreign policy message that needed broad public support.

The journalists should not have been surprised. Trump publicly berated Barack Obama on numerous occasions. While his dislike of Obama was complex, his behavior at the 2011 White House Correspondents' Dinner revealed a potential source of his hostility.

Prior to that event Donald Trump maintained that Barack Obama had not been born in the United States and therefore was ineligible to be president of the United States. When President Obama stepped up to deliver a humorous monologue at the April 11 event, he saw an opportunity to poke fun at the champion of this false claim. Referring to rumors that Donald Trump might run for president someday, Obama pointed to Trump's limited leadership experience as TV host of *Celebrity Apprentice*. Then Obama referred to recently published documentation confirming his U.S. birth. Now that the birther claim was put to rest, Obama teased, Trump could focus on "issues that matter – like, did we fake the moon landing?" Comedian Seth Meyers piled on. "Donald Trump has been saying he'll run for president as a Republican," noted Meyers," which is surprising, since I just assumed he was running as a joke."[83]

Commentators in the national media interpreted the situation as public humiliation. They observed that Trump did not smile. He appeared angry. When asked about the event later, Trump scolded Meyers for being "too nasty, out of order" but said he enjoyed the attention. From that time on, though, Trump's references to Obama became more contemptuous. Trump made several statements in 2011 claiming Obama might attack Iran to boost his chances in the next presidential election.

A suggestion that President Trump's contempt for Barack Obama played a role in America's troubles with Iran is, of course, a matter of speculation. But there is context for considering the idea. Throughout his presidential campaign and years in the White House from early 2017 to early 2021, Donald Trump delivered numerous verbal beatings to supposed villains.

Just about anyone who criticized Trump became a target. President Trump ridiculed Hillary Clinton, Adam Schiff, and Nancy Pelosi. Heroic and much-admired individuals received the president's wrath, as well, including Senator John McCain, aviator, and POW in the Vietnam War, and Khizr Khan, whose son, a U.S. soldier in Iraq, died protecting his men from a suicide bomber. Even the 16-year-old climate activist Greta Thunberg received insults. Thunberg's offense? Staring down President Trump at a UN meeting on climate change. Donald Trump expressed scorn towards numerous people who criticized him, but no public figure was as consistent a mark for contempt as Barack Obama, the former president.

Trump's long record of lambasting Barack Obama evidently revealed deep-seated enmity. Ordinarily, U.S. presidents do not speak much about their predecessors, but when they do, the references tend to be positive. Trump, by contrast, referred to Obama often and in a disparaging way. CNN analyst Daniel Dale calculated that Trump mentioned Obama's name 537 times in the first 10 months of 2019. "For whatever reason," observed Fernando Cruz, who served both Obama and Trump at the National Security Council, "President Trump has fixated on President Obama, and I think that he views President Obama as a metric he has to beat." Peter Nicholas, who covered the White House for *The Atlantic*, said, "a guiding principle of Trump's White House has been simply: 'If Obama did it, undo it.'"[84]

Trump hammered President Obama's domestic initiatives. He tried to terminate Obama's signature achievement, the Affordable Care Act (its popular name, "Obamacare," provided an attractive target). Trump also undermined the Obama administration's environmental initiatives. President Trump reversed Obama's efforts to move energy consumption away from coal, and Trump opened national parks for commercial and mining activity, rejecting the protections Obama promoted. He mocked Obama's support of wind power and rolled back regulations for oil and gas production, including standards for methane gas emission.

In foreign affairs President Trump abandoned his predecessor's efforts to bring nations together to fight climate change, and he rejected Obama's plans for a trans-Pacific trade deal. Trump also scratched Obama's programs for improved relations with Cuba.

The most notable attack on Obama's legacy in international affairs came in May 2018 when President Trump began pulling the U.S. out of the nuclear accord with Iran. Trump ignored advice from members of his national security team that supported the agreement. The accord had been working. Iranians complied with its terms, placing nuclear programs on hold in return for a promise of reduced sanctions. President Trump blasted the accord as "the worst deal ever." His actions led Iran to reinstate nuclear development. In a brief time, Trump managed to smash effective security arrangements that had the backing of the UK, Russia, France, China, and Germany.

The reasons for Donald Trump's major decisions appear shrouded in mystery. Why did President Trump try to obliterate Obamacare but offer no well-conceived substitute? Why did he abandon the Iran nuclear deal but provide no alternative that foreign policy experts considered effective? Perhaps Trump's rejection of these and other important measures did not reflect disagreement about policy details. Maybe Trump objected to them because they symbolized the goals and accomplishments of Barack Obama.

There can be no certainty about the emotional impact of Donald Trump's unpleasant experience at the White House Correspondents' Dinner on April 11, 2011. Musings about the connection must remain speculative. Not even well-trained psychologists or psychiatrists can provide definitive judgments about the significance. Nevertheless, Donald Trump's lengthy and extensive record of negative comments about his predecessor is so unusual that the possibility of a connection to the event of 2011 is intriguing.

Why Did Many Republicans Refuse to Accept the Election Results? Research by a Psychologist Long Ago Suggested an Answer

Surveys taken several days after the 2020 presidential election showed that most Republicans believed Trump really won the election. A Reuters/Ipsos opinion poll reported on November 18, fifteen days after the presidential election, that 52% of Republicans thought Trump won. Later surveys indicated that between 70% and 80% of Republicans did not accept reports of Biden's victory. They thought the election was rigged and claimed fraud tipped the balance in Biden's favor.

Why did so many Republicans refuse to acknowledge overwhelming evidence that confirmed Joe Biden's victory? Millions of Republicans continued to accept myths about a stolen election. Facts did not influence their judgment. Evidence didn't shake beliefs.

Obviously, Trump influenced the thinking of many Republicans. Trump frequently asserted that he won. He claimed there had been a mysterious disappearance of ballots, and manipulation of tallies indicated fraud. Commentators on Fox News and many other right-oriented media sources backed his specious claims. But there may be an explanation from the field of psychology that explains the reluctance of many Republican voters to accept facts related to the election.

University of Michigan psychologist Christopher Peterson referred to this psychological research when discussing a rumor that spread across the Internet in 2011. The message claimed the world would end at 6 PM on May 21, 2011. After the projected date passed without a calamity, several people refused to recognize they'd been duped. "How many folks acknowledge that they were mistaken when the ensuing facts stare them in the face?" Peterson asked. Some do but many do not, he reported. "People will go to great lengths to maintain consistency among their beliefs, even when they prove to be blatantly wrong."

Christopher Peterson based this interpretation on research by a famous psychologist who conducted groundbreaking investigations in the 1950s. Leon Festinger developed the concept of Cognitive Dissonance, which suggested why some people hold firmly to beliefs when confronted with contradictory evidence. An investigation that helped launch his theory related to a group of people that believed a Chicago woman's prediction that a great flood would destroy the world on December 21st. When the disaster did not occur, many followers did not acknowledge they had been misled. They accepted the cult leader's explanation that God spared them because of their devotion, commitment, and actions. Rather than acknowledge they had been wrong, those true believers turned more faithful. They attempted to persuade others, trying to broaden membership in the cult.

Leon Festinger followed up this study (published in a book with other scholars, *When Prophesy Fails*) with several experiments that demonstrated the significance of Cognitive Dissonance.[85] When confronted with contradictory information, Festinger observed, individuals often feel uncomfortable. Their personal beliefs or hopes are contradicted by hard facts. People reduce that dissonance (inconsistency) by avoiding situations or information that intensifies their discomfort. Especially when individuals have deep convictions and take significant actions in support of them, they are reluctant to question cherished ideas. If they are associated with a large group of people committed to the belief, their fidelity often becomes more intense. They find comfort in numbers.

Cognitive Dissonance appears to be a factor in the persistence of belief and loyalty displayed by many Republicans despite hard facts about Joe Biden's victories in the Electoral College and the popular vote. For years after the 2020 election, members of Trump's base enthusiastically accepted untruths disseminated by the admired leader. They were not inclined to challenge Trump's controversial statements and misrepresentations.

Those True Believers heard the former president and his enablers on television, radio, and the internet claiming information reported in the national media was false. To accept facts reported outside the partisan bubble could, indeed, produce the kind of emotional discomfort Festinger described. When dealing with the clash between internal beliefs and external realities, they kept the faith.

Furthermore, as Festinger showed, Trump's hard-core supporters discovered comfort in numbers. They proselytized, hoping to expand the size of their group and build an impression that their favored ideas enjoyed wide-spread acceptance. During the weeks of extensive media attention to Trump's fruitless legal and rhetorical efforts to deny Biden's victory, MAGA members tried to shore up their cause. They shared favorite reports on websites about supposed mischief in the tabulation of ballots, trying to legitimize claims they heard from Trump and the rightwing mass media.

Psychology cannot provide all the answers to an important question that fascinates pundits: Why did so many Republicans refuse to change their minds in the face of abundant factual evidence that contradicted their ideas about the presidential election? Insights developed long ago by psychologist Leon Festinger may explain, to some degree, why this puzzling behavior was prevalent.

A Psychologist's Experiment in the 1960s May Help Explain Why Millions of Trump's Followers Believed His Lies

Why did so many Republicans continue to believe the former president's lies about a stolen election? The most obvious explanations relate to efforts by GOP politicians and media celebrities to promote Trump's fallacious state-ment about the election. There is another, less recognized factor, however, that might provide clues for understanding the ideas and behavior of millions of Americans. Back in the 1960s, psychologist Stanley Milgram conducted experiments that showed ordinary people are surprisingly malleable when an individual playing the role of a figure in authority communicates instruc-tions. Milgram discussed his findings in a 1963 article and explored them in more detail in a book published in 1974, *Obedience to Authority: An Experimental View.*[86]

Stanley Milgram and his research team at Yale recruited volunteers for a "learning" experiment. Participants were males ranging in age from 20 to 50. The researchers asked them to instruct a learner to respond correctly to questions. The participants served as the teacher, and the learner was Milgram's confederate pretending to be a participant in the experiment. The individual directing the study wore a gray lab coat and appeared to be a social scientist. He played the role of a professional researcher.

After the confederate learner was strapped to a chair with electrodes, the faux scientist asked participants to administer levels of shock to the "learner" situated unseen in a separate room. Voltage shocks on a large machine gave the participant opportunities to increase voltage levels from 15 (a light shock) to 450 (danger-severe shock). Milgram's confederate, pretending to be the learner, did not truly receive electronic jolts, but he pretended to suffer from them. Milgram wanted to see how far people would go obeying instructions that seemingly could harm an individual.

Even though the participants could hear the fake learner screaming in pain, they followed orders from the individual pretending to be a social scientist. The man in the lab coat insisted they continue, even when the learner turned silent after pretending to experience great pain from high voltage. Two-thirds of the participants (65%) gave the "learner" the maximum, 450 volts. All participants were willing to apply shocks up to 300 volts.

Milgram and his researchers concluded that people tend to obey instructions if they regard the authority figure as morally right and/or legitimately based. People often act as directed when they perceive the person speaking to them is qualified to lead and takes responsibility for the consequences of decision-making.

In subsequent experiments, Milgram found that ordinary people in the United States of various ages and backgrounds behaved much like participants in his original studies. Additional experiments conducted by social scientists outside the United States brought related outcomes. Conformist behavior in the face of instructions by an authority figure seemed not to be a distinctly American characteristic. The effect occurred in diverse societies.

Do these experiments throw *some* light on the MAGA followers' adoration of Trump and their acceptance of Trump's leadership? Perhaps.

Donald Trump was the adored leader for his grassroots admirers. Millions of Trump's followers viewed him as a venerated authority figure. They approved of his messages, but they were also impressed that he held the nation's highest position, President of the United States. Trump's champions in right-wing television programming, talk radio shows, and internet communications invoked that title often. They identified Trump as *President* to accentuate his importance and legitimate his judgments.

Republican politicians and conservative media personalities were *supporting actors* in this political drama. They played important roles promoting the leader's messages, but they were not the principal *originators* of those communications. Trump was. The power of Trump's position as the GOP's chief authority figure was evident in the way he reacted to the 2020 election. Trump declared it invalid. If he had accepted results of the Electoral College, most Republicans in Washington and his backers in the media would have done the same.

Donald Trump's enormous influence over the right's power brokers and millions of admirers was evident days after the November 2020 presidential election. The electoral count was close, but eventually Fox News declared Biden the winner. For a brief time, Trump brooded in silence. Then he burst out in fighting spirit. Trump claimed the vote was marred by considerable fraud. Victory, he announced, had been stolen from him and the Americans that voted for him. He demanded justice. Quickly, many GOP politicians and right-wing media personalities joined Trump's cause. Recognizing that the former president still had millions of Americans in his camp, they, too, talked about a corrupt election.

By using their bully pulpits to spread false information, GOP officials and media celebrities betrayed millions of Trump's devotees. Authority figures in right-wing politics and news analysis vigorously defended Trump.

Despite his defeat, they enabled Trump to reclaim his position as hero of the masses.

It is not surprising that millions of MAGA followers remained loyal to Donald Trump and accepted his "Big Lie." Like the faux scientist in Stanley Milgram's experiments, Trump had long acted like the GOP's vaunted leader, and numerous right-wing politicians and pundits fortified that perception. Their abundant praise encouraged millions of MAGA enthusiasts to view Trump as the esteemed leader of the United States. In many respects, they identified Trump in the fashion of the faux scientist in the Milgram experiment -- as a legitimate authority figure who assumed moral responsibility for the consequences of his actions. Trump appeared that way in large part because enablers had long characterized him an admirable and successful public servant.

Milgram's findings about "Obedience to Authority" throw some light on why many Americans believed the former president's mendacities.

EIGHT

LITE NEWS ON FOX

Many Americans expressed amazement that so many citizens did not have the same understanding that they had about political facts.

The following analyses focus on a few days when commentators in mainstream news programming gave extensive coverage to President Donald Trump's controversial statements and actions. On those days, millions of viewers that watched Fox News on television heard little or nothing about that news.

Fox's programming often obscured unflattering evidence about Republican politics. It obscured information reported in mainstream sources. Primetime commentaries on Fox often focused on topics that had already been addressed frequently in the network's programming.

These analyses question familiar criticisms of Fox's viewers. The analyses maintain that many Americans in Fox's audience sought a thorough understanding of current events. Programming on the network and in other strongly conservative media often failed to inform those curious citizens. Fox's programs did not expose viewers to facts that were widely presented and discussed in mainstream news media.

FOX MISLED TRUMP VOTERS

When Donald Trump stumbled through his presidency from 2017 to 2021, critics asked why so many Americans continued to back him despite mounting evidence of deeply flawed leadership. Often, those critics expressed frustration with the millions of Americans that constituted Trump's "base." They complained that Trump's supporters refused to acknowledge that the president's lying, ethical lapses, and failed policies harmed the nation. Donald Trump remained in power, those critics argued, because starry-eyed admirers ignore the facts.

Those critics cast blame in the wrong place. Trump's supporters didn't deserve all the censure directed at them. They did not create the pro-Trump narrative. They were its recipients. Conservative media had been influential in promoting glowing assessments of Trump's leadership. Fox News served as command-central for that positive perspective. It reached a large audience. In October 2018, according to Nielson's research, Fox racked up its 28th consecutive month as the No. 1 basic cable news channel. Fox drew more viewers at the time than CNN and MSNBC combined.[87]

Millions of Americans who wished to be informed about current events tuned in regularly to Fox. Once they became regular viewers, they tended to stick with the channel. The hosts and reporters on Fox News encouraged loyalty. Frequently, they made critical references to CNN (a favorite target) as well as CBS, ABC, NBC, MSNBC, the *New York Times,* and the *Washington Post.* They hinted that only Fox could be trusted. Don't look elsewhere for information, they warned, because "liberal" media hawked fake news.[88]

What kind of reporting did the Fox News viewership receive through primetime reporting and commentary?

Consider lessons viewers learned on Thursday, December 20, 2018, an extraordinary day of troubles for Trump's presidency. Leading print and television journalists outside of Fox expressed shock then that Trump suddenly announced plans to withdraw U.S. troops from Syria. They warned that an American exodus from the country could benefit the Russians, Syrians, Iranians, and Turks at the expense of Kurds that fought bravely against ISIS.

Military leaders and foreign policy experts blasted Trump's announcement as ill-advised and dangerous.

General Jim Mattis's decision to resign as Secretary of Defense also received abundant commentary that day. Mattis's letter of resignation communicated strong disagreement with the direction of U.S. foreign policy. General Mattis, in a clear rebuke of the president, noted that during his four decades of "immersion in the issues" he had learned the importance of treating allies with respect and "being clear-eyed about malign actors and strategic competitors." Both American and international leaders were alarmed that the general who seemed capable of taming the erratic president planned to leave his post.

On the home front, President Trump led congressional leaders to believe that a compromise was workable on funding for the government. But Trump suddenly reversed his position, insisting there would be no settlement unless Congress provided $5.7 billion for a border wall. On December 20 the stock market dropped sharply on this news and in response to other developments. The next day Republicans shut down the federal government. Wall Street closed with its worst week since the financial crisis of 2008. The crisis stretched for 34 days, making it the longest federal shutdown in history up to that time.

Mainstream journalists focused on the chaos associated with these developments. Several Republican leaders joined them in expressing concern, including Lindsay Graham and Bob Corker. Senate Majority leader Mitch McConnell backed compromises aimed at averting a government shutdown, but Trump and his backers in the Freedom Caucus made compromise unworkable.

Viewers of Fox News got almost no sense of this emergency when watching prime-time programming on the night of December 20. Shows hosted by Martha MacCallum, Tucker Carlson, Dan Bongino (sitting in for Sean Hannity) and Laura Ingraham directed viewers' attention to other matters. The programs focused on a subject that had already received extensive coverage on Fox in previous months and years: undocumented immigrants. Hosts and guests warned that dangerous foreigners threatened to overrun American society.

Even though the real "news" on December 20 was about struggles in Congress to keep the government running, Fox's prime-time programming highlighted stories about an immigrant invasion. Commentators asserted falsely that Democrats advocated "open borders." The TV hosts accentuated a report about a violent undocumented immigrant in California. In each program they and their guests left viewers with an impression that the big news of the day concerned security threats from dangerous aliens. Speakers praised President Trump for his determination to build a wall.

What other topics dominated the night's discussions on Fox, essentially eclipsing any discussion of the big stories of the day about the president's controversial actions and Republicans' threats to suspend many activities of the federal government?

Martha MacCallum's program featured a lengthy interview with Susan Collins. The senator from Maine talked at length about extremist critics of Brett Kavanaugh's nomination to the Supreme Court. Collins pointed out that some individuals harassed her in disgusting ways.

Tucker Carlson drew attention to the work of Robert Shibley, who maintained that America's universities had been pushing aggressively against free speech. Carlson also took shots at a "Climate Tax" and made fun of claims about Russian interference in American affairs. The main threat, he argued, was China.

Dan Bongino and his guests blasted Deputy Attorney General Rod Rosenstein's defense of the "so-called Russia investigation." Bongino praised a "terrific book" by Gregg Jarrett called *The Russia Hoax: The Illicit Scheme to Clear Hillary Clinton and Frame Donald Trump.*

Laura Ingraham, like the other prime-time hosts, devoted considerable time to immigration, but she encountered problems when a sheriff objected to some of her arguments. In an interview the sheriff acknowledged the difficulty of holding a violent undocumented man in California because of laws pertaining to sanctuary cities, but he noted that many immigrants in his community were good citizens and sought help from law enforcement when criminals troubled them. "That's a lie!" Ingraham responded. She ended the interview quickly by mentioning "violence, rape, burglary, robbery and other offenses against property and people."

A pattern in the reporting and commentary on Fox was evident in these four prime-time programs. By focusing on old news stories that had been red meat for years in right-oriented media commentary, there was little time left for an analysis of important news developments of the previous 24 hours. General Mattis's resignation letter hardly got a nod. The outcry by national and international leaders regarding President Trump's plan to withdraw from Syria received little or no attention. The impact of a government shutdown on the American economy was almost completely ignored. The hosts uttered hardly a word about the stock market's huge slide of recent days and weeks. Instead, viewers heard about scary threats from immigrants, Democrats, university administrators, and Chinese hackers. They were reminded often that President Trump had been fighting tenaciously for ordinary Americans.

Hosts and commentators seemed eager to please their most important viewer, the President of the United States. Most of them endorsed and celebrated Donald Trump's statements and actions. Dan Bongino, substituting as host for Sean Hannity, provided an example of the slant by promoting his co-authored book, *Spygate: The Attempted Sabotage of Donald J. Trump*.

The practice of diverting viewers' attention from news stories that undermined the network's favored narratives had been evident in Fox's broadcasting over many years. A decade and a half before, the channel sounded a drumbeat for war in program after program, convincing many viewers that Saddam Hussein had been responsible for the 9/11 tragedy, threatened the world with WMDs, including nukes, and needed to be removed though U.S. military intervention. On the same channel host Bill O'Reilly devoted considerable time to telling viewers about a "war on Christmas." Anti-religious forces were trying to replace "Merry Christmas" with "Happy Holidays," O'Reilly warned.

Complaints about Donald Trump's enthusiasts are often misplaced. Many citizens that were regular patrons of Fox News and other right-oriented programming wanted to be well-informed about current events. They took civic engagement seriously. Those listeners and viewers should have been more discerning, of course, but they were not fully to blame for making poorly informed judgments about national and international affairs. Fox News and other opinion sources on television, radio, and internet were responsible for some of grassroot Republicans' narrow and skewed viewpoints. Millions of Americans turned to the Fox News Channel and other sources, seeking knowledge about current events. They were betrayed by rightwing manipulators of mass communications.

Fox News Left Viewers Poorly Informed About the Coronavirus

During one of the most serious modern controversies in U.S. political history – debates about President Donald Trump's response to the pandemic -- popular prime-time programming on Fox News largely failed to provide information that explained what the controversy was about. The network's shows were problematic not only because of bias in reporting but also for what they left out. Fox's programs often ignored or obscured major questions that politicians and journalists raised about the president's leadership during a profound health crisis. This approach to the news had implications for American democracy. It left millions of viewers poorly prepared to render judgments about current affairs.

One example of this obfuscation of important controversies appeared in Fox's coverage of President Trump's enthusiasm in 2020 for hydroxychloroquine as a treatment for Covid-19. Trump suggested there were "some very strong signs" that this drug could work against the coronavirus. Hosts on Fox quickly joined Trump in championing hydroxychloroquine. Tucker Carlson described the antimalarial drug as a "potentially life-saving medicine." Laura Ingraham said it could be a "game changer." [89]

Then disturbing evidence came to light. Reports indicated that hydroxychloroquine was not a proven remedy for the coronavirus, and inappropriate use could bring sickness or death. Quickly, President Trump turned away from the subject in daily briefings, and several Fox hosts pivoted, as well. Yet Carlson and Ingraham continued to talk about the drug's potential. Unfortunately, many Americans had already responded to Trump's initial claims. Prescriptions of hydroxychloroquine surged.

Controversy did not end there. Days later, Dr. Rick Bright, director of a U.S. government office responsible for developing a vaccine for covid-19, reported that he had been forced out for complaining about inadequate government responses to his warnings and because he refused to endorse medicines such as hydroxychloroquine. This story received prominent coverage in television news programming. But not on Fox.

The network's most popular prime-time host, Sean Hannity, said nothing about the Bright case in his evening broadcast the day when the immunologist's revelation appeared in the headlines. Instead, Hannity accentuated themes that he addressed numerous times in previous broadcasts. During the hour, Hannity criticized China for its role in the pandemic, praised Trump for engineering a great medical mobilization, and bashed Democrats, especially Joe Biden and Alexandra Octavio Cortez. He devoted several minutes to mockery of Democratic House majority leader, Nancy Pelosi, because she playfully displayed her favorite gourmet ice cream on CBS's "Late Late Show." Viewers that depended only on Hannity's program for news on April 22, 2020, would be unlikely to know that a director of planning for the Covid-19 vaccine had been fired, evidently for political reasons.

President Trump then stepped deeper into political quicksand, and again, Fox ignored or obscured the story. During the president's evening news briefing the next day, Trump talked about injecting disinfectants inside people's bodies to protect them from the virus. Journalists and medical experts judged those comments dangerous. Spokespersons for Lysol and Clorox warned the public not to consume their products. A day later, Trump attempted to walk back his comments, claiming his aim was to express sarcasm toward reporters. It was clear from video recordings that the president was not delivering a truthful characterization of the situation.

The firestorm about injecting disinfectants threatened to undermine public confidence in the president's leadership. Staff at the White House sought to limit the political damage by urging Trump to limit his appearances at daily press events. Trump later tweeted that his involvement in the televised briefings was "not worth the time and effort." But he was soon back at the daily news events, trying to rescue his troubled presidency.

Fox News evaded this controversy when it began its prime-time programming after Trump spoke about disinfectants. The next night Tucker Carlson devoted his hour-long show to praising the president and lambasting Democrats. He didn't discuss the brouhaha over disinfectants, a huge topic in mainstream TV news commentary that day. The *Hannity* show followed with Mike Huckabee as substitute anchor. The show's only reference to Dr. Bright's dismissal took less than a minute and it highlighted the Trump administration's perspective. Correspondent Trace Gallagher reported that White House officials said the President's words had been taken out of context. Then Gallagher featured a brief clip. It showed Trump insisting his words communicated sarcasm.

In those broadcasts Fox's top-ranked prime-time program, *Hannity*, and its second-ranked program, *Tucker Carlson Tonight*, gave short shrift to a major political controversy of the day. *Hannity* evaded the subject and Carlson's program suggested Trump's remarks about disinfectants had not been significant.

Debates about the effectiveness of presidential leadership during the pandemic received extensive coverage in television news programming. Yet Fox News clouded its viewers' understanding of the controversies and sometimes skirted past the topics in prime-time broadcasts. Hosts and commentators denigrated people who raised questions about the president's decisions. They also characterized news media that featured critical stories about the administration's response to Covid-19 as biased and untrustworthy.

Fox's programming left viewers poorly informed about current affairs. The network shortchanged its audience. It also undercut democracy. For the American political system to function effectively, voters need exposure to information about current political controversies.

NINE

RESPONSES TO COVID

By March of 2023, three years after illness from Covid-19 began to appear in the United States, the total number of American deaths from the pandemic amounted to approximately 1.1 million people. Millions more suffered from illnesses caused by the infection. Lots of Americans suffered from lengthy illness called "Long Covid."

Could the United States have emerged from the health crisis with substantially fewer deaths? The following analyses suggest the USA did not handle the challenges effectively.

Several problems were evident when the Covid crisis occurred. America's complex medical system lacked universal health care, a benefit present in many other advanced nations around the world. Republicans had opposed spending for public health years before Covid-19 struck. President Donald Trump failed repeatedly to acknowledge the dangers and mobilize vigorous public responses. Many Republican leaders politicized health issues. They opposed masking and other measures to protect the public. Some promoted vaccine skepticism.

Many lives could have been saved through better leadership.

The Pandemic Exposed a Major Flaw in America's Health Care System

The coronavirus emergency exposed a serious shortcoming in America's healthcare system: insurance provided through the workplace. The U.S. approach to health security, an unusual arrangement among modern societies, did not serve the American public adequately during flush times. It was glaringly inadequate during the pandemic. There was no political opportunity to make substantial adjustments in 2020, despite the crisis brought on by Covid.

Conservative Republicans had opposed government-led initiatives to provide universal health care for decades, and they were not about to change course during the pandemic. They agreed to work with Democrats to produce bipartisan responses during the health emergency. The GOP backed robust spending to aid businesses, industries, and hospitals. Republicans joined Democrats in expanding unemployment benefits and sending checks to the American people. Conservatives in Washington supported temporary emergency measures, but they would not tolerate significant long-term adjustments to America's expensive and insufficient health care system. The goal of reforming American health care became almost exclusively the purview of Democrats.

The United States' largely employer-based insurance arrangement became prominent during World War II. Millions of workers left home to serve in the armed services, creating labor shortages. President Franklin D. Roosevelt worried that inflation would spike because companies needed to raise wages to compete for an inadequate supply of workers. He responded with an executive order in 1942 that froze wages. Employers managed to attract workers nevertheless by offering employer-sponsored health insurance. In 1943 Congress made that benefit tax-exempt, an action that reduced the cost of health coverage for individuals and families. In the prosperous decades after World War II, numerous American businesses provided health insurance as an employment perk.

World War II contributed to the formation of a different approach to health insurance in Europe. Economies were in ruins after the war. The Europeans could not establish employer-based systems in an unstable business environment. Programs that emerged on the European continent and in the United Kingdom varied greatly and sometimes included large components of private insurance. But governments served as the primary organizers of medical insurance. Government-sponsored programs helped bring universal health care to the public.

The Europeans were more aggressive than the Americans in keeping health costs under control. Washington had less political clout than European governments when dealing with medical industries. In the USA special interests, including insurance companies, doctors, hospitals, drug companies, and medical device firms merged, lobbied, and competed tenaciously for profits. In this fragmented, free-market environment spending on medical care surged. Health care in the United States became, by far, the most expensive arrangement of modern developed nations. Health care spending represented 18% of gross national product (GNP) in the USA in the early 2020s. [90]Switzerland, second highest, spent 12% of GNP on medical care.

America's employer-based insurance system served nicely during the booming Fifties and Sixties, but over the years changes in employment practices left more and more Americans with inadequate coverage. Years ago, millions of American workers received impressive medical benefits secured by unions. No longer. Union membership declined substantially. Many Americans now work independently as contract workers or as consultants. They must secure health insurance on their own, often at considerable expense. Others hold temporary positions that provide no coverage or limited coverage.

Then the pandemic hit, making employment less secure. In just a few months, businesses placed numerous workers on furlough or released them completely. Unemployment claims jumped to 38.6 million in nine weeks. Workers in restaurants, retail stores, hospitality industries, airlines, manufacturing, and other fields joined the ranks of America's unemployed. The coronavirus produced more than just a job crisis. It created a health insurance crisis.

A survey in February 2020 revealed that many Americans suffered from medical insecurity *before* the Covid-19 emergency. The NBC News/Commonwealth Fund reported in early 2020 that one in three Americans worried they could not afford health care.[91] One in five respondents said they had problems paying or were unable to pay medical bills during the past two years. Then the pandemic destroyed jobs, making additional millions of citizens insecure.

During the Twentieth Century, reform-minded political leaders in the United States tried to improve health security, but they were unable to achieve what European societies accomplished. Franklin D. Roosevelt wanted to include medical insurance in the 1935 Social Security bill. He dropped the plan to pass the social security bill in Congress. Harry S. Truman sought universal coverage as part of his Fair Deal but encountered enormous push-back from the American Medical Association and other organizations.[92] A huge Democratic victory in the 1964 elections helped Lyndon Baines Johnson and Congress to establish Medicare and Medicaid in 1965, yet those measures targeted only a portion of the total population. In 1994 President Bill Clinton and his wife, Hillary, had to back away from a bold plan to expand coverage after encountering fierce opposition.

The program created by President Obama and Democratic lawmakers in 2010 came under sharp Republican attacks. GOP lawmakers tried to chip away at Obamacare's provisions. Then Republican governors and President Donald Trump threatened to take down Obamacare entirely. On May 6, 2020, Trump said his administration would continue backing a constitutional challenge at the Supreme Court. "We want to terminate health care under Obamacare," Trump declared.[93] The president and Republican legislators had long targeted the Affordable Care Act but never identified a comparable replacement. If the GOP's challenge at the Supreme Court had succeeded at the time, twenty million Americans would have lost medical insurance provided through the Affordable Care Act.

The United States is the only modern, industrialized nation in the world without universal health coverage.[94] Its insurance system, based primarily on employer-sponsored programs, failed to protect the public before the pandemic. When Covid struck, the system was woefully insufficient. In late spring, 2020, the U.S. economy slowed dramatically. The pandemic produced a severe employment problem and a related medical insurance problem.

During that crisis, there was an opportunity for leaders in Washington to deal with America's fragmented and expensive medical system that failed to deliver major improvements in public health. In the political environment of 2020, there was no chance for substantial reform. Conservative Republicans, fundamentally opposed to changing America's arrangements for health care, would not consider changes.

During the 2009-2009 financial meltdown, Rahm Emanuel, President Barack Obama's Chief of Staff, made an insightful comment that was relevant to the America's health care crisis during the pandemic. "Never allow a good crisis go to waste," advised Emanuel. "It's an opportunity to do the things you once thought were impossible." [95]

COVID-19 Vaccines Showed the Value of Scientific Research

In 2021, the first year of Joe Biden's presidency, Republicans said Biden deserved little or no credit for progress in vaccinating Americans during the COVID-19 pandemic. GOP leaders claimed President Donald Trump made Biden's job easy by creating Operation Warp Speed. Vaccinations were available at the time of Biden's inauguration, Republicans argued. Joe Biden benefited enormously from Trump's initiatives.

The GOP's claim grossly distorted the evidence. The Trump administration did what any presidential administration would have done in a national health emergency. It gave pharmaceutical companies incentives to produce quick remedies. But the potential for new vaccines was already in place when Pfizer-BioNTech, Moderna and other companies developed products in early 2020. Those pharmaceutical companies benefited from years of scientific investigation funded by the federal government. Donald Trump was not the creator of these impressive advances in medical science. The true heroes were researchers that made scientific breakthroughs. They did the groundbreaking work on mRNA vaccines that tricked the body into creating proteins.

Republican leaders frequently cited Donald Trump's leadership as key to America's success in battling the pandemic.[96] Trump's White House Press Secretary, Kayleigh McEnany claimed, "President Trump put in place an unprecedented vaccine operation that paved the way for President Biden." Kevin McCarthy, the House Minority Leader at the time, tweeted, "President Biden's plan is to rely on work that has already been done by Operation Warp Speed."[97]

Years and decades before 2020, the National Institutes of Health (NIH) and American universities supported basic scientific research that created these important medical discoveries.[98] When the pandemic became a serious threat early in 2020, the U.S. government provided $10.5 billion for pharmaceutical companies to accelerate vaccine development.[99]

Officials in the Trump administration did not busily engage in vaccine planning after distributing the money. That was the work of experts at pharmaceutical companies. Some firms, such as Moderna, took the financial incentive. Moderna came up with a successful formula in just six weeks. Its vaccine did not reach people's arms until late in 2020 because trials involving many volunteers took months to complete. Pfizer-BioNTech refused government funds. Its leaders recognized they could move forward quickly on their own. The money was helpful in Moderna's case, but most important is what came before. Scientists had already provided discoveries that enabled fast production of vaccines.

Much of the groundbreaking research had been conducted through grants to universities provided by the National Institutes of Health (NIH). Some of the main researchers moved from universities to pharmaceutical companies, such as Katalin Kariko. She had worked at the University of Pennsylvania and later became a senior officer at BioNTech. Dr. Barney Graham conducted essential research at Vanderbilt University and later became Deputy Director of the NIH's Vaccine Research Center. Graham's research team partnered with Moderna to design an effective COVID-19 vaccine.

Donald Trump and leaders in his administration did not deserve extraordinary praise for creating medical solutions to the pandemic. Through much of 2020, Trump and officials in his administration denied the existence of a serious threat. They endorsed phony remedies such as hydroxychloroquine. They ridiculed mask-wearing and social distancing and did little to address Covid testing shortages and the lack of protective equipment for medical personnel. When pharmaceutical companies completed the trials and indicated vaccines were safe and ready for distribution, Trump officials lacked a plan of action.[100]

Getting vaccines into the arms of officials required organizational skill. Trump officials failed to provide it. They concealed important medical information during the two-month presidential transition period. After Biden's inauguration, officials in his administration had to operate almost from scratch. They needed to design a complex plan quickly to vaccinate the U.S. population.

An important lesson in this history relates to the value of basic scientific research and the role of the federal government and universities in fostering it. Years prior to 2020, significant investigations into the application of mRNA vaccines had been carried out through federal grants. Fortunately, scientific breakthroughs occurred just a few years before the Covid-19 crisis began. Illnesses and deaths were horrendous, but, at least, new research was well underway at the time. Those vaccines protected millions of people in the United States and around the world.

To confront future health challenges, more substantial government support will be necessary. America's commitment to basic scientific and medical research declined in recent decades. Researchers had to deal with additional cuts in funding made by Trump's White House. The world's experience with Covid-19 reveals that scientific research can produce huge gains for the economy and save lives. Funding basic medical research is a wise investment. Unfortunately, money for that work often declined when the GOP controlled Congress or the White House.

The Trump Administration Was Not Ready for the Coronavirus

In early 2020 officials at the Centers for Disease Control and Prevention (CDC) said the coronavirus would likely spread to U.S. communities. Unfortunately, federal agencies most responsible for dealing with the virus had been hit previously by funding cuts favored by the GOP. Furthermore, the Trump administration's first efforts in the emergency were chaotic. Washington was poorly prepared to deal with a Covid-19 pandemic.[101]

The first signs of governmental disorganization appeared when authorities in Washington had to decide about sheltering Americans from the Diamond Princess cruise ship. Several passengers tested positive for the coronavirus. Experts at the CDC wanted passengers to remain in Japan. Individuals at the State Department and a health official from the Trump administration overruled the CDC. They allowed more than 300 cruise ship passengers to fly to the United States and then tried to send them to facilities in California and Alabama. Residents in the selected communities objected vigorously. Citizens of Costa Mesa, California pointed out, for example, that a field outside a Development Center where the cruise ship passengers would be housed was a popular playground for neighborhood children.

These botched efforts to provide care for just a few hundred people revealed the Trump administration was grossly mismanaging the pandemic in its early days.

The president's public comments had not been helpful. Trump likened the coronavirus to the common flu, predicting it would fade away when spring arrived. Even though CDC officials urged the American government to prepare for likely outbreaks in the U.S., Trump declared the virus "is very well under control in our country." He claimed, "very few people" have been infected, and "they're all getting better." At a press conference Donald Trump suggested the United States was "very close" to developing a vaccine. Medical professionals said a widely available vaccine was probably 12 to 18 months away.

Years before, President Barack Obama demonstrated how a smart, coordinated governmental reaction to a health threat can yield impressive results. Obama made Ronald Klain, a talented Washington staffer, America's "epidemic czar." Klain coordinated the work of numerous federal agencies to contain a deadly Ebola virus outbreak in West Africa. His work helped prevent Ebola's spread across the globe.

In 2020 health officials found it difficult to launch a fast and effective response to the coronavirus, because the Trump administration had been undermining their programs. The White House cut $15 billion in national health spending and slashed the global disease-fighting operation budgets of the CDC, the Department of Homeland Security, and the Department of Health and Human Services.[102] Staff layoffs at the CDC's global health section were so great that the number of countries in which the agency was working had to be reduced from 49 to 10. In 2018 the Trump administration disbanded the National Security Council's global health security unit and reassigned the Rear Admiral that was coordinating its efforts.

When the Covid crisis first appeared, American society was poorly prepared to deal with the emergency. Republicans in Congress had undercut important health care agencies in previous months, and the administration handled a case involving infected cruise ship passengers ineptly. President Trump made the situation worse by minimizing the seriousness of Covid's threat to public health. The Trump administration lost valuable time when dealing with a pandemic in the late winter and early spring of 2020. Its lethargic response ultimately cost many American lives.

During the Covid Crisis, Trump Talked Like President Roosevelt but Acted Like President Hoover

When the Great Depression threatened the wellbeing of millions of Americans, President Franklin D. Roosevelt acted swiftly. In his administration's first "hundred days" new initiatives restored public confidence and set the nation on a road to recovery. In contrast, President Donald Trump reacted slowly and inadequately to the mounting threat from Covid-19. Trump invoked language that resembled Roosevelt's, saying he would deal with the pandemic as a "wartime president." Trump seized the opportunity to boast about his bold leadership in a "medical war," but he did not back the words with strong action. Like Herbert Hoover, the troubled president who preceded Franklin D. Roosevelt, Trump was reluctant to exercise federal power in a crisis.

Herbert Hoover supported some initiatives by the federal government during the Great Depression, but he opposed extensive federal intervention. Hoover favored voluntarism and individual efforts. When markets crashed, he asked corporate leaders to maintain production and employment. His appeals failed to arrest the downturn. By the last days of his administration, Hoover's reputation was in tatters.

When FDR took the oath of office on March 4, 1933, unemployment approached 25%, and the financial system of the United States was near collapse. Roosevelt's inaugural address excited hope with a message that "the only thing we have to fear is fear itself." FDR explained how he intended to combat the depression. He asked Congress for "broad executive power to wage war against the emergency, as great as the power that would be given to me if we were in fact invaded by a foreign foe." During the next "hundred days," the New Deal initiated numerous major legislative programs.[103]

Roosevelt and the Congress rescued troubled banks, provided jobs for millions of unemployed Americans, raised depressed farm prices, and created the TVA, which stimulated the southern economy. Broad-based recovery took years, but the New Deal's actions quickly improved public confidence. Days after Roosevelt's inauguration, citizens deposited cash in banks that they had been hoarding.vThe stock market then surged with its largest one-day increase in history. In the 1936 presidential election Americans registered their judgment about FDR's leadership. They gave Roosevelt a 523-8 electoral victory.

Mimicking Franklin D. Roosevelt language, President Donald Trump announced in the spring of 2020 that he was taking command of a "big war" against the coronavirus. Trump congratulated his administration for mobilizing resources. In televised news conferences he claimed enormous progress securing test kits, masks, and gowns for health care workers. When journalists cited reports about huge shortages, Trump offered vague or dismissive responses.

Dr. Anthony Fauci, a respected medical expert, provided candid assessments of serious health risks at these televised events, but the president contradicted him and other medical professionals. Trump underestimated the danger of Covid-19, promoted unproven drug remedies, and questioned the need for extensive and prolonged social distancing. Health professionals were especially alarmed when the president said he wanted to "open up" businesses across America during the second week in April 2020 and fill churches on Easter Sunday.[104] Experts warned that millions of Americans would likely be infected by that time. An explosion of new cases would create a huge burden for overwhelmed doctors and nurses.

President Trump wanted to get Americans back to business activity so that the economy recovered quickly, stock markets flourished, and his reelection prospects improved. But the Covid-stimulated financial crash was not triggered by a weak economy. Markets and businesses fell because the global health crisis forced millions of people into isolation. Flattening the curve of new infections could aid economic recovery. But, if millions of Americans followed Trump's recommendations and abandoned social isolation before the virus came under greater control, the U.S. economy could take a more painful beating.

President Trump remained hesitant about dealing forcefully with the health risks. Rather than create a robust central command in Washington to coordinate the nation's medical actions, Trump practiced a version of laissez faire. He left responses to the crisis largely to corporations, state governments, and local hospitals. Then, in the manner of Herbert Hoover, Trump slowly changed course. He reluctantly agreed to put new federal measures in place as troubles mounted. Yet he refused to use his presidential authority boldly as Franklin D. Roosevelt did.

U.S. intelligence agents warned in January and February 2020 that the coronavirus could devastate American society. Trump, his administration, and GOP leaders in Congress saw their reports. Some senior administration officials urged the president to act quickly, but as one of them noted, "they just couldn't get [the president] to do anything about it."

The threat that worried intelligence officials became abundantly evident by mid-March 2020, and still the president hesitated. Rather than direct a robust *national* response, Trump let state and local governments handle the challenges. Doctors and nurses complained about huge shortages of protective gear. Trump referred the matter to state governors, saying, "we're not a shipping clerk."

Absent direction from the White House, the medical response lacked organization and guidance. During the first three weeks in March 2020, there were huge differences in the way states, communities, and businesses dealt with the pandemic. Health officials warned emphatically that cruise travel was dangerous, yet ships filled with thousands of passengers, including many vulnerable senior citizens, were still at sea. San Francisco, New York, and other cities locked down while thousands of young people celebrated Spring Break in Florida's nightclubs.

Republican and Democratic lawmakers urged Trump to invoke the Defense Production Act so that major industries could shift quickly from manufacturing consumer products to making protective clothing for doctors and nurses, ventilators for patients, and other medical equipment. One physician complained that his colleagues were on the front lines "at war with no ammo." Trump refused to invoke the act's broad powers. He pointed to the risk of giving the federal government direction over business affairs. Such an extraordinary action is only appropriate in a "worst-case scenario," he argued. As often happened during the pandemic's buildup, Trump later backpedaled. Eventually, FEMA invoked the Defense Production Act to order medical supplies.

Like Herbert Hoover, Trump relied considerably on voluntary efforts. He praised the CEOs of major corporations for promising aid in the emergency. Trump preferred a free market approach. He opposed strong federal intervention in business affairs. Advocates of leadership from Washington disagreed. They pointed out that *temporary* federal coordination did not represent an assault on free enterprise. It was an emergency measure. Lacking coordination from Washington, state governments competed against each other in desperate efforts to obtain medical supplies.

The contrast is striking between President Trump's clumsy, haphazard, and hesitant response to the health crisis and Franklin D. Roosevelt's all-hands-on-deck approach to the Great Depression. FDR's New Deal cooperated with state and local governments when administering programs, but leadership and planning came largely from Washington. President Roosevelt understood that the federal government needed to assume primary responsibility for directing responses during an extraordinary crisis. FDR did not simply talk about waging "war against the emergency." He mobilized the nation for combat.

Programs initiated in Washington during FDR's first hundred days did not solve all problems of the Great Depression. Nor could immediate and well-planned mobilization managed by Washington stop Covid-19 in its tracks. But Roosevelt's example of broad-based action showed that strong presidential leadership could improve conditions quickly and lift the spirits of an anxious people. In early 2020, the American people truly needed a "wartime president."

Did the Virus Come from the Wuhan Lab? Republicans Tried to Make the Answer Political

Republicans were running victory laps and giving each other high-fives in response to growing evidence that the Wuhan Institute of Virology in China could have been the source of the COVID-19 outbreak that killed millions of people worldwide and devastated economies. Republicans said their leaders speculated that the virus originated in the Wuhan, but the liberal news media pooh-poohed that idea because President Donald Trump mentioned it when he criticized China. Partisanship colored the analysis, Republicans argued.

Politicians on the right raised legitimate questions about the origins of the coronavirus, but so did many others, including scientists. Facts, not politics, eventually changed judgments about the Wuhan lab's possible importance. New evidence appeared in 2021 indicating Covid-19 could have emerged first from the virology lab in Wuhan rather than the city's "fresh market" that sold wild animals. Information about efforts by Chinese authorities to conceal information and the inadequacy of investigations conducted by the World Health Organization (W.H.O.) led to demands for new research into the virus's origin. By politicizing this topic, conservative politicians and their supporters in the national media complicated the search for the truth.

Republicans (and many commentators on Fox News) argued that the Wuhan lab was the likely source of trouble. GOP Senator Tom Cotton of Arkansas, Secretary of State Mike Pompeo, and President Donald Trump said there could be a connection with the lab in 2020, but the "mainstream" news media characterized their ideas as a foolish conspiracy theory. Two conservative-oriented columnists with the *New York Times* summarized the Right's criticisms in op-eds. Ross Douthat accused journalists of practicing "media groupthink."[105] They refused to accept the possibility that Trump's ally, Tom Cotton, might be correct, Douthat argued. "Think what you will about the Arkansas Republican," wrote the *Times's* conservative columnist Bret Stephens. Cotton offered "reasonable observations warranting impartial investigation." Stephens complained that "media gatekeepers" exhibited "rank partisanship" and "censorship" by dismissing Republicans' claims as conspiracy mongering.[106]

When Cotton, Pompeo, and other Republicans suggested the Wuhan lab was largely to blame for the pandemic, their charge served President Trump's election-year efforts to focus media attention on China rather than the Republican administration's flawed efforts to deal with the coronavirus. Many news analysts did not place much confidence in their statements because of the truth-challenged behavior of the President and his backers in Washington. Republicans praised the president or remained silent in the face of Trump's blizzard of untruths. It is not surprising that in 2020 journalists lacked confidence in Republicans' claims about the Wuhan lab.

Information about the source of the outbreak was limited when Covid became a major news story in February and March of 2020. Much discussion in the media was devoted to questions about the scourge's impact on health, how individuals could avoid infection, and when effective vaccines would become available. At the time, the Chinese government said the virus originated from animal to human transmission at the Wuhan fresh market. In early 2020 President Trump praised the Chinese government for its cooperation.[107] Trump promoted friendly relations with Xi Jinping, because he was seeking a new trade agreement with China.

The World Health Organization backed the Chinese government's explanation about Covid's origins in the fresh market early in 2020, but some reporters questioned the decision. They noted that U.S. embassy officials criticized the Wuhan virology lab for failing to implement robust safety and security measures.[108] News stories also revealed that representatives from W.H.O. were unable to investigate conditions at the Wuhan lab independently. W.H.O. received funding and support from nations that worked with it, including China. The Chinese government controlled essential information about the Wuhan lab.

Demands for a more thorough study of the laboratory surged in late March 2021 when a group of specialists chosen by W.H.O. released a report in collaboration with Chinese scientists. It called the possibility of a lab leak "extremely unlikely." That investigation, conducted without independent efforts to obtain interviews and data, provoked criticism from medical experts. Dr. David A. Relman, a professor of medicine and microbiology at Stanford University, complained that W.H.O.'s investigation appeared "biased, skewed, and insufficient."[109] It had been conducted without full transparency and without researchers' access to important information.

In May 2021, the Chinese government refused to participate in a new investigation by W.H.O., and President Joe Biden responded by asking the U.S. intelligence community to complete a 90-day review of details about Covid's origins. Biden wanted to get ahead of escalating criticism of the Chinese government's obstruction. The Democratic president noted that two important theories about the virus's origins had become prominent – that it came from the Wuhan market or from the Wuhan lab. Biden sought a "definitive conclusion."[110]

After President Biden's announcement, discussions about the Wuhan lab's possible role in the pandemic's origins received considerable attention in the national media. On June 6, 2021, CBS Television's program *60 Minutes* featured a hard-hitting report on the controversy.[111] It suggested the Wuhan lab was a likely source of the pandemic.

If President Trump, Republican politicians, and conservative pundits had established an impressive record of candor when the pandemic emerged, they could have contributed to discussions about the Wuhan lab, but they chose to politicize the subject instead. They attempted to divert attention from Trump's inadequate response to the crisis by blaming China for the pandemic. The Wuhan lab may have been a source of the outbreak, but Republican rhetoric made it difficult to engage in serious study of the evidence. Eventually, facts, not politicking, made the lab-leak theory appear worthy of investigation.

Why Were Many Republicans Resistant to Vaccination? Look to History for Some Answers

By 2021, new vaccines provided impressive protection from the coronavirus. Yet many people in the United States were hesitant or adamantly opposed to getting a shot. Resistance was concentrated in America's rural districts, among people with low incomes, and with citizens that did not have a college education. But the most distinctive characteristic of anti-vax sentiment related to politics.[112] Republicans were far more suspicious of vaccination than Democrats. In the 2020 presidential election Donald Trump won 17 of 18 states that had the *lowest* vaccination rates. Joe Biden won in the 22 states that had the *highest* adult vaccination rates.

Why was the contrast between red and blue regions stark? Most explanations presented in the news media focused on current events. Commentators noted that Donald Trump did little to promote vaccination before and after leaving the White House. Commentators also mentioned that Republican officials and hosts and guests on Fox News often questioned the vaccines' effectiveness and safety. Many of those individuals criticized efforts by the Biden administration to encourage vaccinations. They characterized the vaccination campaigns as assaults on individual liberty.[113]

These explanations are relevant, but there is also a deeper explanation for vaccine resistance that receives less public attention. It relates to the way leaders in the Republican Party had been bad-mouthing science and promoting pseudoscience for years. The denigration of science and scientists occurred notably under the leadership of presidents Ronald Reagan, George W. Bush, and Donald Trump. Their administrations appointed industry-affiliated personnel to federal agencies, individuals that questioned the validity of professional research. Many of those officials supported policies that pleased ideological, business, and religious interests. Misrepresentation of scientific evidence in those years became a familiar practice in Washington. In the context of that history, it is not surprising that in the years of the Trump administration many Republican leaders tolerated or championed arguments that contradicted scientific knowledge.

President Ronald Reagan's statements about environmental matters alarmed scientists.[114] Reagan questioned reports about dangers from air pollution. He suggested trees produced more air pollution than automobiles, a comment that inspired jokes about "killer trees." Reagan prevaricated when dealing with evidence that a buildup of chlorofluorocarbons in the atmosphere could produce holes in the ozone layers.

The Reagan administration abruptly changed the established practice of appointing leaders to federal regulatory agencies that were sympathetic to their stated missions. Reagan's team staffed the federal government with several individuals that vigorously defended the industries subject to regulation. The President's choice of Anne Gorsuch Burford as head of the Environmental Protection Agency was a significant example. Burford, a corporate lawyer, had opposed the Clean Air Act. She attempted to purge the EPA of scientific experts and enforcement agents responsible for minimizing toxins in the air and water. Burford's interference with a superfund designed to clean toxic waste sites earned her a contempt citation from Congress. [115]

President George W. Bush's administration staffed many federal agencies with individuals chosen for ideological conformity rather than expertise. Working inside the government, those officials undermined enforcement of the Clean Air Act. They also expelled an eminent cell biologist from the President's Council on Bioethics who supported embryonic stem-cell research. Responding to pressure from religious groups, the administration required the National Cancer Institute to post information suggesting connections between abortion and breast cancer. When the World Health Organization and the Food and Agricultural Organization recommended limits on consumption of fat and sugar because of increases in obesity-related diseases, an official in the Bush administration who disagreed with the conclusion informed WHO that in the future scientists working in the organizations' committees needed to be approved first by his office.[116]

Some of the most troubling assaults on science in the Bush administration related to suppression of evidence about climate change. One of the administration's first important acts was to abandon commitments to the Kyoto Protocol of 1997, which sought international cooperation to reduce greenhouse gas emissions. Revelations later reported that the administration of President George W. Bush welcomed active involvement by Exxon executives in the formulation of climate policy. In 2008 Jason Burnett, a former EPA official, informed the U.S. Senate that Vice President Dick Cheney and the White House Council on Environmental Quality attempted to censor vital information about the impact of climate change.[117]

Donald Trump put the politicization of science on steroids when the pandemic created an extraordinary health crisis in 2020. His administration blocked reporting by major agencies in the government, insisted on conformity to the President's outlook, and diminished the role of scientists and medical professionals in the creation of coronavirus policies. Strategists and lobbyists appointed by the administration pressured the Centers for Disease Control (CDC) repeatedly, demanding the agency's announcements conform to the President's public statements, including Trump's claims that the virus was under control and did not constitute a major health threat. When Trump foolishly promoted an anti-malarial drug, hydroxychloroquine, as an effective treatment for Covid, medical experts objected strongly, but to little effect. Trump disagreed with analyses by the renowned infectious disease expert, Antonio Fauci, and he eventually diminished Fauci's public role.[118]

The administration then appointed Scott Atlas as a special White House adviser on the coronavirus. Atlas, a radiologist, proposed letting younger people get the virus so that the public could obtain "herd immunity." Epidemiologists objected, warning that Atlas's plan would likely produce more infections, hospitalizations, and deaths. Like many actions by the administration, Trump's affinity for Atlas related to the president's interest in reopening the economy quickly to improve prospects for his reelection.

Dr. Anthony Fauci said it was "quite frustrating" that a large percentage of Republicans were hesitant about receiving a Covid vaccine.[119] Deciding to get vaccinated is "not complicated," Fauci declared. "We're not asking anybody to make any political statement one way or the other. We're saying, try and save your life. And that of your family and that of the community."[120]

Many Americans and medical experts shared Fauci's frustration. They could not understand why opposition to vaccination was so intense among Republicans. When searching for answers, a broad historical perspective can deliver some insights.

The situation was not new. Over four decades, Republican presidential administrations contradicted scientific information to achieve policy goals. Conservative presidents, legislators, and pundits rejected and sometimes ridiculed the findings of scientists and medical experts. Against this historical background, resistance toward vaccination in America's red states during the Covid pandemic was not surprising. Republican leaders had been dismissing the recommendations of scientific and medical experts for a long time.

The GOP's Vaccine Skeptics Should Have Followed George Washington's Example

During the Covid crisis, health officials welcomed celebrity endorsements of immunization, because approximately 30% of Americans were hesitant or opposed to getting the vaccines. Stars from the world of entertainment promoted the government's vaccination campaign, including Lin-Manuel Miranda, Dolly Parton, Patrick Mahomes, and Oprah Winfrey. Former presidents Bill Clinton, George W. Bush, and Barack Obama pitched vaccination as well. Yet it remained difficult to influence the holdouts. Promoters of vaccination might have made greater progress convincing skeptics by citing the achievement of George Washington, a much-respected "celebrity" from history. During the American Revolution, General Washington required his troops to be immunized against smallpox. Using the mass media to enlighten the public about Washington's example might have aided the government's education programs.

George Washington knew the horrors of smallpox from personal experience. In 1751 he accompanied his brother on a trip to the Caribbean.[121] Washington hoped the tropical airs would aid his sibling's recovery from "consumption" (tuberculosis). George Washington contracted smallpox in Barbados. He survived but carried scars from the illness for the rest of his life.

When Washington was Commander in Chief of the Continental Army, he learned how the scourge could damage a fighting force. A smallpox epidemic struck American troops that invaded Canada in 1775-1776. On the way to Quebec, about 30% of those soldiers dropped out of action because of sickness. Eventually, with about 50% of troops infected, the Americans retreated. Smallpox, as well as blizzards and British troops, damaged the campaign to bring Canada into the revolution.

General Washington was disturbed by reports about the American army's troubles in Canada and smallpox epidemics in Boston, Philadelphia, and other cities. Soldiers under Washington's command lived and trained in close quarters. If smallpox spread among them, wrote Washington, "we shall have more dread for it, than the Sword of the Enemy." Washington acted swiftly in 1777 to prevent infections among his soldiers. He required inoculation of all army recruits that had not developed immunity from previous bouts with smallpox.[122]

The procedure for inoculating individuals at that time was risky. "Variolation" involved the lancing of pustules from a smallpox victim followed by insertion of the infected knife under the skin of a healthy person. In about two weeks, the patient typically became sick, but the illness was less severe than in a naturally acquired infection. Years later, in 1796, British scientist

Edward Jenner created a true vaccine from cowpox that made immunization easier to administer and less dangerous.

When General Washington made his controversial decision, several political leaders in the colonies opposed variolation. They feared the process could spread infections rather than minimize them. Washington dismissed these concerns. He wisely endorsed medical intervention. After mass inoculation, all but about fifty soldiers in his army survived the epidemic.

This history carried a lesson for holdouts against Covid vaccines. America's revered "Founding Father" applied the rudimentary medical science of the 1770s when confronting a dangerous outbreak. Washington's leadership saved the Continental Army and quite possibly rescued the cause of American independence as well.[123]

In the 2020s Americans had much better access to medical information than Washington had when he required mass immunization. New vaccines had brought infectious diseases under control, including polio, measles, and mumps. Then came mRNA vaccines, which triggered immune responses that could protect millions of people from Covid-19.

Despite impressive scientific advances, public opinion surveys showed that many Americans were reluctant to get Covid shots.[124] Polls indicated that more than 40 percent of Republicans were hesitant.[125] Resistance was especially intense in rural areas and in the southern states.[126] Distrust of the vaccines was widespread geographically, however, and not confined to a few specific groups, noted Tara Kirk Sell, a senior scholar at the Johns Hopkins Center for Health Security.[127] People that distrusted vaccines came from many different backgrounds and had diverse reasons for rejecting vaccination.[128]

Leaders in President Joe Biden's administration recognized that many Americans resisted vaccination because they did not believe claims about safety made by government officials, medical experts, former presidents, and celebrities. To overcome that distrust, White House strategists encouraged doctors and pharmacists to answer questions, provide confidence-building information, and administer shots. The Biden team hoped vaccine skepticism could be reduced through assurances from people in local communities that were familiar, respected, and trusted.

Efforts to deal with vaccine hesitancy could have been advanced, too, if administration officials noted the achievement of one of the most familiar and admired leaders of the Revolution. George Washington protected his troops from a deadly epidemic by organizing the first large-scale immunization campaign in American history. Washington's bold action enabled the patriots to continue fighting and eventually win their struggle for independence from the British empire. General Washington applied the best medical science of his times when confronting a major health crisis. Modern-day vaccine skeptics should have learned from Washington's example. They needed to apply the best current medical science to protect themselves and their communities.

TEN

THE EXTREME COURT

A Pew Research Center Report released on July 21, 2023, showed the American people's confidence in the U.S. Supreme Court was fast declining. Just 44% of Americans queried had a favorable view of the Court, while 54% expressed an unfavorable view. Favorable views had dropped by 26 percentage points since 2020. Pew's research found a stark divide between the opinions of Democrats and Republicans. Just 27% of Democrats and Democrat-leaning independents had a favorable view of the Court, while 68% of Republicans and Republican-leaning independents gave the Court favorable marks.[129]

Pews' findings were troubling. Years before, most Americans felt confident that justices on the Court interpreted the law in objective and fair-minded ways. Positive views of the Court enhanced respect for the Constitution.

Why has public trust in the justices' work been eroding? These analyses point especially to judicial overreach on the part of justices nominated by Republican presidents.

Republicans Have Been Packing the Court for Decades

When Democrats reacted to conservative overreach at the Supreme Court and talked about expanding the number of justices, Republicans accused Democrats of advocating "court packing." Yet GOP presidents and legislators have been packing the Supreme Court for years, not by increasing the number of justices but by nominating fervent ideologues. They appointed robustly conservative judges that took partisan positions on numerous issues. The rulings of those jurists often clashed with mainstream public opinion. At the country's highest court, just one or two individuals, operating with the extraordinary authority of lifetime tenure, managed to negate major legislation. Progressives worried that justices on the Supreme Court would take extremist positions on major issues well into the future.

Court "packing" carries a negative connotation in American political discussions. The term implies disrespect for the tradition of nine-justice membership that has been in place since 1869. Packing invokes references, as well, to Franklin D. Roosevelt's efforts to increase the high court's membership in 1937 when it appeared that a staunchly conservative majority was about to nullify the New Deal's social and economic reforms. Facing a barrage of criticism, Roosevelt backed away from his plan. But FDR's gambit seems to have influenced the Court. In a "switch that saved nine" some conservative justices did not overturn some of the New Deal's welfare and regulatory measures.[130]

Since the 1980s, Republican presidents have been politicizing the Supreme Court by nominating sharply conservative individuals even though the American people are not as strongly committed to conservatism as those nominees. A 2021 Gallup Poll reported that 37% of Americans surveyed identified as moderate, 36% as conservative, and 25% as liberal. An impressive majority -- 62% of Americans queried by Gallup identified either as moderate or liberal – not conservative).[131]

In *Neither Liberal nor Conservative: Ideological Innocence in the American Public* (2017), political scientists Donald Kinder and Nathan Kalmoe reported that only a minority of voters are deeply engaged in political life and are ideologically committed to the right or the left. The U.S. population *appears* to be divided along ideological lines, they acknowledge, but research shows that most Americans are ideologically "innocent." Kinder and Kalmoe updated an influential finding that political scientist Philip Converse reported in the 1960s. Converse discovered that many voters lack consistent opinions about burning issues of the day. Their views are not based on coherent ideologies.

Even though most Americans are not ideologically committed to conservatism, Republican presidents and their key advisers have aggressively promoted strongly right-oriented judicial candidates since the 1980s. President Ronald Reagan's ideological push became immediately evident with his nomination of Antonin Scalia in 1986. A year later Reagan nominated Robert Bork, setting off a huge controversy that divided the Senate and the nation. Bork revealed extreme perspectives when questioned by senators. Those radically conservative judgments eventually killed his chances for a seat on the Court. Years later, when Bork published *Slouching Towards Gomorrah: Modern Liberalism and American Decline*, he sounded like a militant culture warrior.

Subsequent Republican presidents continued packing the Court with radicals in robes. President George H. W. Bush nominated Clarence Thomas, another fervent conservative. Rather than govern from the political center because of his controversial victory in 2000 (aided by the intervention of conservative justices on the Supreme Court), George W. Bush pleased the Right by nominating Samuel Alito, Jr. President Donald Trump continued the practice of selecting ardent conservatives by nominating Neil Gorsuch, Brett Kavanaugh, and Amy Coney Barrett.

Brazenly, without embarrassment, the Supreme Court's conservative justices have acted in ways that undermined democracy. Election reforms were quickly dismantled. In 2010 the conservative majority in a 5-4 ruling produced a controversial decision in *Citizens United V. Federal Election Commission*. That ruling enabled corporations and other organizations to spend unlimited funds on elections. Soon after, "dark money" from undisclosed wealthy donors and business interests wielded enormous influence in U.S. elections. In *Shelby County v. Holder* (2013), again in a 5-4 ruling, the conservative majority undermined an important reform that Congress had created. The Voting Rights Act of 1965 protected citizens from laws and policies of state and local governments that denied equal rights to vote based on race. The Court gutted a key provision of the law. Numerous actions followed that led to the suppression of voting by African Americans.

In an important case related to same-sex marriages, conservatives on the Court lost, but the addition of three justices at the Court by President Donald Trump might someday overturn that important civil rights achievement. *Obergefell v. Hodges* (2015) dealt with marriage by same-sex couples. A *Washington Post/ABC* poll near the time of the ruling indicated that 59% of respondents supported same-sex marriages, and only 34% opposed. Yet four conservatives, Roberts, Scalia, Thomas, and Alito, dissented. Justice Anthony Kennedy, who retired from the Court in 2018, provided the swing vote that guaranteed same-sex couples equal marriage rights. In October 2020, Justices Thomas and Alito blasted the 2015 *Obergefell* decision. They left an impression that the decision on same-sex marriage was not as settled as many believed.

Since the 1980s, nomination of many strongly rightist jurists by Republican presidents has resulted in much closer Senate votes to confirm than had been characteristic of the Senate's handling of nominees in the past. Prior to the Eighties, most individuals recommended by the presidents received confirmation with substantial bipartisan support. Reagan's nomination of Robert Bork upset that tradition. The Senate rejected Bork by a vote of 42-58. President George H. W. Bush's choice, Clarence Thomas, squeezed by with a close 52-48 decision in the Senate. John Roberts, Jr., nominated by George W. Bush, fared better, winning an appointment by a count of 78-22. Since then, the selection of ideologically inclined figures provoked substantial party-line voting. Samuel Alito, Jr. won confirmation by 58-42, Neil Gorsuch by 54-45, Brett Kavanaugh by 50-48, and Amy Coney Barrett by 52-48. The Senate's decision on Barrett's nomination lined up almost exclusively in terms of party affiliation. Votes in the Senate have been closely divided largely because individuals nominated by Republican presidents were transparently partisan choices. Individuals recommended were associated with far-right perspectives, not majoritarian sentiments.

Court-packing has been abundantly evident in the actions of Republican presidents and White House staff, GOP legislators, and state and local

Republican officials since the 1980s. It can be seen in nominations for the U.S. Supreme Court and in controversial decisions at the Court made by Republican-appointed justices. This situation has created enormous problems for the American political system. Millions of Americans, including independents and disillusioned Republicans, sense that just five or six opinionated individuals on the Supreme Court have the authority to impose their opinions on the American public for decades to come.

Those few men and women can wield enormous power over the society even though Republican presidents that nominated them received fewer popular votes than Democratic candidates that lost the presidential elections. In the twenty-first century George W. Bush's close victory over John Kerry in 2004 constitutes the *only* case of a GOP presidential candidate winning a popular vote majority up to the time of Joe Biden's presidency. Since 2000, Republican presidents have been promoting ideologically minded jurists on American society despite the failure of GOP candidates to secure popular mandates from the American people.

Four decades of Republican court-packing by nominating extremists have created significant problems for democracy. Partisan appointments to the Supreme Court and partisan decision-making at the Court undermined the judicial system's reputation for fairness, integrity, and legitimacy.

In a Case About Covid Restrictions, Conservatives on the Supreme Court Acted Like Culture Warriors

Years ago, when conservatives were unhappy about the influence of liberals on the United States Supreme Court, they complained bitterly about "activist judges." They called for "judicial restraint," urging justices on the high court to refrain from interfering excessively in public affairs. These complaints were rarely heard after conservatives achieved majority influence on the Supreme Court. They often applauded when right-oriented justices make controversial rulings that overturned decisions by elected officials.

One of the notable examples of judicial overreach by conservatives occurred in a decision at the Supreme Court in November 2020. By a vote of

5-4 the conservative justices ruled against New York state's efforts to limit religious gatherings in sections of New York City that had been troubled by high incidence of Covid infections. Strongly opinionated judgments by justices Neil Gorsuch and Brett Kavanaugh hinted that conservatives at the Court might overturn other efforts by government officials to protect public health.

"Activist Judges" is an appropriate label for Gorsuch and Kavanaugh. Their written opinions in the New York case reflected partisan judgments. Gorsuch and Kavanaugh attempted to demolish rationales used by New York's governor and others in the state government. New York officials were struggling to protect the public during a fast-spreading pandemic. They established rules for large public gatherings based on recommendations by medical experts. Gorsuch and Kavanaugh overturned their decision by presenting a *political* argument favored by many conservatives. They judged New York state's Covid restrictions unconstitutional, claiming they established unfair limitations on religious liberty.

Gorsuch's and Kavanaugh's written statements had the character of op-ed columns in the partisan media rather than thoughtful inquiries into significant constitutional issues. The justices tried to undercut the logic behind New York state's actions. Gorsuch opined, "So, at least according to the Governor, it may be unsafe to go to church, but it is always fine to pick up another bottle of wine, shop for a new bike, or spend the afternoon exploring your distal points and meridians. Who knew that public health would so perfectly align with secular convenience?" Kavanaugh added, "The State must justify why houses of worship are excluded" from liberties accorded to some businesses to continue operations during the pandemic.

Is it the job of Justice Gorsuch to act like final arbiter when public officials all over the nation were struggling to match conflicting goals? Those officials wanted to prevent the spread of the coronavirus *and* let citizens earn a living and engage in leisure activities. Efforts to find the right balance between these interests required careful study and attention to local conditions. It involved complex decision-making. It was not the job of Supreme Court justices to tell those officials how to deal with crowded gatherings during a severe health crisis.

It is surprising that these conservative justices viewed the New York situation as an assault on religious liberty. The state's management of the pandemic did not reflect intolerance toward religion. As Justices Sonia Sotomayor and Elena Kagan explained, religious groups were not being treated with specific prejudice in New York's rules. Distinctions made by the state were based on the recommendations of scientists. Medical experts reported that "large groups of people gathering, speaking and singing in close proximity indoors for extended periods of time" can "facilitate the spread of COVID-19." Sotomayor and Kagan pointed out, too, that "New York treats houses of worship far more favorably than their secular comparators" by "requiring movie theaters, concert venues, and sporting arenas subject to New York's regulation to close entirely but allowing houses of worship to open subject to capacity restrictions."

During a time when complicated public health issues (including mask-wearing) were cannon fodder in the culture wars, the justices acted like culture warriors. Five conservatives on the Court, Justices Thomas, Alito, Barrett, Gorsuch and Kavanaugh, chose to lecture government officials about governing during a pandemic. In doing so, they rejected science and invoked partisan talking points. Their engagement as "activist judges" soiled the Court's image of impartiality.

Decades ago, Supreme Court justice Louis D. Brandeis said, "the most important thing we do is not doing." Whenever possible, recommended Brandeis, "a statute should be construed in a way to avoid constitutional issues." Brandeis encouraged the justices not to "formulate constitutional rules broader than required by the precise facts in the case." Unfortunately, five conservatives on the Supreme Court took a different approach. In the New York case they engaged in a highly controversial form of judicial activism.

ELEVEN

RACIAL POLITICS

When Barack Obama won the presidential election in 2008, many Americans viewed the outcome as a sign of significant social progress. They thought the election of an African American to the nation's highest office signaled major improvements in race relations.

Progress has been made on some fronts since that time. As one of the following analyses shows, the removal of Confederate stars and bars from Mississippi's state flag was a significant development. It reflected growing recognition that America's Civil War began primarily because of disagreements about slavery. Also, in the early 2020s Americans of diverse backgrounds came together to protest the brutal death of George Floyd. Many whites displayed signs proclaiming, "Black Lives Matter."

Yet racial tensions did not diminish substantially. Dog Whistle politics remained a problem. Furthermore, Republicans promoted false impressions about threats from Critical Race Theory and the 1619 Project, and Donald Trump appealed to whites' resentments. Troubling, too, were public opinion polls that showed many Americans believed race relations were turning worse in the 2020s, not better.

Dog Whistle Politics

When Republicans practice dog-whistle politics, they make indirect appeals to white voters who are critical of racial, religious, ethnic, and national minorities. Pundits identify the practice as a "dog whistle" because it refers to ultrasonic whistles that dogs hear but not humans. Politicians that employ the "whistle" use coded language that avoids terms that are likely to be attacked as hateful, prejudiced, or racist. GOP politicians have been sounding dog whistles for decades to excite voters' anxieties and drive them to the polls. Often those soundings helped Republicans win local, state, and national elections.

During the 1964 presidential campaign, GOP candidate Barry Goldwater did not make direct racist appeals (and, arguably, he was not a racist), but Goldwater's rhetoric drew white Democrats away from their party. Goldwater opposed the Civil Rights Act of 1964, complaining that it allowed federal intrusion in local affairs and that businessmen had a right to deal with customers as they wished. Occasionally, Goldwater offered more obvious appeals to whites' anxieties. He told the Georgia State Republican Party, "We ought to forget the big cities. . . I would like our party to back up on school integration." Goldwater's appeals brought considerable support from white voters and helped the GOP achieve gains in the southern and southwestern states. Yet President Lyndon Johnson was an overwhelming favorite of voters that year. He won the presidential election by a wide margin.

Richard Nixon won the 1968 presidential election, in part, by promoting a "Southern Strategy." That, too, was an example of dog-whistle politics. The Republican candidate blamed many of America's problems on blacks, but not through specific language. H.R. Haldeman, Nixon's close adviser, said "The key is to devise a system that recognizes this while not appearing to." Rather than refer directly to blacks, Nixon called for "law and order" and respect for "states' rights."

Many elements factored in Ronald Reagan's presidential victories; indirect references to race were only part of the mix. Reagan defended his positions on principle, not prejudice. He had opposed the Civil Rights Act and the Voting Rights Act, arguing against federal intervention in states' affairs. Reagan launched his 1980 campaign for the White House near Philadelphia,

Mississippi, the place where three civil rights workers had been slain years before. During his visits around the United States, Ronald Reagan spoke often about an exploitative "welfare queen," and listeners understood that the lady was a black woman. Reagan convinced many white Democrats, including southerners, to abandon their party and register as Republicans.

Lee Atwater, a master at dog-whistle politics, assisted Reagan in 1980 and 1984 and then proved helpful to George H. W. Bush. In the 1988 presidential contest Democrat Michael Dukakis had a strong early lead in the polls. Then Atwater's strategy took effect. Lee Atwater's most noteworthy contribution to Bush's campaign was the Willie Horton ad. It reported that Dukakis allowed a furlough for a murderer when he was governor of Massachusetts. Horton, while free to roam, attacked a couple. He beat the young man and raped the woman. Lee Atwater said he was going to make Willie Horton the "running mate" of Michael Dukakis. The TV spot accentuated fears about crime and violence.

By the early Twentieth Century, American demography was changing in significant ways, and political leaders needed to adjust their campaign strategies. The new electorate included more Latinos, East Asians, South Asians, people with ties to the Middle East, and others. The electorate also included more young voters, single women, and Americans that rejected traditional religious affiliations. Yet the GOP did not go after these emerging constituencies as aggressively as the Democrats. Republican leaders continued to concentrate on whites, including many evangelicals.

The electoral impact appeared in the 2008 and 2012 presidential elections. Minority voters supported Barack Obama by 80% in both elections. Latinos backed Obama in 2012, 71% to 27% over Republican candidate Mitt Romney. Obama carried the women's vote by 55-44 in 2012 and won the single women's vote that year by 67-31. He won 60% of voters from 18 to 29 years of age.

In the 2012 presidential contest a large field of Republican contenders tried to rally partisans by criticizing "illegal" immigrants. Voters understood that the candidates' references to undocumented aliens referred mainly to Latinos and especially to Mexicans. Mitt Romney signaled appreciation for the issue in a televised debate. He called for "self-deportation" of undocumented immigrants living in the United States. Romney's impractical idea drew laughs from the audience.

In the race for the GOP's presidential nomination in 2016, several Republicans criticized candidate Donald Trump for making dog-whistle appeals to voters' prejudices. Yet candidates that ran against Trump that year practiced their own dog-whistle appeals. Many of them demanded that President Barack Obama acknowledge "radical Islamic terrorism." Presidential candidate Ted Cruz said, "As long as we have a Commander-in-Chief unwilling to utter the words 'radical Islamic terrorism,' we will not have a concerted effort to defeat these radicals . . ." The many Republican leaders who backed this demand appeared unable to understand President Obama's reluctance. Including the word "Islamic" with each reference to terrorism offended Islamic citizens who viewed terrorism with the same disgust as most Americans. The three words, when combined, associated decent individuals and families with crimes against humanity.

Republican leaders could have aided American society's adjustment to momentous demographic and cultural shifts. By the 2010s and 2020s, many students in public schools were non-white. For the first time in the nation's history, white Christians were less than half the national population. Democrats responded to these demographic and cultural shifts, turning their party into what Ronald Brownstein called a "coalition of transformation." The Democratic Party offered a broad tent that accommodated diverse groups. But Republicans favored a "coalition of restoration," Brownstein noted. They appealed to nostalgic longings for an idyllic American past in which white Christians were the dominant group.[132]

Movers and shakers within the GOP could have aided their constituents' adjustment by encouraging a positive response to America's social evolution. Instead, many of them exploited fear of demographic changes and promoted wedge politics. They stressed the politics of fear, suspicion, and division. Their tactics helped the GOP win some elections, but it also deeply fragmented American society.

The Controversy Over Mississippi's Flag was About History

In 2020, a time of lively debates about Confederate symbols, a significant change occurred. Mississippi, the last southern state with a flag that featured stars and bars of the Confederacy's battle flag, gave its banner a makeover. The protests for racial justice, especially after George Floyd's death that year, made an impact. It takes more than a design change in the flag, however, to alter personal sentiments. Lots of Mississippians, and Americans as well, do not think the Civil War occurred primarily because of slavery. Absent an informed understanding of the Civil War's principal cause, it is difficult for them to make sense of the brouhaha over Confederate symbols.

A huge portion of the U.S. population – about half of Americans surveyed in recent years -- traced antebellum divisions to disagreements about "States' Rights," economic and cultural differences, and conflicts between industrial and agrarian interests. A public opinion survey by the Pew Research Center in 2011 reported that 48% thought the Civil War occurred primarily because of concerns about states' rights. Only 38% thought slavery was the primary reason. 9% thought both factors were important in about equal measure.[133]

"States' Rights" is a vague term. It relates to constitutional issues, but it had deeper significance as well. In the antebellum period, southern leaders associated the concept with a "right" to defend slave property. This supposedly principled stand was contradictory. When Northern legislatures passed Personal Liberty Laws, seeking the "right" of their citizens to protect runaway slaves from capture and return to their "owners," southern leaders in Congress objected strongly.

Many historians now question "states' rights" and other vague explanations for the coming of war. James M. McPherson, a prominent author of books about the Civil War, estimated that 90% or more of serious scholars agree the war came because of "increasing polarization of the country between the free states and the slave states over the issue of slavery, especially the expansion of slavery." An examination of major clashes from 1850 to 1860 supports this perspective. Arguments about slavery were central in the Compromise of 1850, the Fugitive Slave Act, "Bleeding Kansas," the Dred

Scott decision of the Supreme Court, the Lincoln-Douglas Debates, John Brown's raid, and Lincoln's election.

Southern ordinances of secession made the point clear. South Carolina, Virginia, and other states called for separation because Abraham Lincoln was "hostile to slavery." Alexander H. Stephens, Vice President of the Confederacy, tied the slavery issue to race relations in his "Cornerstone Speech" of March 21, 1861. He said the Confederacy's "foundations are laid, its cornerstone rests, upon the great truth that the negro is not equal to the white man; that slavery, subordination to the superior race, is his natural and normal condition."[134]

When the shooting began, other concerns quickly replaced talk about slavery. President Lincoln abhorred the institution, but he understood the need for caution. Northern opinion was sharply divided on matters of slavery and race. Furthermore, Lincoln could not afford to alienate leaders in the border states. He said, "I hope to have God on my side, but I must have Kentucky." Lincoln made saving the Union the principal cause when fighting began. He committed to emancipation later, not only for humanitarian reasons but also to undermine the Confederacy's war effort. Jefferson Davis and other southern leaders also moved away from discussions about slavery after the war started. They called for armed resistance to the Union's plans to recruit soldiers and attack the South. Confederate leaders accentuated patriotism, requesting enlistment to protect homes and land from Yankee invaders.

In the decades after the Civil War and especially in the early Twentieth Century, many politicians, historians, journalists, and citizens downplayed slavery in their explanations for disunion and war. They pointed out that many Confederate soldiers did not own slaves. Promoting a spirit of reunion, nationalism, and racial solidarity, they attributed the conflict largely to factors other than slavery. "States' Rights" often served as a generic term that represented several different explanations. Scholarly analyses that identified slavery as the paramount issue did not become the prevailing viewpoint until the second half of the Twentieth Century. But outside of academia, traditional interpretations continued to attract a broad following. Authors of school textbooks, teachers, reenactors, and others gave short shrift to slavery when explaining secession and war.

It should not be surprising that many Americans have downplayed the unpleasant subject of slavery in their discussions about the Civil War. It was unappealing for southerners to acknowledge that the cause for which ancestors fought originated in a defense of "owning" other human beings. Acknowledgement was uncomfortable for Americans from other regions, too. The diminution of stories about slavery resembled, in some ways, presentations of American history that gave limited attention to injustices against Native Americans, Asians, Hispanics, and others. Popular media often communicated this storytelling. It was not until after the Second World War that many Hollywood movies portrayed African Americans, Native Americans, Asians, and Hispanics more favorably.

Americans obscured the darker aspects of their history, but they were not unique. In other nations, too, the people were hesitant about acknowledging injustices from the past. Germans soft-pedaled teaching about the Holocaust until the late 1970s, and some Japanese politicians still want to downplay accounts of the Imperial Army's use of "Comfort Women" (Korean sex slaves) and their military's involvement in China, particularly the "Rape of Nanking."

Recent debates about Confederate symbols in the United States were part of this broader story of challenges many societies faced. Now citizens must deal with unpleasant chapters in their history. Mississippi's state flag, featuring Confederate iconography, was obviously offensive to many people in the state. The flag should inspire all citizens' pride. Statues and monuments are objects of criticism, too, but they are not typically official state emblems, like a flag, which more directly represents the government and its people.

Replacement of the state flag and other Confederate symbols may produce only superficial progress. It will be difficult to achieve major adjustments in attitudes if many people still believe that states' rights and other nebulous issues were the principal reasons for secession and war. Mississippians and all Americans can better understand what controversies over

Confederate iconography are about if they acknowledge the prevailing opinion of professional historians.

One group in Mississippi, representing 37% of the state's population, has long accepted the scholars' perspective. Most African Americans in the state recognize that the war started over slavery and ended with freedom for their ancestors.

The Debate Over Critical Race Theory Was a Ruse

In the early 2020s, conservatives and progressives engaged in vigorous debates about "Critical Race Theory." They criticized or defended the concept as if it were a major subject of study in universities and a program that is implemented widely in public schools. Yet until very recently, Critical Race Theory (CRT) was not discussed broadly in universities or incorporated frequently in school curricula. CRT was a rather obscure academic concept until media personalities and politicians on the Right invoked it to excite the Republican base. Rightwing promoters of Critical Race Theory employed the term to advance the party's prospects in elections.

Can the strategy work? Can exploitation of this emotion-laden topic stir conservative voters to cast their ballots in elections? A look back at the 2004 presidential election suggests the scheme has a potential to make an impact. Attention to hot-button social issues sometimes brings numerous conservative voters to the polls.

In 2004 Republican incumbent George W. Bush and Democratic challenger John Kerry were in a close race. The situation changed when Republican strategists placed statements on eleven state ballots that defined marriage exclusively as the union between a man and a woman.[135] Resistance to gay marriage brought a huge increase in Republican turnout compared to the 2000 election. Bush won the critically important swing state of Ohio and the presidency thanks to his 136,000-vote advantage there. If just 70,000 Ohio voters supported the Democrat instead, John Kerry would have won the state's electoral votes and the presidency.[136] In a related way, conservatives hoped Critical Race Theory would excite Republicans to cast their ballots.

CRT was not a prominent topic in national conversations until recently. Back in the 1970s and 1980s, writers such as Derrick Bell and Kimberle Crenshaw helped to launch ideas about Critical Race Theory. A core idea was that racism is not simply a matter of individual prejudice. Proponents of the concept said racism was pervasive in subtle and complex ways in the nation's legal systems, institutional structures, and social norms. In 2019, a related argument undergirded this concept. The *New York Times* published a lengthy article describing the 1619 Project. The Project reframed the country's history. It accentuated the importance of slavery in the formation of the American nation, and it drew attention to the contributions of Black Americans in the county's development.

In 2020 Christopher Rufo, an obscure right-oriented speaker and writer, countered these arguments in a manner that appeared to be unprejudiced.[137] As Rufo later confessed, CRT served as a "perfect villain." In some presentations Rufo claimed the idea had radical, even Marxist roots. On September 2, 2020, Christopher Rufo appeared on Fox's Tucker Carlson Show and quickly succeeded in turning Critical Race Theory into a household term. Carlson gave Rufo an enthusiastic introduction. The TV host claimed CRT "has pervaded every aspect of the federal government" and warned it "is an existential threat to the United States." The next day White House Chief of staff, Mark Meadows, called Rufo and told him President Donald Trump liked his comments and wanted "action" against CRT. Discussions about Critical Race Theory in the national media expanded greatly. [138]

Later, in March 2021, Rufo explained the value of treating this little-known concept as the "existential threat" Carlson described. Identifying CRT as an influential ideology affecting university thought and school teaching allowed Republicans to "drive up negative perceptions" and make CRT appear "toxic," Rufo explained. He said the "goal is to have the public read something crazy in the newspaper and immediately think 'critical race theory.'"

CRT became a new example of conservative strategists' familiar tactic of employing language that excites the Republican base. During Barack Obama's presidency, strategists on the right renamed the Affordable Health Care Act "Obamacare." The term suggested an overreaching black president was threatening to replace citizens' medical insurance with his own radical plan. When Hillary Clinton emerged as the Democratic candidate for the White House, conservative strategists pinned the word "Benghazi" on her. Republican-led committees failed in several tries to identify a Benghazi-related scandal involving the former Secretary of State. That, too, was a con. During the 2020 election season, strategists on the right accused Democratic candidates without evidence of being "socialists" and "radical" and advocates of "defunding the police." They also associated racial justice protests with "antifa" without evidence that a large, well-organized, and violent black group by that name was orchestrating the demonstrations.

These terms were never intended to illuminate public understanding. They aimed to provoke anxiety, fear, anger, and resistance.[139] In a related way, Christopher Rufo invoked Critical Race Theory. CRT, said Rufo, was a catchall term that symbolized "the entire range of cultural constructions that are unpopular in America."

The debate over Critical Race Theory was a ruse designed to stoke white resentment toward blacks and energize whites' participation in elections.[140] Conservative strategists wanted voters to focus on CRT and pay less attention to important issues such as the pandemic, health care, income inequality, climate change, and other subjects that affected the daily lives of Americans more directly than the phantom CRT menace stressed by the Right.[141] By elevating CRT's importance in the public mind, Republicans managed to distract voters from issues that mattered.

Attacks on History Teaching by State Legislators Threatened Free Speech

Back in the 1920s, politicians in several states banned the teaching of evolution in public schools. Those controversial actions drew national attention in the notorious "Monkey Trial" of 1925. Novels, stage performances and movies about the event delivered an important message. They showed that politicians' efforts to prohibit learning, knowledge, and thought undermined education. Until recently, most Americans understood lessons from this dark chapter in American history. Recently, though, a new movement for censorship in education gained momentum. In several states Republican legislators proposed bills that prevented teachers from addressing topics in the classroom related to slavery and racism. These legislative measures threatened cherished principles of free thought and free speech.

American society has long been committed to freedom of expression. Supreme Court Justice Oliver Wendell Holmes, Jr. stated the idea notably, saying the ultimate good in society "is better reached by free trade in ideas -- that the best test of truth is the power of thought to get itself accepted in the competition of the market . . ". Holmes objected to government efforts to limit speech. His words have been cited numerous times in America's courts. They are invoked to reject censorship. Modern jurists often use the term "marketplace of ideas" to epitomize Holmes's idea.[142]

The Republican state legislators' attempts to guide and control students' understanding of the American past constituted a dangerous assault on this ideal. Commentators in the national media did not give adequate attention to the threats to free speech implied in legislators' efforts to define what could be taught in public schools. Discussions in newspapers, the internet and television concentrated, instead, on arguments about whether Critical Race Theory, the 1619 Project (that dealt with slavery and its legacy), and other interpretations of history illuminated the public's understanding of the past or damaged it. Some commentators pointed to political goals associated with the burst of state legislation, noting that strategists on the right believed popular resistance to teaching about slavery and race would benefit Republican candidates in the elections. These discussions were useful, but there is another important issue to consider.

As historian Timothy Snyder explained in a *New York Times* article, the war about history teaching related to a war on democracy. Authoritarian figures in the Soviet Union falsified or concealed information about wars, famines, and purges during Joseph Stalin's regime for political purposes. In recent years, "memory laws" have been promoted in the USA, Snyder pointed out. Legislators and governors asserted "a mandatory view of historical events, by forbidding the discussion of historical facts or interpretations or by providing vague guidelines." [143]

These rules, prohibiting teachers from addressing troubling topics from U.S. history, could have a chilling effect on instruction. Public school teachers, working for modest salaries, understood that complaints about their instruction from parents or school administrators could lead to their dismissal. The new state rules had the potential to cultivate a fearful instructional environment that resembled Senator Joseph McCarthy's deleterious impact on public education in the Fifties.

Republican politicians applied enormous pressures on teachers. In Florida, the State board of Education restricted instruction in Critical Race Theory and other topics from classes on history and civics. The state prohibited teachers from sharing their personal views or attempting to "indoctrinate or persuade students to a particular point of view" that contrasted with state standards. In Tennessee a proposal prohibited teachers from treating the rule of law in America as "a series of power relationships and struggles among racial or other groups."[144] Republican officials in Arkansas, Texas, Idaho, Iowa, and Oklahoma pushed related measures. Some bills threatened financial penalties against teachers that engaged the prohibited subjects.

Teachers were aware that a parent, politicized by comments heard in rightwing media, could charge them with brainwashing students. Nebulous terms that appeared in the state mandates such as "indoctrinate," "persuade" or teaching a "particular point of view" could easily be invoked to attack an educator's statements or reading assignment. These indistinct rules ensured that history teaching in many states would become whitewashed, bland, and boring. They were likely to promote superficial analysis of the past, instruction that concealed unpleasant realities. Timothy Snyder succinctly identified the problem when he said, "History is not therapy, and discomfort is part of growing up."

Long before Oliver Wendell Holmes, Jr. defended the "free trade in ideas" philosopher John Stuart Mill made an influential argument against censorship. In *On Liberty* (1859), Mills championed the free flow of ideas. No one alone knows the truth and no one idea alone embodies the truth, he argued. Ideas that go unchallenged can become dogma. Open competition between ideas is the best way to separate falsehoods from fact.

Republican legislators moved into dangerous territory when they interfered directly in education and told school systems what could and could not be said in history and civics teaching. The legislators' knee-jerk reactions to disputes about Critical Race Theory and other academic concepts fostered censorship in American education. Politically motivated legislators and governors undermined cherished American freedoms to achieve popularity with their base and secure temporary political advantages. They made a Faustian bargain that threatened American ideals.

TWELVE

GUNS, IMMIGRATION, AND CLIMATE

These three important and controversial issues continue to roil American politics. The American people are sharply divided in their opinions about them, and the two major political parties are split, as well.

The analyses in this chapter reveal that the extremist rhetoric of radical Republicans made it exceedingly difficult for American society to make progress on these matters.

Long Ago, There Was a Chance to Make America Safer from Gun Violence, but We Failed to Act

When a mass shooting occurs like the attack at an elementary school in Uvalde, Texas that killed 19 students and two teachers, commentators in the national media often discuss the motive of the killer, how the shooter entered the building, the training of school personnel, and the response of law enforcement authorities. These analyses are helpful for understanding how the massacre occurred, but they do not identify the central cause of trouble: guns. Shootings at schools represent just one among numerous examples of violence with firearms. Each day, on average, 321 people are shot in the United States.[145] More Americans died from gunshots between 1968 and 2017 than in all American wars.[146]

Long ago, I published a book that examined the origins of the gun problem in modern American life. I noted that firearms-related deaths and injuries had been a minor problem in the mid-twentieth century, but during ten years from the mid-Sixties to the mid-Seventies gun-related injuries and fatalities surged. I traced the troubles to "firearms democracy." In the United States, far more than in other advanced societies, guns could easily be obtained by just about anyone that wanted them.[147]

Revolvers and rifles were accessible at cheap prices in those years. "Saturday Night Specials," small, inexpensive handguns, were available for as little as $12. In 1963 Lee Harvey Oswald assassinated President John F. Kennedy with a mail-order Italian rifle that he bought for $21.45. Americans owned an estimated 125 million firearms at the time (the current estimate is 400 million).

Attacks with firearms were escalating at an alarming rate at that time, and very little was being done to confront the problem. Violent crime continued spiraling out of control. I predicted: "As long as the [gun] cult remains strong, and its popularity seems to be growing rather than waning, gun controls will lack abundant political friends and the idea of Firearms Democracy will continue in vogue. In this environment even the most cockeyed warning about the danger of gun control will be accorded great respect. Thus, the great debate will go on and on."

In the Sixties and Seventies, like today, gun enthusiasts fiercely resisted attempts to regulate firearms. They said the Second Amendment guaranteed the right to bear arms. "Guns don't kill people; people kill people," asserted critics of regulation. Firearms were essential for personal security, they argued. Guns protected law-abiding citizens from criminals.

A strategy applied then by gun enthusiasts remains effective for blocking regulation. Gun enthusiasts in the Sixties and Seventies objected vehemently to even the most moderate efforts to keep firearms out of the hands of people who might engage in criminal activity. Defenders of gun possession took an absolutist position. They said gun ownership was a fundamental right of free citizens.

The fragmented political system aided the cause of gun ownership. There were more than 20,000 federal, state, and local gun laws on the books at the time. Superficially, the United States looked like the most firearms-regulated society in the world. Yet the plethora of laws across wide geographic areas made enforcement difficult. Firearms could easily be marketed and transported across political boundaries.

In one notable way, gun-related violence today is strikingly different. In the Sixties and Seventies there were few reports about mass murders. The most shocking news story of the time related to Charles Whitman's 1966 shooting spree from a tower at the University of Texas. Whitman shot 38 people, killing 14 before lawmen gunned him down.

These days events like the Whitman shooting are familiar. In recent years there have been numerous attacks on groups of people. They are frequently committed by emotionally unstable young men wielding semi-automatic weapons. The attackers create mayhem in diverse places, including schools, colleges, shopping centers, dance halls, houses of worship, movie theaters, and outdoor concerts. Some are driven by prejudice toward people of a particular race, ethnicity, religion, or gender. Others strike at random.

Americans often respond to news about gun violence by purchasing weapons. They think the weapons will make them more secure. But the expansion of gun ownership makes American society less safe. Opportunities to use guns in nefarious ways increase. *New York Times* columnist Charles M. Blow described the outcome: "In our gun culture, 99 percent of gun owners can be responsible and law abiding, but if even 1 percent of a society with more guns than people is not [responsible], it is enough to wreak absolute havoc. When guns are easy for good people to get, they are also easy for bad people to get."

Applying numbers to Blow's thought experiment, if 1% of Americans might endanger the society if they possess a gun, there are three million, two hundred and fifty thousand potentially dangerous people in the country.

Is gun regulation just a pipe dream, or is it feasible? Evidence from other English-speaking countries suggests regulation can work.[148] When a gunman in Britain killed 16 in 1987, the nation banned semiautomatic weapons, and after a 1996 school shooting, lawmakers banned most hand-guns. Britain now has one of the lowest gun-related death rates in the developed world. After a massacre in 1996, Australia initiated gun buy-backs and acquired about a million firearms. Soon after, the number of mass shootings plummeted. Canada and New Zealand have tightened gun laws, too, after mass fatalities from shooting incidents.

The problems that emerged in those English-speaking countries resemble problems that appeared in the United States during the 1960s. Guns were not as prevalent in Britain, Australia, Canada, and New Zealand as they were in the United States during the 1960s, but they were abundant. Yet citizens and political leaders in those countries managed to change direction. American society went the other way when signs of escalating gun violence began to appear. Political leaders blocked most bills to regulate guns. Possession of firearms multiplied. It should not be surprising that the outcomes are markedly different. Today the rate of deaths by gun violence in the United States is nearly 100 times greater than in the United Kingdom.[149]

In the early 1960s, Americans lost an opportunity. They could have taken vigorous action to promote gun safety when troubles associated with "firearms democracy" appeared. Instead, political leaders chose a hands-off approach. Now there are more guns than people in the United States, and Americans are much more fearful about shootings than citizens in other developed countries.

In 1934 Congress Passed Major Gun Regulation. Here's Why It's Much More Difficult to Regulate Firearms Now

May 22-23, 2021, was a particularly bloody weekend. A dozen mass shootings occurred in the United States (defined by CNN as gunfire that wounds or kills four or more people). A few days later, a distraught employee at a transportation facility in San Jose, California shot and killed nine co-workers. Americans are disturbed by these reports, but the federal government is not likely to take meaningful action to reduce gun violence. Conservatives in Congress and the Supreme Court established formidable obstacles to firearms regulation. It is useful, however, to recall a time in American history when the federal government dealt effectively with gun violence. The National Firearms Act of 1934 reduced murders involving "machine guns." Political conditions at the time made gun reform workable.

During the 1920s, the American public became deeply concerned about a crime wave. The Prohibition law that blocked production, distribution, and sale of alcohol created opportunities for gangsters. Crime syndicates provided illegal alcohol. When they sought territorial control in America's cities, sometimes they fought with competitor gangs. Innocent civilians, including children, died in the firefights. Law enforcement officials tried to arrest the criminals, but they were greatly disadvantaged. Gangsters had faster cars and greater firepower. Some criminals wielded a Thompson submachine gun ("Tommy Gun") that sprayed numerous bullets per minute.

Newspapers featured stories about gun-toting gangsters, including John "The Killer" Dillinger, Arthur "Pretty Boy" Floyd, George "Machine Gun" Kelly, and Bonnie Parker and her lover, Clyde Barrow. The news media complained about the criminals' easy access to automatic weapons. "Why should desperadoes, brazen outlaws of the period, be permitted to purchase these weapons of destruction?" an editorial in the *Waco* (Texas) *News-Tribune* asked. Critics of these firefights often called for new gun regulations.

Franklin D. Roosevelt became President in March 1933 and responded quickly to the violence. He declared a "New Deal on Crime." FDR's Attorney General, Homer Cummings, demanded action. "A machine gun, of course, ought never to be in the hands of any private individual," argued Cummings. He called the gangster problem "a challenge to American civilization." It was a war for the "soul" of the county. "We have got to win that war . . . We shall," declared the Attorney General.[150]

The Second Amendment was not a great obstacle to passing gun control legislation in 1934. The principal difficulty was the limitation on Congress's power to regulate commerce. The New Dealers came up with a clever solution. They designed a $200 tax (equivalent to about $3500 today) on the purchase or transfer of defined firearms, which included Tommy Guns and sawed-off shotguns, and they required those weapons to be registered.[151]

The National Firearms Act, passed by a strongly Democratic-controlled Congress in 1934, established the first comprehensive federal gun-control law. The legislation taxed high-powered automatic weapons virtually out of existence.

In 1939 the Supreme Court accepted the law's constitutionality in *United States v. Miller*. Focusing on the Second Amendment's opening words -- "A well regulated Militia, being necessary to the security of a free State" – justices ruled that a sawed-off shotgun, the weapon identified in the appeal, did not have "a reasonable relationship to the preservation or efficiency of a well regulated militia." For the next six decades, advocates of firearms reform cited this decision to reject challenges to regulation.

Today's advocates of gun regulation will be wise to recognize striking differences between political conditions in the Thirties and those of the present. In 1934 Democrats benefited from a huge 1932 election victory for FDR and the party's candidates for Congress. Democrats wielded enormous clout in the U.S. House and the Senate. In the early 2020s power in the two houses was closely divided. Democratic President Joe Biden favored gun reform, but he recognized the difficulty of passing legislation. Democrats needed a much larger majority in Washington to achieve progress. They were also stymied by a conservative majority on the Supreme Court.

Both the National Rifle Association (NRA) and the Supreme Court operate differently today than in the Thirties. During discussions about the 1934 firearms legislation, the National Rifle Association gave Democrats qualified support. The NRA's president, Karl Frederick, said the "promiscuous toting of guns" ought to be "sharply restricted and only under licenses." Today's NRA, tainted by scandals, remains adamantly opposed to meaningful gun regulation. In 2008 conservatives on the Supreme Court swept away gun restrictions in *District of Columbia v. Heller*. The justices said the Second Amendment to the Constitution confers an individual's right to possess a firearm for traditional lawful purposes of self-defense.

Polls show most Americans want federal action to deal with endemic gun violence. The American people have good reason to seek legislative support. In 2019 there were 14,400 gun-related homicides in the United States and 23,941 suicides involving guns. Mass shootings were especially shocking. Emotionally troubled individuals gunned down many people at the Sandy Hook Elementary School (2012), in Orlando (2016), in Las Vegas (2017), and at a high school in Parkland, Florida (2018). Despite public outcries, leaders in Washington failed to take significant action.

The history of the National Firearms Act of 1934 and the Supreme Court's ruling in 1939 carries lessons. A meaningful response to endemic gun violence is unlikely to occur until advocates of regulation secure impressive majorities in the U.S. House and Senate, control of the White House, and majority influence at the Supreme Court. Achieving that combination in today's political environment is a tall order. Unusual political circumstances in the Thirties made reform possible. It will take extraordinary political circumstances in the future to reduce gun violence substantially.

If Republicans Truly Want to Crack Down on Immigration Law Violators, They Will Have to Arrest Millions of American Citizens

When President Donald Trump and Attorney General Jeff Sessions explained why they wanted to revoke the DACA program that gave temporary protection to over 800,000 undocumented young immigrants that were brought to America by their parents, they hammered a point that other critics of DACA echoed in the national media. Trump and Sessions argued that these minors were in the United States *illegally*. They did not draw attention, however, to the illegal behavior by millions of American citizens who employed their parents. The hiring of undocumented immigrants did not just involve violations of the law by large businesses. Millions of individuals in the United States employed undocumented workers to repair their roofs, cut their lawns, and clean their homes. Those American citizens engaged in unlawful behavior. Politicians and pundits gave almost exclusive attention to the approximately eleven million "illegal" immigrants in the country and the 800,000 immigrant minors that could lose protection from DACA. Many other "illegals" were involved, U.S. citizens that eagerly employed undocumented workers.

Attorney General Jeff Sessions placed the legal issue front and center when defending his call to end Deferred Action for Childhood Arrivals (DACA). "As Attorney General," explained Sessions, "it is my duty to ensure that the laws of the United States are enforced and that the Constitutional order is upheld."[152] President Donald Trump argued that change was necessary "because we are a nation of laws." When discussing the subject on CNN, Ed Martin, a pro-Trump commentator, made a related point. Immigrants "broke the law," argued Martin. "They are lawbreakers."

In recent decades, the federal government tried to crack down on employers that hired undocumented workers. The Immigration Reform Control Act of 1986 made it illegal to hire or recruit illegal immigrants knowingly. Nevertheless, employers, large and small, knowingly or neglectfully, violated the rules. When members of Congress advocated stricter workplace enforcement, business owners objected strongly. Political leaders in Washington discovered it was easier to increase funding for border security than to fund a more robust monitoring of hiring practices. During the administrations of Presidents Bill Clinton and Barack Obama, the federal government improved surveillance of employment. A system called E-Verify simplified an employer's search for information about prospective employees. But a 2013 report from the Migration Policy Institute revealed that less than 10% of seven million or more employers had enrolled in E-Verify.

The parents of minors affected by DACA migrated to the United States because they found plenty of jobs in the booming economy. An article in the *Texas Tribune* (December 16, 2016) identified the situation in an informative headline: "In Texas, Undocumented Immigrants Have No Shortage of Work."[153] Texans readily hired immigrants for labor at distribution centers, in fast food service, in the hospitality and agricultural industries, and numerous other kinds of work. The employment scene in Texas did not simply involve a group of poor law violators seeking jobs from well-meaning families and company managers that were determined to obey the law. Everyone involved, citizen and non-citizen, participated in the ruse. All benefited.

Defenders of immigration needed to move beyond references to the hardships "Dreamers" faced and to the contributions undocumented immigrants made to the U.S. economy and military. Immigrants' advocates needed to challenge deceptive arguments about upholding the law and requiring "illegals" to leave the country. If Republicans wished to stand on principle, they needed to deal with the behavior of millions of Americans who violated the nation's immigration laws with a wink and a smile.

Few Responses to "Now Hiring" Signs? Welcome Immigrants

In 1979 a family left the Soviet Union and emigrated to the United States. A bright young boy in the family, Sergey Brin, attended school in Adelphi, Maryland and earned an undergraduate degree in computer science at the University of Maryland. He then began graduate study at Stanford University. In the 1990s Brin worked on an advanced internet search engine with his classmate and friend, Larry Page. Eventually, the two young men launched a company named Google. You know the rest of the story.[154]

This is just one example among many of immigrants' contributions to America's economic progress. A 2019 report showed that 45% of Fortune 500 companies had been founded by immigrants or their children. Presently, one-fourth of all new firms are created by immigrants.[155] Many newcomers to America are job-creators.

From the 1960s, when restrictions against immigration began to loosen, until 2016, the U.S. economy soared. Immigrant families played major roles in that progress. America's corporate innovators included South African Elon Musk, a founder of PayPal, Space-X, and Tesla and Steve Jobs, Apple's creator, and the son of a Syrian immigrant. Katalin Kariko, a Hungarian-born biochemist worked with other foreign-born scientists to create mRNA technology at Pfizer that produced Covid vaccines.[156]

Other newcomers to the United States did not steer research and development at major corporations but nevertheless contributed significantly to economic advancement. Immigrants and their families gave valuable service to America's farmers, construction companies, hospitals, nursing homes, and other businesses and institutions. They worked at jobs that many native-born Americans avoided.

Beginning especially in 2017, however, Washington slammed the doors shut on many foreigners. From the start of his presidency, Donald Trump criticized immigrants and promoted major restrictions on their entry.[157] His administration slowed down legal immigration proceedings. Wait times doubled for green-card applications. U.S.-based companies that were accustomed to hiring foreign-born computer engineers, scientists, and medical researchers faced difficult obstacles obtaining H-1B for skilled workers.[158] Companies in China, India, and Canada benefited from these actions. Their managers hired talented people.[159]

There was a shortage of job applicants in the early 2020s. The United States had a record 5 million openings.[160] Declines in immigration were a much-overlooked factor in this labor shortage. Throughout the USA, stores post signs indicating, "Now Hiring." Agricultural firms were desperate for workers, as were retailers, fast-food operators, managers of food markets, housing contractors, and factory owners. Supervisors in restaurants and coffee shops limited business hours because they could not hire adequate staff.[161]

Why didn't numerous people show up to take employment opportunities that offered good pay?

Years ago, many analysts attributed the lack of job applicants to a "Great Resignation." They noted that many workers quit their jobs during the Covid pandemic. Some employees decided to retire because they were unhappy about their work environment, low wages, and few benefits. But, as economist Paul Krugman demonstrated, labor participation later surged. By early 2022, employment had climbed to pre-Covid levels. Many workers that had quit jobs moved into better positions, Krugman reported. There was more "reshuffling" than "resignation."[162] Yet job shortages persisted. Why?

Declines in immigration were part of the problem, argued Krugman. Foreign workers' participation in the U.S. economy plunged during Trump's presidency. Their disappearance hurt the nation's job markets. The United States needed to attract many more foreigners, both skilled and unskilled.

If immigration to the U.S. becomes tightly restricted, the United States could experience troubles that resemble Japan's labor problems. In the 1980s,

Japan's economy grew rapidly, but progress slowed in later decades. Declining birth rates and a lack of immigration made it difficult for Japanese businesses to replace lost workers. Japan's population aged significantly. The country lacked adequate workers for the electronic and motor vehicle industries and for agricultural production. The declining labor force also created trouble for Japan's social security system. Not enough workers contributed funds to it. Immigration could provide valuable assistance, but the Japanese had long been reluctant to open their country to foreigners.[163]

In the United States related dislocations began to appear. Four years of immigration restriction by the Trump administration and some continuing restrictions maintained by the Biden administration produced obstacles to progress that resembled difficulties in Japan.

There were no easy fixes. Immigration was a volatile issue, and not just because of broad Republican hostility. Thousands of migrants appeared at the border with Mexico. They left their native lands because of sagging economies, ravages from climate change, and the danger of criminal violence. By the thousands, they sought opportunity in the USA.

The United States cannot handle a totally unrestricted influx of immigrants, but the USA needs many foreign settlers to keep its economy growing. Compromise is necessary. America's employment problem in boom times – a shortage of available workers – could have been alleviated. The nation needed skilled and unskilled foreign-born workers.

Reactions to *An Inconvenient Truth* Revealed Lost Opportunities to Deal with Climate Change

When the documentary film *An Inconvenient Truth* opened in May 2006, former Vice President Al Gore, who is the central figure in the film, hoped the movie would increase public awareness of climate threats and arouse bipartisan political support for action. Two years after the movie's release, prospects for cooperation looked promising. The nominees for President of the United States by both major political parties called for ambitious climate programs. Later, intense partisan division on climate issues grew. Political leaders failed to take meaningful action. In recent years the recurrence of floods, droughts, and heat waves convinced world leaders that a shift to green energy is necessary. The hour for adjustment is late, however. Secretary-General Antonio Guterres summed up the dangers in a 2023 scientific report issued by the United Nations. "Humanity is on thin ice," warned Guterres, "and that ice is melting fast."[164]

An examination of *An Inconvenient Truth's* place in this history illuminates the history of lost opportunities in struggles to protect the planet. GOP politicians were largely responsible for the failure to deal aggressively with climate threats.

The idea for creating the movie emerged when producer Laurie David saw a film excerpt of Gore's lecture about global warming. She thought a feature-length production could inform the public about environmental threats. Davis Guggenheim soon joined the project as director. He faced a challenge trying to turn Gore's lectures and slideshow into compelling entertainment. To excite the interest of moviegoers, Guggenheim made Gore the central character in the narrative.

The production drew attention to Al Gore's longtime work as a climate activist. Gore became concerned about warming temperatures when he took a class at Harvard taught by Roger Rovelle, a scientist who recorded the buildup of carbon dioxide in the atmosphere. Later, as a new member of the House in 1976, Gore held the first congressional hearings on climate change. In 1992 he published a bestseller, *Earth in the Balance.* As Vice President in the 1990s, Al Gore promoted the 1997 Kyoto Protocol, a UN initiative to reduce greenhouse gases. After he lost the presidential election in 2000, Gore devoted considerable time to lecturing on climate change in the United States and around the world.

An Inconvenient Truth was a surprising hit for a documentary film. It received considerable praise, won a prestigious award, and influenced public opinion. David Edelstein, reviewer for *New York Magazine*, called the film "One of the most realistic documentaries I've ever seen – and dry as it is, one of the most devastating in its implications."[165] The movie won an Academy Award for Best Documentary Feature. In 2007, Gore and the Intergovernmental Panel on Climate Change received the Nobel Peace Prize. That year a 47-country survey on the impact of *An Inconvenient Truth* conducted by the Nielsen Company and Oxford University reported 66% of respondents who saw the movie indicated it changed their minds about global warming.[166]

When an interviewer asked President George W. Bush if he would watch the film, Bush replied, "Doubt it."[167] Relations between Bush and Gore had been strained since the 2000 presidential campaign. The tension was due partly to Gore's criticism of Bush in 2000 for failing to address global warming.[168]

Some Republicans in Washington blasted the film and Gore. Senator Jim Inhofe of Oklahoma, a prominent climate denier, compared *An Inconvenient Truth* to Adolf Hitler's book, *Mein Kampf.* Inhofe said every claim in the movie "has been refuted scientifically."[169] Congressman Lamar Smith of Texas claimed the science was flawed because of "exaggerations, personal agendas and questionable predictions."[170] Republicans also complained that Al Gore's prominence in the movie damaged the film's potential for attracting bipartisan support. Gore, they noted, had been the *Democratic* candidate for president. They said Gore's abrasive personality hurt the environmental cause.

Intervention by powerful business interests magnified political divisions. In the years after *An Inconvenient Truth*'s release officials at coal, oil, and gas companies bankrolled communications that questioned the validity of climate science. These well-financed campaigns delivered political dividends. One of the most productive strategies involved requests in 2010 for "No Climate Tax" pledges from congressional candidates.[171] Of 93 new members in Congress that won their races, 83 signed the pledge.

President Barack Obama tried to implement climate initiatives by giving the Environmental Protection Agency greater authority to regulate carbon emissions and by promoting electric cars and batteries, but the next president took a different approach. Donald Trump promised to "save coal" during the 2016 campaign. He denounced climate change as a hoax. Shortly after moving into the White House, Trump pulled the United States out of the Paris climate accord. Trump's administration also scrubbed references to "climate change" from government websites.

Climate denial was prominent in GOP politics, but there had been several Republicans that were willing to advocate climate action in the first years after release of *An Inconvenient Truth*. In 2008 the Republican Party's candidate for president made the case for renewable energy. John McCain called for mandatory limits on greenhouse gas emissions, supported a "cap-and-trade" program that gave companies incentives to invest in clean alternatives, and pledged to challenge the globe's biggest polluters, including China and India, in efforts to protect the earth. In a major speech on the topic, McCain urged action rather than "idly debating" whether climate change was man-made. McCain said, "We need to deal with the central facts of rising temperatures, rising water and all the endless troubles global warming will bring."[172]

In recent years some Republican officials have demanded responses to the kind of "endless troubles" John McCain described. They recognized the threats to communities, evidenced by storms, floods, droughts, and melting ice. Several Republican leaders in southern Florida demanded climate action because of rising waters and flooded streets. Jim Cason, the mayor of Coral Gables (which is adjacent to Miami) said, "I'm a Republican, but this is a non-partisan job . . . You have to deal with facts, deal with risks and probabilities, you can't keep putting your head in the sand."[173]

Unfortunately, a head-in-the-sand approach is still favored by many Republican officials and legislators. In 2021 twelve states with Republican attorneys general sued President Biden because of his efforts to implement rules aimed at reducing greenhouse gases. That year 109 Republican representatives and 30 Republican senators in the 117th Congress refused to acknowledge the scientific evidence of human-induced global warming.[174] In 2023 the House Republicans' debt ceiling proposal aimed to repeal major policies designed to incentivize deployment of green energy.

Al Gore made a significant contribution to public awareness of climate issues through his central role in *An Inconvenient Truth*, but Gore could have done more for the environmental cause if he had won the 2000 presidential election. George W. Bush joked about his opponent in that campaign, saying Gore "likes electric cars. He just doesn't like making electricity."[175] Al

Gore, who realized long ago that electric cars could play an important role in protecting the planet, lost that presidential election by just a few hundred ballots in Florida.

Progress toward reducing greenhouse gases might have come earlier if the count in Florida had gone the other way. It seems likely that efforts to raise public awareness of climate threats would have been more robust in a Gore presidency.

Beijing Profits from Renewable Energy While Washington Argues About It

At the beginning of the documentary film, *China's New Silk Road*, the managing director of Changan, one of China's top carmakers, proudly shows off the company's sleek new electric vehicles. He boasts that they can sell for only $30,000 and possibly less because the government provides incentives and subsidies. Chagan is just one of many companies in China that benefited from government support. President Xi Jinping's "Made in China" program, created in 2015, aimed to turn his country into the world's top creator of products that rely on green energy.

The government of the United States also tapped those opportunities. President Barack Obama's administration and Democrats in Congress directed funds to businesses relying on renewable energy. The "stimulus" bill achieved a lot, but conservatives opposed it aggressively and blocked subsequent efforts. That obstructionism had consequences. China is now far ahead of the United States in creating products that the world needs to reduce climate change.

Chinese progress in the development of electric vehicles (EVs) involves more than just financial support for assembly plants such as Changan's. Years ago, China's leaders recognized that electric vehicles require rare materials. Lithium, a key component in batteries for EVs, was in short supply. The Chinese government responded by inducing local firms to acquire lithium mining operations in the Democratic Republic of Congo. That African country holds a substantial portion of the world's lithium deposits. China's government also kick-started the complex manufacturing that transformed lithium, nickel, cobalt, and manganese into electrodes for batteries. Beijing provided generous subsidies to CATL, the company that now dominates the manufacture of batteries used in the electric vehicles of General Motors, BMW, and other companies.

The Chinese were not ideologically restrained when fostering new technologies. Taking a pragmatic approach, they achieved enormous progress. China encouraged a symbiotic relationship between the government and private enterprise. That cooperative approach paid off handsomely.

Around the time President Xi Jinping was supporting the green revolution, President Barack Obama endorsed a related initiative. Responding to the Great Recession, his administration and Democrats in Congress passed the American Recovery and Reinvestment Act, popularly known as the "stimulus." Sections of the $831 billion program aimed to jump-start projects in clean energy. It sought reduced dependence on fossil fuels. The Act promoted innovations in the manufacture of car batteries and electric vehicles. It supported "capturing" carbon, reducing pollution, weatherizing homes, building a "smart grid," and expanding solar and wind power. The Recovery Act constituted America's largest single investment in clean energy.

Republicans responded by denigrating the bill. They characterized it as a political boondoggle, a waste of the taxpayers' money. Congressman Darrell Issa, a leader in the GOP's resistance declared, "A green jobs fueled recovery is a theory and is yet unproven." Issa organized a committee hearing on the bill's clean energy initiatives with a hyper-partisan title, "How Obama's Green Energy Agenda is Killing Jobs."

When news surfaced that an American manufacturer of solar panels received stimulus money and later filed for bankruptcy, Republicans acted like they found political gold. Solyndra's troubles, they asserted, proved government intervention was a foolish idea.

Democrats countered, saying the stimulus program assisted 21 large projects and numerous smaller ones. There are always some business failures when new companies appear, they argued. Solyndra ran into difficulties because of the recession, declining oil prices, and cheap, subsidized solar panels manufactured in China.[176]

Republicans and their backers in the national media devoted considerable time to highlighting Solyndra's problems but said very little about another U.S.-based company that received financial assistance through the stimulus program. Tesla, an electric car manufacturer, received a $465 million federal loan to build a plant in Fremont, California. Tesla repaid the federal loan early. In 2020, Tesla became the world's most valuable automobile company.

During the administration of President Donald Trump, Republicans put the kibosh on renewable energy projects. Trump said climate change was a "hoax." He claimed wind turbines caused cancer. The Trump administration stymied projects that supported wind and solar innovations. It also rolled back automobile fuel efficiency standards that had been established during Obama's presidency.

In recent years the United States and China have taken different approaches to the emerging revolution in green technologies. China's government consistently pushed for innovations with planning and financial support. In contrast, the United States government operated inconsistently. When Democrats were influential in Washington, funding for research and development in renewable energy expanded. Republicans were much less flexible when responding to the opportunities. Committed to laissez faire, they've resisted even modest efforts to prepare U.S. firms and workers for the future.

Donald Trump's Most Troubling Legacy

If you ask people to name Donald Trump's worst impact on America and the world, many will identify his actions that undermined democracy. When future historians look back on the record of Donald Trump's presidency, however, a different legacy may rank as more important. Trump's position on climate change could stand as his most concerning influence. Donald Trump consistently dismissed scientists' warnings. The U.S. and the world lost precious time in the struggle to protect life on earth during Trumps years in the White House from 2017 to 2021.

On numerous occasions, President Trump labeled climate change a "hoax." He claimed Chinese leaders promoted the idea to make U.S. manufacturing less competitive. Trump lambasted the Paris Climate Agreement, saying it "hurts Americans and costs a fortune." He said climate change was "mythical;" evidence for it was nonexistent. "It's freezing in New York," Trump reported. "Where the hell is global warming."

Decades from now, historians will ask where the hell was the American president when floods, droughts, fires, and other calamities showed a major environmental crisis was brewing.

THIRTEEN

GLOBAL THREATS

When the Soviet Union collapsed and the Cold War with Russia ended, many observers hoped a more peaceful and cooperative era in international relations was about to begin. In the 1990s, Francis Fukuyama, an influential commentator on global affairs, wrote about the "end of history." He noted that leaders in many societies recognized liberal democratic capitalism was the most successful framework for creating political and economic progress.[177]

News events soon undercut that hope. Conflicts around the world broke out over tribal and ethnic rivalries. Russia and China, rather than engaging cooperatively in a "New World Order," turned aggressively nationalistic under authoritarian leaders. After 9/11, the U.S. engaged in occupation and warmaking in Afghanistan and Iraq. Both interventions are now judged fiascos that cost the U.S. greatly in blood and treasure.

This analysis contrasts Republican and Democratic responses to these and other international matters from the 1990s to the present.

It Matters Who's in Charge: Lessons from the Iraq War

Years ago, historian Timothy Naftali appeared at my university to talk about his recently published book. Naftali had completed an analysis of the Cuban Missile Crisis with a Russian scholar. The co-writers based their interpretation on formerly classified Soviet archives as well as newly released U.S. sources. The title of their book, *One Hell of a Gamble: The Secret History of the Cuban Missile Crisis*, suggested how close the world had come to nuclear holocaust in October 1962.

During the Q & A after Naftali's presentation, one of my History Department colleagues asked Naftali what lessons could be drawn from his investigation. Timothy Naftali said we should think carefully when supporting a candidate for the presidency. In a crisis, it is helpful to have a skilled leader at the White House. Naftali's reply suggested the outcome of the Missile Crisis might have been different if an inept Commander in Chief had been in charge in Washington instead of John F. Kennedy.

Timothy Naftali's message was on my mind when I read Robert Draper's informative book, *To Start a War: How the Bush Administration Took America into Iraq* (2020).[178] Draper's history reveals that many top officials in Washington were responsible for the mistakes in judgment that took the United States unnecessarily into the Iraq War and the costly occupation that followed. One individual, though, was the principal architect of the fiasco, Draper argues: President George W. Bush.

Robert Draper shows that Bush, an amiable Texan with little knowledge about international affairs when he won the 2000 election, appeared directionless in the early months of his presidency. Bush spent considerable time away from Washington in those months, cutting brush at his Texas ranch. The shocking events of 9/11 transformed him. Suddenly, Bush acted like a man with a mission. He expressed determination to go after the "bad guys." Brimming with self-confidence, the President encouraged officials in his administration to create plans for action.

If Bush had focused most of his efforts on the capture of Osama bin Laden, his energetic commitment would deserve kudos. But some top and middle-level officials suggested Saddam Hussein, President of Iraq, had connections to al Qaeda. They claimed Iraq was developing chemical, biological, and nuclear weapons. Quickly, Bush bought into this idea. In the first days after the 9/11 tragedy, he demonstrated keen interest in poorly documented assertions that Iraq's government had ties with terrorists. Bush encouraged further investigation. Figures in his administration gave the "First Customer" what he wanted.

Those officials had a variety of reasons for supporting action against Iraq. Deputy Defense Secretary Paul Wolfowitz had been advocating regime change in Iraq for years. Vice President Dick Cheney went along because of his fears about terrorism and interest in expanding America's global power. Defense Secretary Donald Rumsfeld saw an opportunity to test ideas about new modes of warfare. He thought combat with high tech weaponry could substantially reduce the need for boots on the ground. George Tenet, the CIA director, according to Draper, meekly backed the Commander in Chief, seeming eager to provide information that supported Bush's impressions.

Draper identifies George W. Bush's lack of curiosity as a key leadership flaw. One of Bush's most serious errors related to an alarming report presented to him on August 6, 2001. The title was "Bin Laden Determined to Strike in U.S." President Bush did not raise serious questions about this briefing or demand a major investigation of the threat. The individual that prepared the report thought at the time, "So what is this – you're not even *curious?*"

President George W. Bush was not curious about many things, notes Draper, and that approach to management affected deliberations at the White House and in government agencies from September 11, 2001, until the bombing and invasion of Iraq began in March 2003. False claims about Saddam's weapons programs and ties to al Qaeda quickly gained currency. Iraqi individuals with questionable credentials and experience, such as Ahmed Chalabi, achieved extraordinary influence with the Administration's key strategists.

Errors in judgment mounted after the war with Iraq began. Most notable among poor decisions made after the bombing and invasion was L. Paul "Jerry" Bremer's determination to exclude Baath Party officials from participation in the new Iraqi government and his decision to disband the Iraqi army. Chaos followed Bremer's actions. Many of the former Baath Party and army officers joined an insurgency that menaced U.S. troops in Iraq for years.

President Bush was slow to recognize the mistake. He was not inclined to ask questions about people in his administration that managed projects in Iraq.

Some people in the federal government did question policies, including intelligence officials inside the CIA. But they had great difficulty getting the attention of powerful figures. Leaders in the Bush administration did not take the dissenters' concerns seriously.

Secretary of State Colin Powell had doubts about the case for war, too, but promoters of military action armed him with inaccurate information. They encouraged Powell to deliver a speech at the United Nations that made a case for war. That UN address, coming from a popular military officer with a reputation for integrity, was influential. When it later became evident that the information Powell received was flawed, Powell's reputation to a hit.

The point Timothy Naftali made in his discussion about the Cuban Missile Crisis is relevant to the history Robert Draper presents in *To Start a War*. Selecting a President of the United States is serious business. During the Missile Crisis, a skilled president led the United States away from a dangerous precipice. A much less competent President during the 9/11 tragedy led the nation into a disaster. More than 4400 U.S. soldiers perished in Iraq and hundreds of thousands of Iraqis died. The U.S. invasion created instability in the Middle East and triggered violent clashes in the region. Mistakes produced by a flawed president and officials in his administration continue to threaten global peace.

What Did Hillary's Vote in Favor of the Iraq War Really Signify?

During the race to win the Democratic Party's nomination for president in 2016, candidate Bernie Sanders delivered a persuasive response to Hillary Clinton's claims about her broad experience and knowledge in foreign policy. Sanders pointed out that Hillary Clinton erred in October 2002 when, as a senator, she backed President George W. Bush's request for authorization to take military action in Iraq. Bernie Sanders reminded audiences that he opposed that resolution when he was a congressman from Vermont. Sanders claimed his stand demonstrated greater wisdom in dealing with international problems.

Did Hillary Clinton's decision to back President Bush in 2002 reveal deep flaws in judgment? Or was the situation at the time of the vote more complex than Sanders and other critics of Mrs. Clinton acknowledged?

Neither Hillary Clinton nor many other Democrats in the Senate were pleased when President George W. Bush thrust a war-authority resolution in front of them shortly before the congressional elections of November 5, 2002. Dick Gephardt, the Democratic House Minority Leader and Tom Daschle, the Democrats' Senate Minority Leader, accused President Bush of "playing politics." They complained that the Bush Administration put Democratic legislators on the spot. If they rejected the president's request, they would look like appeasers. President Bush seemed to justify their criticism when he spoke on behalf of Republican candidates for Congress shortly before the November elections. Bush denounced Democrats in Congress for trying to deny presidential authority to confront major security threats.

Senator Hillary Clinton found decision-making difficult when evaluating the president's request. She had opposed the Vietnam War when she was an undergraduate at Wellesley and as a law student at Yale. Senator Clinton spent considerable time in the fall of 2002 examining evidence presented by the Bush Administration. She said the vote was "probably the hardest decision I've ever had to make." But she made it with conviction. Hillary Clinton warned that Saddam Hussein was developing biological and chemical weapons. She expressed concern that Iraq might develop nuclear capabilities. Clinton said Saddam Hussein threatened to "alter the landscape of the Middle East."

Did Hillary Clinton expect the vote in Congress would lead to war? She and other prominent Democrats said they hoped their support for President Bush would increase pressure on Saddam Hussein and produce a diplomatic solution. Yet the language of the resolution they backed indicated clearly that military intervention was an option on the table. The resolution authorized the President to use the armed forces of the United States to deal with threats from Iraq.

Years later, Hillary Clinton acknowledged that her vote "got it wrong" but she added, "I wasn't alone in getting it wrong."[180] She was correct on that point.

In 2002 many other Democrats in the Senate backed the resolution. Support for war-making authority came from senators with liberal credentials, including Tom Daschle, Byron Dorgan, Diane Feinstein, Harry Reid, Jay Rockefeller, and Chuck Schumer. Senator John Kerry, a Democrat who ran for President in 2004, voted for the Iraq resolution, as did Joe Biden, who was Barack Obama's running mate in 2008. Other Democratic senators opposed the resolution, including Paul Wellstone, Dick Durbin, Russ Feingold, Robert Byrd, and Edward Kennedy. Democrats that were not in Congress and not required to vote on the resolution were freer to express their disapproval. Al Gore, speaking as a private citizen, offered a blistering critique of President Bush's policy in Iraq. Barack Obama, a state senator in Illinois, also spoke forcefully against the resolution.

Why did several Democratic senators, including Hillary Clinton, accept President Bush's request for war-making authority?

Sensitivity to the political risks associated with opposition may have been a factor. When George W. Bush's father, President George H. W. Bush, asked for congressional support for military intervention in the Persian Gulf in 1991, many Democrats in the House and Senate opposed him. Some of those Democrats paid a price. An international coalition led by the United States handily defeated Saddam Hussein's forces and freed Kuwait. The Persian Gulf War was enormously popular in the United States. In the 1992 and 1994 Congressional elections several Democrats that had opposed that war lost their seats. Republican candidates prevailed for a variety of reasons – not just because of Democratic politicians' stance on the resolution -- but Democrats saw a lesson in the election results.

Opposing a president's patriotic-sounding request for authority to stand up against aggression could harm a politician's career. Democrats that were eager to achieve higher office, including the presidency, tended to back President Bush in 2002. Hillary Clinton, Richard Gephardt, John Kerry, and Joe Biden were among them. Mrs. Clinton won election as U.S. senator in

2000. She did not need to face voters in November 2002, but she was aware of long-term political risks associated with a vote to oppose the president during an international crisis.

Hillary Clinton's speech explaining her decision characterized Saddam Hussein as a severe threat to peace in the Middle East. In October 2002 many prominent people in American society agreed with her assessment of the threats and dangers. Journalists in the national media failed to ask enough tough questions about the Bush administration's claims that Iraq was developing weapons of mass destruction and charges Saddam Hussein had a hand in in the tragedy of 9/11. Later, the *New York Times* and other newspapers came under fire for publishing articles that placed excessive credence in the administration's assertions.

In October 2002 many Americans were fearful about the possibility of another terrorist attack. In March of that year the Department of Homeland Security unveiled a color-coded terrorism threat advisory scale. Those notices put the public on edge. Homeland Security raised the alert level from yellow to orange in September 2002, just a month before the congressional vote on Iraq. Under the circumstances, the President's request for authority to confront a supposedly dangerous threat had considerable public support.

An investigator in search of evidence revealing the pervasiveness of nervous public sentiment can find relevant information in a video on *YouTube*. It shows filmmaker Michael Moore receiving an Academy Award for his documentary, *Bowling for Columbine*. The date is March 23, 2003 -- four days after U.S. bombing of Iraq had begun. When Moore first appears on the stage, the audience cheers loudly. Then Moore uses the occasion to berate President Bush for starting a war in Iraq with flimsy evidence. Suddenly the crowd explodes in loud protests. The band strikes up and the provocative filmmaker is quickly ushered off the stage. This incident, occurring several months *after* the historic congressional vote of October 2002, shows that support for U.S. military action remained strong. Numerous members of the generally liberal Hollywood community objected fiercely when Michael Moore dared to criticize the president and his program of military intervention. [181]

In the months and years after the invasion of Iraq it became clear that the Bush Administration failed to plan adequately. Defense Secretary Donald Rumsfeld grossly underestimated the number of troops needed to subdue the Iraqi population and establish control over the country. Paul Bremmer, who governed U.S. activities in Iraq in 2003 and 2004, quickly disbanded Iraq's military security forces and intelligence infrastructure. That was one of the biggest mistakes of America's occupation, for it stoked a powerful Sunni-led insurgency. Cruel treatment of Iraqi prisoners by U.S. personnel at Abu Ghraib embarrassed the Administration. The number of injured and killed Americans escalated, as did the cost of the war. By November of 2005, political backing for the U.S. intervention in Iraq was beginning to crumble. Pennsylvania congressman John Murtha of the House defense appropriations committee called for a quick pullout of U.S. troops from Iraq. Soon after, many other political leaders joined the call for a substantial withdrawal of U.S. forces.

In short, the authorization for military action backed by Hillary Clinton and other Democratic leaders in October 2002 appeared more strikingly mistaken *after* the Bush Administration's ineptitude in managing the war and occupation became manifest.

NATO Was Right to Expand its Membership to Countries on Russia's Border

Support for NATO used to be bipartisan. Republicans as well as Democrats, backed NATO enthusiastically. That situation changed in recent years. Donald Trump bad-mouthed NATO frequently and complained that several member nations were "delinquent" in contributing funds to the organization. At one point in his presidency Trump reportedly wanted to withdraw U.S. troops from NATO, but he backed off when it became clear the idea lacked support in Congress. After Trump left the White House, Republican criticism of NATO intensified. In the spring of 2022, shortly after Russia invaded Ukraine, 63 House Republicans voted against a symbolic resolution that reaffirmed U.S. support for NATO and its principles. When explaining their opposition, some GOP leaders said NATO was at fault for provoking

Vladimir Putin. They repeated an argument Putin frequently made – that NATO's expansion near and on the border with Russia constituted an aggressive, provocative act.[182]

Debates have been raging since the 1990s about the wisdom of NATO's eastward expansion. Critics of that enlargement warned it would arouse the Russians' distrust of the West and damage prospects for improved relations. Those who championed NATO's expansion wanted to protect the sovereignty of European countries and promote freedom, democracy, and peace across Europe. Over the years, leaders in American politics, diplomacy, and journalism made persuasive arguments for each position. Events in recent years, however, make the debate appear less balanced. One of the two conflicting positions now appears considerably more persuasive.

Historical background is useful for understanding how and why American judgments about this controversy changed.

In the decades after the Soviet Union collapsed, American presidents reached out, attempting to improve relations. President George H.W. Bush showed restraint when the Soviet Union disintegrated. He refused to gloat or declare a victory over America's long-term adversary. President Bill Clinton nurtured a warm and friendly relationship with Boris Yeltsin, Russia's president in the 1990s. When President George W. Bush met Vladimir Putin, he claimed to see into the Russian leader's "soul." Bush described Putin as "straightforward and trustworthy." President Barack Obama attempted to "reset" relations with Russia, reduce tensions, and establish common goals that could benefit the citizens of both countries.

In the 1990s and early 2000s some prominent observers of international relations warned that NATO's inclusion of countries situated close to Russia's borders could undermine prospects for good relations. They said expansion could make the Russians suspicious, fearful, and insecure. Russia's leaders would view NATO's enlargement as a form of exploitation. Russia was economically and militarily weak after U.S.S.R.'s demise. It could not effectively protest NATO's growth. American analysts warned that NATO's expansion across eastern and southern Europe would sow long-term Russian distrust. George F. Kennan, architect of Cold War "containment," expressed this concern. So did Defense Secretary Robert Gates and the *New York Times* 's influential columnist, Thomas Friedman.

President Bill Clinton's Secretary of Defense, William J. Perry, almost resigned because of his disagreement about NATO's expansion. Perry later explained, "At the time we were working closely with Russia, and they were beginning to get used to the idea that NATO could be a friend rather than an enemy... but they were very uncomfortable about having NATO right up on their border and they made a strong appeal for us not to go ahead with that."

These critics of NATO's expansion had good reason to recommend caution. Opportunities for amicable relations with post-Soviet Russia looked promising. During his early years as Russia's president, Vladimir Putin welcomed improved commercial and cultural exchanges involving the United States and Europe.

In 2003, during that hopeful period, Michael McFaul, who later served as President Barack Obama's ambassador to Russia, published an analysis of the situation for the Carnegie Endowment for Peace. McFaul offered a realistic assessment. He said Russia could be troublesome if it lapsed back into dictatorship. But McFaul also recognized opportunities for progress if Russia consolidated into a liberal democracy. "I have no doubt," wrote McFaul, "that [a democratic] Russia will develop into a reliable and lasting ally of the United States in world affairs."[183]

Many other observers of international affairs shared McFaul's judgment at the time. They thought Russia had the potential to become a valuable contributor to global peace and progress.

Later, Michael McFaul had a strikingly different impression of Russia and Putin. He became a harsh critic of the nation and its leader. Advocating a hawkish position on aid to Ukraine during its war with Russia, McFaul wrote, "More Western military assistance, especially weapons that can shoot down Russian airplanes and rockets or destroy artillery, is immediately needed for ending this war."[184]

The reasons for McFaul's harsh judgment are obvious. Like many others who expressed hope for good relations years ago, McFaul reacted to recent history. Putin's nefarious intentions became manifest in 2014 when he seized Crimea and promoted military intrusions into eastern Ukraine. Then came Russia's destructive invasion of Ukraine in 2022. That aggression showed Putin's complaints about NATO's expansion were a ruse. By lashing out at NATO for expanding to Russia's borders, Putin aimed to arouse Western feelings of guilt, make NATO appear the aggressor, and distract attention from his territorial ambitions.

For many years Vladimir Putin blasted NATO for intruding on Russia's sphere of influence and threatening his nation's security. In view of Russia's brutal invasion of Ukraine, Putin's charges about NATO 's belligerence appear fallacious. Russia, not NATO, is the true threat to peace and progress in Europe.

Unfortunately, many Republicans did not acknowledge Putin's deceptions. They endorsed the idea that NATO's eastward expansion had been an unnecessary provocation that wrecked opportunities for friendly relations between the United States, Europe, and Russia. Disturbing news events did not shake their judgments. When Finland and Sweden abandoned neutrality and asked to join NATO in the early 2020s, most informed Americans understood why those two nations changed course. Putin's decision to attack Ukraine revealed he was a major threat to peace and progress. Yet facts about the Ukraine War did not change the judgment of many Republicans. They embraced Donald Trump's position on NATO, which resembled Putin's interpretation of history.

Was there a Russia Connection in Trump's Concealment of Government Documents at Mar-a-Lago?

One of the great mysteries about ex-President Donald Trump's hoarding of sensitive government documents at his residence at Mar-a-Lago relates to motives. It is not clear why Trump kept important government papers at his private residence. Those documents were supposed to be housed at the National Archives. It is also not apparent why Trump's representatives lied when the FBI collected boxes of government papers from Trump's Florida property. Those agents, obviously acting on Trump's behalf, claimed they provided all the missing information. Later, in a raid at Mar-a-Lago, FBI agents retrieved additional documents, including several marked classi-fied. Some of the folders reportedly contained information about nuclear weapons.

Journalists asked why Trump attempted to hide voluminous informa-tion, including details related to national security.

Some of Trump's defenders responded by claiming a mix-up occurred during the hectic days before Joe Biden took up residence at the White House. They speculated that Trump and his aides unintentionally stored government papers in boxes that contained personal items. This explanation lost credibil-ity, however, when Trump insisted the papers were rightfully his.

Others suggested nefarious motives. They noted that Trump's business empire was overextended and heavily in debt. Perhaps Donald Trump wanted to sell access to interested parties, domestic or foreign. Another possible motive concerned Trump's interest in protecting his reputation. The folders might contain embarrassing information.[185]

There is another explanation for Trump's fierce resistance to surrender-ing the documents that received little attention in the news media. Donald Trump's longtime friendly relationship with Vladimir Putin could be a factor. Ties to Putin were not identified in news reporting about the documents. Details about their contents remain sealed. Yet Trump's record of persistent kowtowing when dealing with Putin's and Russia's interests is puzzling. In that context, reports the some of the top-secret documents related to national security are concerning. Those papers would be of considerable interest to the Kremlin.

Donald Trump had been obsequious toward the Russian leader. He consistently spoke about Putin with admiration. When Valdimir Putin engaged in aggressive actions that challenged the security of the European Union, NATO, and Ukraine, Trump refused to criticize the Russian leader and often defended him.

Valdimir Putin appeared to have considerable leverage with Trump. The sources of that influence are mystifying. Only a few clues have emerged. Years ago, one of Trump's sons acknowledged that Russia provided considerable money for the family's real estate investments. Putin's sway with Trump might relate, as well, to Russia's intervention in the 2016 U.S. presidential election. Russian hacks released Democratic leaders' emails and secretly inserted negative propaganda about presidential candidate Hillary Clinton in American social media.

There could be a connection between the two mysteries -- Trump's submissive relationship with Putin and Trump's efforts to stockpile classified U.S. documents. Here are just a few among numerous comments and actions by Trump that raise questions about his relationship with Putin and the Russians.

Campaigning for president in 2016, Trump praised the Russian leader often. He said Putin was "so nice" and "a strong leader." Trump claimed Putin did "a really good job outsmarting our country." He also promised that, if elected, he would "get along very well" with Putin. Trump honored that promise during his years at the White House.

During the 2016 campaign, Trump suggested Russia could keep Crimea. He said, "The people of Crimea, from what I've heard, would rather be with Russia than where they were."

At a news conference in 2016 Trump encouraged the Russians to hack Hillary Clinton's emails. He said, "Russia, if you're listening, I hope you're able to find the 30,000 emails that are missing."

Shortly before the 2017 inauguration, Trump announced he was open to lifting sanctions against Russia. He said, "If you get along and if Russia is really helping us, why would anybody have sanctions if somebody's doing some really great things?"

In a 2017 meeting at the Oval Office, Trump shared highly classified documents with two senior Russian officials.

Trump attacked NATO frequently when he was president. He claimed the organization was "obsolete" and said he would not commit to NATO's defense pledge. Trump considered withdrawing from NATO, and he considered ordering U.S. troops out of Germany.

Donald Trump spread Russian disinformation about Ukraine and temporarily froze U.S. aid to the country. His actions contradicted U.S. foreign policy and benefited Moscow's interests.

Intelligence reports in 2019 and 2020 indicated the U.S. government believed Russia paid bounties to Afghan militants to kill American soldiers. Trump called these reports a "hoax" presented by "fake news."

These are just a few examples that suggest Donald Trump valued support from Putin or feared Putin's influence. *Something* must explain Trump's abundant efforts to please the Russian leader. *Something* ought to illuminate why Trump shocked U.S. intelligence officials on numerous occasions by acting in ways that benefited Russia and harmed interests of the United States and its allies.

We can only speculate about motives. No evidence has come to light so far that ties Trump's concealment of government papers to his relationship with Putin. Investigation of materials that had been hidden at Mar-a-Lago may show that Trump's desire to control the documents had nothing to do with Putin and Russia.

Nevertheless, news reports have featured bits of information that showed the documents could be of great interest to the Russians. Some of the folders contained top-secret information about nuclear weapons.

The mystery remains. Why did Trump consistently excuse, admire, and praise Vladimir Putin when the Russian leader was obviously the free world's nemesis?

President Biden's Speech on Afghanistan Signaled the Potential for a Major Shift in America's International Relations

In 2022, a year after the rushed U.S. exit of military personnel from Afghanistan, Republicans in the House Foreign Affairs Committee issued a 121-page report that lambasted the Biden administration for its handling of the evacuation. The report said President Biden ignored recommendations from U.S. military commanders to keep a small U.S. military presence of approximately 2500 troops in Afghanistan. Biden's flawed decision-making, the report argued, led to "Taliban battlefield gains."[186]

Republicans that crafted the report as well as many pundits that echoed their criticisms failed to appreciate President Biden's broad perspective on the history of U.S. intervention in Afghanistan and lessons that could be drawn from it. Biden's identified his outlook in a speech delivered in early July 2021. The president's comments had relevance beyond the specifics of U.S. involvement in Afghanistan. They reflected Joe Biden's long-held judgment that there must be limits to America's military interventions abroad. Biden's address pointed to new challenges that were not getting the attention they needed because of commitments in Afghanistan and elsewhere. President Biden referred to terrorist threats in South Asia, the Middle East, and Africa. Problems related to the pandemic, climate change, and cyber security required action, too, he argued. Furthermore, the United States needed to be at the cutting edge of technological development to compete globally.

President Joe Biden responded in that speech to people that disagreed with his decision to pull American troops out of Afghanistan. "I ask them to consider the lessons of history," he counseled. The U.S. military had been in Afghanistan for 20 years. America committed a trillion dollars to actions in Afghanistan. 2448 Americans were killed there and 20,722 wounded. Remaining in Afghanistan several more years would continue losses in blood and treasure. The United States did not go into Afghanistan to nation-build, Biden emphasized. "No nation has ever unified Afghanistan . . . Empires have gone there and not done it." He identified projects at home that received inadequate funding because of America's costly military engagements abroad.[187]

President Biden's message resembled an argument historian Paul Kennedy made in his 1987 book, *The Rise and Fall of the Great Powers*. Kennedy observed that powerful nations of the past, including Spain, France, and England, got bogged down in overly ambitious military pursuits. When the cost of those vast operations mounted, national debts spiraled. Rather than making these countries more powerful, military overstretch eventually weakened them. Kennedy's history lesson offered a warning to the American people in 1987. President Biden's speech regarding the Afghanistan pullout presented an update of the Kennedy thesis. In 2021 the U.S. was vastly over-committed abroad.

In recent years several historians and journalists have drawn attention to problems that resulted from overly ambitious military interventions. They noted that operations in foreign countries – fighting, occupying, and keeping the peace – have been undertaken by the United States far more than by other countries.[188] Freakonomics, using a broad definition of military operations, reported that "America has been at war 93% of the time – 222 out of 239 years – since 1776."[189] Washington maintains troops in about 800 military bases in more than 70 countries.[190] The U.S. engaged in a dozen *major* wars since its creation: the Revolutionary War, the War of 1812, the Mexican War, the Civil War, the Spanish-American War, World War I, World War II, the Korean War, the Vietnam War, Operation Desert Storm, the Iraq War, and the war in Afghanistan.[191]

President Biden's speech hinted at broader questions that emerged from an examination of this history. Is it time to end what Biden called the "forever wars"? Since the United States spends more on defense than the next eleven nations combined, is this single country assuming too much responsibility for international security?[192] After the United States failed at nation building in several troubled societies, should U.S. leaders approach foreign missions more cautiously in the future? Is military overreach limiting funding for schools, housing, and health care in the United States?

In a 1953 speech before the American Society of Newspaper Editors, President Dwight D. Eisenhower identified problems associated with the last question:

Every gun that is made, every warship launched, every rocket fired signifies, in the final sense, a theft from those who hunger and are not fed, from those who are cold and are not clothed. The cost of one heavy bomber could build modern schools in 30 communities, or two fine, fully equipped hospitals. We pay for a single destroyer with the money for new homes that could have housed 8000 people.

President Biden, like Dwight D. Eisenhower and historian Paul Kennedy, was concerned about the impact of military spending on the domestic economy and society. But there is another consideration that drove Biden's interest in reducing America's military footprint around the globe. Military intervention placed thousands of uniformed Americans in harm's way.

President Biden mentioned this concern in a speech on May 28, 2021, at Joint Base Langley-Eustis in Hampton, Virginia. He reminded service men and women in the audience that he had visited Afghanistan and Iraq about 25 times and met soldiers that were on their fourth, fifth or sixth mission in the war zone. Biden described his late son's military service and conjectured that Beau's death was related to service in Iraq. Beau "went as an incredibly healthy young man and came back with a severe tumor because his hooch was just downwind from those burn pits."[193]

President Biden told the audience of military personnel that he kept information on-hand every day that listed the total number of troops lost in Afghanistan and Iraq. "Every one of these lives is a tragedy, an empty seat at the dinner table, a missing voice at the holidays," said the President. He linked those tragedies to his decision to change the U.S. relationship with Afghanistan. Biden said the first thing he did after announcing plans for withdrawal was to visit Section 60 at Arlington National Cemetery. That region of the cemetery is dominated by the Afghanistan and Iraq war dead.

From personnel experience, Joe Biden understood the sorrow parents feel from the loss of a son or daughter in a theater of war. Biden did not want to see more grave markers at Arlington. His emotional commitment to military families evidently gave him courage when dealing with generals, politicians, and pundits that objected vigorously to the policy shift. After America's 20-year war in Afghanistan came to an end, there was an opportunity to transform America's role in global affairs.

Leaving Afghanistan: Short-Term Pain, Long-Term Gain

The rushed conclusion to America's 20-year experience in Afghanistan excited many angry criticisms of President Joe Biden's leadership. Pundits and politicians blamed the president and top officials in his administration for the United States' final chaotic weeks in Afghanistan. They drew attention to the betrayal of Afghan allies, the plight of Afghan women, damage to America's international reputation, and prospects for terrorist activity in a Taliban-run country.

The critics' focus on the rushed exit was understandable, but a broader view of America's twenty-year activity in Afghanistan produces better appreciation of the case for withdrawal. Fortunately, an important book appeared that provided this wide-lens perspective: *The Afghanistan Papers: A Secret History of the War*. Author Craig Whitlock drew conclusions from more than 1000 interviews with participants in the war and from secret reports of the U.S. military and intelligence agencies.[194]

Whitlock's investigation showed it was much easier to enter a war than to leave it. During the twenty years of U.S. military engagement in Afghanistan, numerous officials in Washington recognized the mission was mistaken and failing. Yet they were reluctant to reveal those judgments to the American people. Instead, they released upbeat reports about steady progress. With so much blood and treasure committed, presidents and officials knew a decision to pull out would have severe repercussions. President Joe Biden's troubles with Afghanistan illustrate the political risks. Critics attributed America's "defeat" to his decision-making. Biden, they charged, "owned" the disaster.

The Afghanistan Papers: A Secret History of the War showed that numerous presidents, strategists, advisers, legislators, and military personnel played a role in the fiasco. They failed to identify clear, achievable goals. Leaders defended military operations in Afghanistan to stop terrorism, kill al-Qaeda's leader, perform nation-building, promote democracy, and accomplish other objectives. The vague and frequently changing goals made success illusive. No specific achievement represented substantial progress or signaled the moment had arrived to send troops back to the USA. Eventually, the fight in Afghanistan became "America's Longest War." More ominously, some referred to it as an "Endless War."

Afghan society modernized and liberalized thanks to the presence of U.S. military and civilian personnel, but cultural resistance remained strong. Locals saw the Americans, Europeans, and others as unwelcome foreigners.

Corruption surged after U.S. dollars flowed into the society. Afghan loyalties remained fragmented along tribal lines. The government was unable to function effectively on its own. Rebels made large territorial gains. Kabul's position looked increasingly precarious. Back in 2006 a Taliban leader notably described the long-term situation, saying, "You have all the clocks, but we have all the time."

The war created enormous damage. Approximately 241,000 people died in Afghanistan's twenty-year conflict, including about 71,000 civilians. Thousands of American service personnel died or were injured. The financial cost was enormous. Estimates of U.S. spending in Afghanistan range between one and two *trillion* dollars.

Some of President Biden's critics said the U.S. could have maintained a low level of troop commitment in Afghanistan for a long time to prevent Taliban dominance. That would have been difficult. Afghanistan's civil conflict was dynamic, not static. The Taliban warriors were gaining. Rebels seized considerable territory in years and months before the U.S. exit.

The Trump administration gave the Taliban an attractive peace deal that promised U.S. forces would depart by May 2021, and it drew down U.S. troops from about 13,000 to 2,500 prior to Joe Biden's inauguration. Trump's negotiators also gave the Taliban a green light to release 5000 fighters from prison. Some of those individuals were ISIS terrorists. They may have engaged in the tragic suicide bombing at the airport gate that killed several Americans and Afghans.

Propping up the Kabul government with a small American presence was unlikely to produce lasting success. If the Taliban continued to advance, as expected, the U.S. would need to send thousands of additional troops to prevent the government's collapse. Joe Biden acknowledged this problem in a speech on August 31, 2021. "There's nothing low grade or low risk or low cost about any war," he stressed. The United States would have to expand commitments if Taliban advancements continued.

Many of Biden's critics viewed events from a short-term perspective. They blamed him for "losing" the war and damaging the United States' international reputation. But America's engagement in Afghanistan, like its long involvement in Vietnam, was never, in a broad sense, a confrontation that was America's to win or lose. In the long term, it was the responsibility of people in those countries to repel enemies. The United States was not going to engage forever in a local, civil conflict.

President Biden deserved praise for making a difficult but necessary decision. Doing the right thing – changing course in Afghanistan after twenty years of American engagement – was inevitably going to excite recriminations. It took courage to announce the pullout. Biden made his principal judgment about the need for change shortly after the last U.S. military plane left Kabul. He said, "I was not going to extend the forever war."[195]

President Biden's critics characterized the situation in language that communicated gloom and doom. It was not surprising that angry detractors employed sullen language when describing the chaotic scenes in Kabul. They were disappointed that many more Afghan allies and their families could not be airlifted before the last U.S. military plane departed. Yet there is cause for praise, as well. The President, officials in Washington, military officers, and U.S. troops rescued thousands of Americans, Afghans, and others under extremely dangerous conditions during the final weeks of August 2021. They deserve recognition for heroic work under extremely difficult circumstances.

War Between the U.S. and China? Beware of Thucydides's Trap

In 2017 Harvard political scientist, Graham Allison, published a provocative book, *Destined for War: Can America and China Escape Thucydides's Trap?* Allison explored lessons from the writings of Thucydides, the Athenian historian and general who chronicled the Peloponnesian War that began in 431 BC. The rise of Athens and the fear it instilled in Sparta contributed to the outbreak of a devastating military conflict between these city-states of ancient Greece. Allison and his research team considered whether similar conditions often lead to war, situations in which a rising power threatens to displace a dominant one. Of the 16 cases studied in which a major nation's rise threatened the position of a leading state, 12 resulted in war. The U.S.-China relationship had related characteristics, Allison noted.[196] Leaders in the United States had been troubled by China's rising wealth and military buildup. Many Americans wondered if the rivalry could someday turn into a clash of arms. Could yet another Thucydides's Trap be in the making? Judging by the bellicose language in discussions about the United States and China, Allison's question is relevant.[197]

Earlier in the twenty-first century, conversations in the national media about U.S.-China relations focused primarily on commercial rivalry. The Chinese were building a manufacturing dynamo and beginning to assert influence over Asia-Pacific affairs. China was a strong competitor in business activities, pundits acknowledged, yet the two nations had a mutual interest in economic progress. The Americans and Chinese bought and sold from each other. This symbiotic relationship appeared to promote peaceful relations.

Then the situation changed. Recent discussions about U.S.-China relations had a hawkish tone. Some observers spoke about a new "Cold War."[198] Others warned about a hot war. Military conflict was not inevitable, they said, but it was possible. A clash involving ships or planes in the South China Sea, for instance, could escalate, producing a catastrophe. Also, war might break because of Chinese aggression against Taiwan.

Republicans became especially bellicose in their statements about China. During the 2016 presidential campaign, Donald Trump complained that Beijing had been allowed to "rape our country." During his four years in the White House, Trump railed against China and called for "trade wars."[199] Numerous conservative politicians and pundits added their voices to the tough rhetoric. On Fox News, Tucker Carlson asserted that America's "main enemy, of course, is China."

Headlines in articles published in 2020 and 2021 identified the potential for an outbreak. "The Cold War Between the U.S. and China Just Got Hotter," indicated *CNBC*[200] "The Risk of China-US Military Conflict is Worryingly High," reported the *Financial Times*.[201] "Coming Storms: The Return of Great-Power War" stated *Foreign Affairs*.[202] "Short of War: How to Keep the U.S.-China Confrontation from Ending in Calamity" in *Foreign Affairs* suggested ways to mute the war drums.[203]

Journalists and politicians may be exaggerating the danger of armed conflict. The United States and China are competitors in economic, cultural, and military realms, but warfare would wreck their goals, not advance them. Both nations have powerful military organizations backed by high-tech weapons of mass destruction. War between the countries would paralyze global trade, produce financial wreckage in the warring countries, and cause great human suffering.

Why was there so much discussion about the possibility of "war" even though armed conflict would harm both sides substantially?

China's ambition under President Xi Jinping was a factor. The Chinese engaged in unfair business practices and theft of intellectual property. They also crushed human rights of the Uighurs in the Xinjiang region and the rights of citizens in Hong Kong. China continued to threaten Taiwan and take aggressive military actions in the southern Pacific.

War-talk emanated considerably from the United States. In terms of the Thucydides Trap, it is the United States, the globe's dominant power for more than seven decades, that seemed threatened by the upstart nation.

Bellicose rhetoric in the USA was due, partly, to the Trump administration's aggressive relationship with China. President Trump initially praised China's president, Xi Jinping, but his rhetoric later turned bellicose. Trump vilified China and slapped tariffs on its commerce. His tough language characterized China as a global villain. Trump alluded often to the "China virus." He made criticism of China a major talking point during his campaign for reelection.[204] Secretary of State Mike Pompeo added his voice to Trump's attacks.[205] In 2020 Pompeo sounded like he was calling for an overthrow of the Chinese Communist Party. He urged America's allies to "induce China to change."

Later, President Joe Biden and his diplomatic team faced enormous challenges. After years of insults hurled at the Chinese by Republican lawmakers, President Trump, and officials in his administration, Biden could not easily tone down the rhetoric. Biden recognized the political cost of appearing soft when talking about China. Republicans would pounce if a

Democratic president expressed interest in more peaceful and cooperative relations.

With so much distrust fomented in the Trump years, it is not surprising that tensions rose when the new Biden administration began talks. In a meeting at Anchorage, Alaska between Chinese and American diplomats. Biden's Secretary of State, Anthony Blinken, and his National Security Advisor, Jake Sullivan, criticized China's practices, and the Chinese responded with charges about American hypocrisy. China's representatives claimed American leaders treated them with "condescension."[206]

The Anchorage meeting would have been more productive if discussions occurred in the manner diplomacy typically works, in private. Beginning the first major conference between American and Chinese officials in front of the television cameras created opportunities for dramatics. The diplomats postured like verbal combatants for home audiences. Instead of reducing tensions, the discussions exacerbated them.

During Biden's years in the White House, China's actions under Xi's leadership became even more threatening. Construction of man-made islands that could serve as military bases expanded. Chinese warplanes buzzed the waters near Taiwan. China's One Belt and Road Initiative burdened numerous poor nations with huge debts. Fears about China's military buildup and ambitions intensified in Pacific countries. Worries about theft of intellectual property led many company leaders to relocate manufacturing operations to other nations. Also, China's warming relations with Russia were concerning.

There are many reasons for the growing hostilities between the United States and China, but Graham Allison's ideas about Thucydides's Trap likely played a role. After World War II, the United States emerged as the globe's dominant economic and military power. The United States promoted a framework for international relations. American planners organized global agreements on trade and tariffs and sponsored the growth of diplomatic and military alliances such as the United Nations and NATO. The U.S. encouraged multilateral interventions to stop communist expansion, preserve peace, advance economic development, or enhance security. Sometimes the U.S. acted like the world's "policeman" Now China is in the rear-view mirror, gaining rapidly in economic and military strength. Americans worry their nation may soon be bumped out of its dominant position by the fast-rising competitor.

The American people would be wise to view this challenge as worthy competition that, hopefully, can be handled peacefully. It would be foolish to fall into Thucydides's Trap, concluding the rivalry can only be settled through a clash of arms. This competition is not a zero-sum game. The Americans and the Chinese have huge stakes in each other's future.

FOURTEEN

BIDEN'S PRESIDENCY

The Biden administration acted swiftly to deal with current and future challenges. The American Rescue Plan supported Covid vaccination and provided direct cash relief for American families and businesses. A huge infrastructure bill invested billions. The administration's proposals addressed climate and energy needs, and the CHIPS and Science Act supported high-tech development in the United States.

These initiatives jump-started economic growth. U.S. productivity soared, the nation's unemployment rate dropped significantly, and jobs became plentiful.

Nevertheless, many Americans expressed disappointment in Biden's leadership. They worried especially about inflation.

Analyses in this chapter examine controversies in the years of Biden's leadership. They show the Biden administration's accomplishments were greater than many Americans realized. This interpretation notes that the nation's first Republican administration (in Lincoln's time) boldly implemented wide-reaching infrastructure projects that stimulated economic growth. Republicans could have found useful lessons in the record of their party's actions in the 1860s. But many Republicans refused to consider evidence that suggested an activist federal government could energize long-term economic and social development.

The final piece looks at Biden's low popularity rating 12 months and six months before the presidential election of 2024. Public opinion polls indi-

cated many potential voters thought Biden was too old to govern effectively in a second term. The analysis asks whether Democrats would have been wise to seek a different candidate under the circumstances.

Republicans in Lincoln's Time Had a More Sophisticated Understanding of Infrastructure than Today's Republicans

When President Joe Biden announced programs to modernize the American economy and create jobs for the future, Republicans objected to the plan. They backed only a small fraction of the proposed spending, principally for the repair of roads and bridges. Republicans denounced other initiatives, claiming they did not fit into traditional definitions of infrastructure.

Those Republicans failed to examine the origins of their own political party. In the early 1860s, Republicans in Abraham Lincoln's administration and Congress endorsed a multi-faceted approach. They had a broad view of infrastructure. Their actions created a dynamic economy. The Biden administration's plan for modernizing American society aimed to boost long-term economic growth as well.

Biden and congressional Democrats wanted to upgrade and expand road and bridge construction, actions identified with traditional infrastructure, but they had broader plans to improve conditions in the USA. The proposals included environmental efforts to fight climate change, incentives for expansion of renewable energy, improvements in the nation's electric grid, aid for seniors facing health-care expenses, programs to lower prescription drug prices, improvements in childcare, aid for clean water projects, and access of high-speed internet in areas of the country that lacked digital connectivity.

Many GOP legislators rejected this expansive application of the infrastructure idea. Sam Graves, the top Republican on the House Transportation and Infrastructure Committee insisted, "A transportation bill needs to be a transportation bill, not a Green New Deal. It needs to be about roads and bridges." Scott Sloofman, a principal aide to Senate Minority Leader, Mitch McConnell, complained that President Biden sold the proposal as an infrastructure plan but it "actually intends to reshape the U.S. economy and other parts of American life." Republican senator Shelley Moore Capito of West Virginia warned Biden's proposal included social programs that would reengineer "our own social fabric."

These objections revealed a myopic conception of infrastructure. To better prepare Americans for challenges in the future, leaders in Washington needed to think broadly and imaginatively about ways government action could stimulate development and improve the lives of the American people.

Abraham Lincoln and his fellow Republicans demonstrated that broad vision when they took control of the federal government in a time of crisis. With eleven Confederate states out of the Union, Lincoln and Republicans in Congress sought reforms that had long been blocked by southern obstructionists. A burst of Republican-led initiatives jump-started economic transformation in the early 1860s.

Republicans supported initiatives designed to transform American society. They created a Homestead Act that provided settlers in the west with 160-acre parcels and potential title to the land if they remained and developed it. The Morrill Act promoted "institutions of agricultural and mechanical instruction." Many state-run public universities grew out of that program. Republicans created a system of national banks to foster economic stability and provide a national currency. Lincoln's Republican-led government financed Civil War military operations, in part, through a new federal income tax. They tried to protect America's emerging manufacturing industries from foreign competition with a protective tariff. Republicans in the time of Lincoln's leadership also supported construction of the transcontinental railroad. Through land grants and financing schemes (some of which produced scandals), Congress stimulated the growth of commerce and passenger travel. These and other programs improved opportunities for American individuals, families, and businesses. Through a wide range of programs, President Abraham Lincoln and Republican legislators made the federal government a catalyst for change.

In 2021 Biden and the Democrats recognized, like Lincoln and the Republicans of 160 years before, that narrow-minded, special interest politics had long-hindered economic progress. Democrats believed Washington had an important role to play preparing American society for challenges ahead. Unfortunately, many Republicans in Washington did not share that outlook. They supported limited spending on traditional "infrastructure" projects and opposed broad programs that focused on future needs. Republicans failed to consider the broad vision of their party's founders. During the Civil War, President Lincoln and Republicans in Congress recognized the federal government's potential to advance modernization.

Programs of the Biden Administration Were Not Singularly Responsible for Inflation

When Joe Biden began his presidency, the U.S. economy was in trouble. The Covid pandemic had slowed economic growth dramatically. Prospects for a quick recovery did not look promising. Biden, his economic advisers, and Democrats in Congress anticipated the problems. They acted swiftly to get ahead of them. The Biden administration proposed bold investments to deal both with current and future challenges. The administration's American Rescue Plan supported broad-based Covid vaccination and provided direct cash relief for American families and businesses that had been hard hit by the pandemic. The administration's huge infrastructure bill invested billions throughout the country to promote high-speed internet, safe roads and bridges, modern wastewater systems, clean drinking water, and reliable electricity. The Inflation Reduction Act promoted huge investments regarding climate and energy needs. The CHIPS and Science Act boosted investment in high-tech research and production. It aimed to bring back semiconductor manufacturing in the U.S.

These spending initiatives jump-started economic expansion. In the following months and years U.S. productivity soared, the nation's unemployment rate dropped to historic lows, and jobs were plentiful.

Inflation accompanied this growth, but that price spiral was only partly related to federal spending for these programs. Price rises occurred because of dislocations caused by the coronavirus, lockdowns in China, and the war in Ukraine. Inflation was a global problem at the time, not a distinctly American one. Throughout the world, societies struggled with inflation, and in many countries the inflation rate was higher than in the United States. Those nations never had a series of rescue and stimulus measures such as the ones advanced by President Biden, the Democrats, and some Republicans. Global developments, not specifically American ones, pushed up prices. Especially important, the American people realized extensive benefits from government programs that invested in the present and the future. Economic growth was far more impressive in the United States than in most other nations that were troubled by inflation.

Democrats that defended the spending plans when they were under consideration in Congress, including Jared Bernstein, an economist and long-time adviser to Biden, worried about the nation's shaky economic situation when Biden became president. In January 2021 a U.S. government report indicated the U.S. economy lost 140,000 jobs the previous month. Joblessness appeared likely to persist until 2024. Despite substantial spending for Covid relief in 2020, more bold measures seemed necessary. Bernstein and other advisers recalled that back in 2009 the Obama administration cut the size of its planned stimulus to satisfy conservative critics. That trimmed-down bill was inadequate. Recovery was painfully slow. It took six years to bring jobs back to pre-recession levels.

Mark Zandi, Chief Economist of Moody's Analytics, viewed the Biden administration's programs in terms of "good" and "bad" inflation. The good kind, he argued, came in from U.S. government stimuli that reduced unemployment. The "bad" type occurred because of international developments such as the global pandemic, lockdowns in China, and the war in Ukraine. "Bad" inflation was difficult to control.[207] In the early 2020s bad inflation related primarily to global problems.

Economic downturns in the U.S. often have global connections. The Panic of 1873 and subsequent "Long Depression" affected numerous countries as did the Great Depression of the 1930s. The Great Recession of 2008-2009 was a worldwide phenomenon as well. Economic problems the Biden administration inherited were evident in many other counties at the time.

Prices climbed substantially in many advanced nations, the Pew Research Center reported in June 2022.[208]

The pandemic created a huge economic shock throughout the world. Governments spent vigorously to aid citizens during the emergency. When global health improved in 2021 and 2022, consumers were eager to spend again on goods and services. Supply chain breakdowns complicated recoveries. Production facilities, transportation networks, and labor forces could not keep up with fast-growing demand. Those difficulties exacerbated when China, the world's manufacturing dynamo, mandated lockdowns in various sections of the country as part of its zero-Covid program. China's policies created huge trade disruptions.

Another important international shock that spiked inflation occurred in late February 2022 when Russia's military invaded Ukraine. A series of actions and reactions followed. The United States, NATO allies, and other countries backed sanctions. Russia responded by cutting back oil and gas sales to Europe. Energy prices surged in global markets. The invasion also affected food prices. It disrupted agricultural production in Ukraine, a major producer of grain products.

When energy and food prices climbed rapidly, consumers in the UK, Belgium, Pakistan, Zimbabwe, Ecuador, and other countries protested. They blamed political leaders for the fast-rising cost of living, even though the officials had little ability to control it. In related ways, frustrated citizens in the United States blamed leaders in Washington for the rising cost of living.

GOP leaders seized the opportunity to slam their opponents. They attacked President Biden and Democrats in Congress, blaming them almost solely for the inflationary spiral. Republican Senate Minority Leader Mitch McConnell attributed inflation to federal stimulus spending promoted by President Biden and the Democrats. "There's no relief in sight," McConnell charged. Inflation was "a direct result" of Democrats "flooding the country with money.[209] Chairwoman of the House Republican Conference, Elise Stefanik said "inflation is skyrocketing because of Democrats' reckless and wasteful spending."[210] Senator Rick Scott of Florida, chairman of the National Republican Senatorial Committee, revealed, unintentionally, why he and fellow Republicans placed most blame at the feet of Democrats. Scott said public concern about rising prices produced a "gold mine" for his party.[211]

Scott, McConnell, and other Republicans typically ignored their party's involvement in spending to deal with the Covid crisis. More than $3 trillion of the approximately $5 trillion total in U.S. financial commitments related to the pandemic occurred during Donald Trump's presidency. Republicans in Congress, especially in the Senate, vigorously supported that emergency spending to assist businesses and the public.

Americans were appropriately upset by the elevated prices seen at the food market and the gas pump, but they were misled in conversations about the source of troubles. Republican politicians, many pundits, and some economists focused largely on spending by the federal government when explaining the problem. Yet spending advocated by the Biden administration was not the largest cause of the inflationary spiral troubling Americans. Furthermore, the Biden administration's economic initiatives created considerable "good" inflation, the kind that delivered robust economic growth. It was a factor in the record-matching 3.5% unemployment level achieved as quickly as 2022. A much greater impact on prices related to "bad" inflation affecting much of the globe because of the Covid pandemic, supply-chain issues associated with lockdowns in China, and the war in Ukraine.

It was difficult to deal with inflation when conversations about it ignored major causes of the price spirals that affected economies throughout the world, not just in the United States.

Biden or Some Other Democrat for President in 2024?

I featured the op-ed below on my website on November 6, 2023, a year before the 2024 presidential election. Writing this piece was difficult. Even though I suggested Democrats would be wise to nominate a different candidate for president, I felt Joe Biden did not deserve a recommendation to retire. He had been an effective national leader. His administration achieved a great deal in domestic and international affairs. Public opinion was the chief factor influencing my judgment. The president's approval rating was embarrassingly low in November 2023. Changing the numbers seemed extraordinarily difficult.

A Biden loss in the 2024 presidential election was not a certainty, but Biden's candidacy put the Democratic Party at a disadvantage. Donald Trump appeared vulnerable. Many voters, including numerous Republicans, were suffering from "Trump Fatigue." The Democrats' prospects for taking the White House and the House of Representatives in the 2024 elections looked good. Achieving control of the Senate was more challenging but possible. If Democrats had a popular presidential nominee, other Democrats in state and local elections could reap the benefits. But Joe Biden's low numbers diminished those opportunities.

In the months after I wrote the piece many pundits expressed related concerns. Commentaries by Ezra Klein and Fareed Zakaria were particularly influential.

Ezra Klein, a *New York Times* opinion writer, argued that the Democrats had better options than Joe Biden. He explained the judgment in a February 2024 podcast that provoked considerable discussion in the mass media. Klein suggested Democrats ought to wait a few months to see if Biden's poll numbers improved. If they didn't register progress by May 2024, Democrats would be wise to seek a different nominee. Klein recommended a selection process that the party applied years before. They could choose the nominee at the Democratic National Convention.[214]

Three months later, in May 2024, Fareed Zakaria, an influential commentator on public and international affairs at the *Washington Post* and CNN, assessed Biden's situation. Zakaria expressed concern about Donald Trump's improved popularity. Polls showed Trump leading in almost all the swing states. Behind those numbers were "even more troubling details," Zakaria warned. An NBC poll asked voters whom they trusted more to deal with the economy. Respondents gave Donald Trump a 22-point lead. Biden was 35 points behind Trump on a question about who could better handle immigration. Only 33% of respondents approved of Biden's leadership regarding the Israel-Hamas war. On a crucially important question about competence, Trump led Biden by 16 points. Also troubling for Joe Biden was the presence of several third-party candidates in the presidential race that were likely to cut deeper into Biden's support than Trump's. Fareed Zakaria concluded that voters' concerns about Biden's age led them to question his capacity to govern. There was "very little that Biden can do to change that perception," Zakaria pointed out.[215]

The perception Zakaria identified, voters' concern about age, constituted a major problem for Biden's candidacy. Ezra Klein demonstrated the difficulty by demonstrating two of Biden's speeches in his podcast – one from 2019 and a recent one. Klein observed that Biden sounded notably less energetic in the later speech. Those who worked with Biden maintained that he remained alert and in command in their private meetings, Klein acknowledged. But Biden's public image as an elderly gentleman who walked slowly and haltingly was prominent in the minds of many Americans. That mental picture was especially influential with young voters, a group that was vital in the Democrats' election strategy.

A central theme in this book's analysis is that the Republican Party became less democratic in its internal operations over the decades. GOP leaders provided fewer opportunities for dissent, debate, negotiation, and compromise as the years passed. Democrats engaged more energetically in political discussions during that time. Yet in dealing with President Biden, Democrats did not respond aggressively to a looming crisis. Trump's candidacy posed serious dangers for America and the world. To confront that threat effectively, Democrats needed to nominate an individual that was likely to inspire enthusiastic support from a broad swath of the American electorate. Rather than decide which nominee could best serve that goal, Democrats allowed Biden to make the decision for them.

Many Democrats recognized Joe Biden's vulnerabilities, but they concentrated their hopes for victory on an improved economy and missteps by the deeply flawed Republican candidate. On both counts that strategy had shortcomings. Persistent discontent over inflated prices and high interest rates undermined the Democrats' economic argument. Despite numerous indictments and several court cases involving Trump, prospects for guilty verdicts quickly diminished. By late spring of 2024, only one court procedure involving charges of violating campaign finance laws in a matter related to "hush money" offered the potential of a conviction and diminished support for Trump from swing voters.

A related threat lurked, as well. If scandals suddenly brought Trump's candidacy to an end, Republicans might replace him with someone possessing mainstream credentials such as Nikki Haley. A more broadly popular GOP candidate would likely pose an even bigger election challenge for Democrats.

It was not surprising that leaders in the Democratic Party continued to favor Biden despite troubling evidence in public opinion polling. As President of the United States, Joe Biden exercised tremendous influence in the Democratic Party's affairs. Leaders in the organization feared that late-date resistance to Biden's nomination could produce huge intra-party divisions. Furthermore, Democratic politicians that questioned Biden's nomination and failed to secure a replacement would quickly lose favor with their Democratic colleagues. They might wreck their future political opportunities in the party. Consequently, most prominent Democrats announced Biden had their enthusiastic support.

Joe Biden gave the United States impressive leadership, and he deserved recognition for notable achievements. But when he insisted on running for a second term, voters recognized that he would be 86 years old in late 2028. Many Americans were unsure about Biden's continued management as a senior citizen. Some worried he might not live long enough to complete a second term. These concerns and others made his candidacy a risky bet for Democrats.

Millions of Americans hoped Joe Biden would come away with a victory in November 2024. I shared their hope. But hope is not a strategy. The anxieties of many Americans -- Democrats, independents, and numerous Republicans, as well -- could have been alleviated significantly if the Democratic Party selected a presidential candidate with broader national support.

The following article shows the challenges that Biden and the Democrats faced were abundantly clear a full year before the elections. If Democrats were to change candidates, a year prior to the elections was a much better time to make the adjustment than in the summer of 2024.

The Latest Polling of Voter Opinion Shows Democrats Need to Find a New Presidential Candidate

November 6, 2023

The results of the *New York Times* and Siena College Polls became public yesterday, and they are alarming. They show Donald Trump leading President Joe Biden in five of six important battleground states a year before the 2024 presidential election. Trump is ahead of Biden by 4 to 10 percentage points among registered voters in Arizona, Georgia, Michigan, Nevada, and Pennsylvania.

Voters' judgments about Biden are shockingly low. Biden's approval rating is only 38.9%, while his disapproval rating is 54.8%. In the recent poll 71% said Biden was "too old" to be an effective president. 62% thought Biden does not have the "mental sharpness" to be effective. Especially disturbing for Democrats, voters under 30, a group Biden won handily in 2020, say they trust Donald Trump more on the economy by a whopping 28 percentage points. The polls show Americans across all income levels feel Biden's policies hurt them personally.

There is evidence from history, too, that suggests Biden's candidacy in 2024 could be in deep trouble. Voters' attitudes about their economic well-being and their judgments about a candidate's charisma weigh heavily in their decision-making. On both counts, Biden looks weak. Yet he refuses to acknowledge mounting evidence of his vulnerabilities.

President Biden can benefit the Democrats and the nation by announcing plans to retire after his current term in office. If he chooses not to run again, he will likely become recognized as America's most successful one-term president. But if he campaigns again, loses the election, and influences the defeat of numerous Democratic candidates, millions of Americans will blame him for the party's and the nation's troubles.

A Biden defeat in 2024 is not inevitable, but the long-term evidence of Biden's weak appeal with voters suggests his run in 2024 is a risky proposition. A victory by Donald Trump, which data suggest is a real possibility, could significantly undermine American democracy. Of course, Trump's presence on the GOP presidential ballot is not certain. If Trump is convicted for criminal behavior in the coming months, Republicans might nominate a different presidential candidate. That person could have even greater appeal with the voters than Donald Trump.

If Biden takes himself out of the race, the Democrats have plenty of attractive political leaders on their bench to take his place. California governor Gavin Newsom, Michigan governor Gretchen Whitmer, and Connecticut senator Chris Murphy are popular. A more obscure figure, Dean Phillips, a U.S. representative from Minnesota, announced in October 2023 that he will seek the Democratic presidential nomination. In an engaging interview on Bill Maher's HBO show, Phillips demonstrated impressive communication skills. These individuals and others could improve the Democratic Party's prospects enormously.

President Biden's supporters dispute the voters' negative impressions about the state of the economy. They think appreciation of Bidenomics will become clearer during the leadup to the election. They are correct in pointing to Biden's economic achievements, but voters' judgments about them may not change much in the next twelve months.

Comparatively speaking, the U.S. economy is in considerably better shape that the economies of other advanced nations. U.S. manufacturing revived during Biden's presidency, investment in technology and infrastructure surged, and the job market became robust. Inflation declined faster in the United States than in Europe.

Yet the voters' *perception* is different. Many Americans recall that inflation and interest rates were lower during Trump's presidency. They give little attention to evidence that inflation spiked throughout the globe in recent years because of the Covid pandemic, supply chain delays, the war between

Russia and Ukraine, and other factors. Furthermore, interest rates climbed globally when central banks combatted inflation by increasing the cost of borrowing.

Most voters do not have the economic chops to recognize the complex international factors influencing inflation and interest rates. They are focused on the economy's impact on their daily lives such as the cost of purchasing food for the dinner table or the interest rate on loans they take out to purchase cars and homes. They revealed their discontent in the polls. The recent survey showed voters across all income levels thought Biden's policies hurt them personally and Trump's policies helped them.

Charisma plays an important role, too, in voters' perceptions about presidential candidates. The 1960 presidential election provided a demonstration. Americans that saw John F. Kennedy on television were impressed with his youth, vigor, and verbal skills. In recent decades two charismatic Democratic presidents served double terms. Bill Clinton and Barack Obama were talented communicators in the age of mass electronic communications. Joe Biden did not captivate voters through personal magnetism in 2020. He succeeded by coming across as a responsible, centrist, mainstream politician who could rescue the nation from the tumultuous leadership of Donald Trump.

Democrats that are frustrated with Biden's low standing in the polls are urging him to campaign more vigorously though personal appearances around the country, and they want him to participate in more televised interviews. That kind of engagement might hurt rather than benefit the campaign. Biden does not project energy in his speaking engagements, and his age shows. The President's formal speeches are well-crafted and fortified with details about achievements. Nevertheless, his oratory does not resonate with many listeners. Biden is far from an ideal candidate in the age of personality-driven campaigning that involves numerous appearances in the mass media.

Democrats cannot rely comfortably on evidence from the party's 2020 presidential victory. Joe Biden won with nearly seven million more popular votes and 74 more Electoral College votes than Trump received, but Biden's margin of victory in six important swing states was miniscule. He squeaked past Trump in Arizona, Georgia, Wisconsin, Michigan, Nevada, and Pennsylvania. If Trump had received a few thousand additional votes in some of those states, he could have won a second term in the White House. The situation in November 2024 may be quite different than it was in November 2020, as recent polls suggest.

Democratic leaders are now in the horns of a dilemma. They know that a political party often loses an election when an internal rebellion undermines the incumbent president. An intense battle in the Democratic primaries could facilitate a Republican victory in 2024. Sticking with Biden could also facilitate a GOP victory.

The prospect of a Trump win in 2024 is so troubling that the choice between the alternatives should be clear. Biden's and Harris's poll numbers have been low for months, and Donald Trump's numbers have been climbing. Another Trump presidency would be disastrous for the nation and the world. If Democrats are going to deal responsibly with the troubling numbers, they will have to act swiftly. They will need to face the daunting task of thanking the elderly, decent, and effective man in the White House. They have to muster the courage to tell Biden he can serve his party and the nation by clearing a path for a different nominee.

As many pundits point out, nothing is inevitable in American politics. Conditions can change dramatically. Biden might prevail in the 2024 election. In view of statistical evidence mounting a year before the election, however, gambling on that outcome seems a risky proposition. Selecting a younger and more popular candidate looks like a safer bet.

EPILOGUE

REFORMING THE GOP

Is the GOP victimized by its past? Has the party's extensive involvement in extremism made it virtually impossible for moderate Republicans to bring their party back to the center-right? Will the current trajectory continue, producing greater extremism in the future?

The Republican record is concerning, as articles in this book attest, but deterministic predictions that the party's future will resemble its past could be mistaken.

A reckoning with extremists has been postponed, largely because the American constitutional system provides inordinate influence for minorities. Two political analysts at Harvard, Steven Levitsky and Daniel Ziblatt, identified this condition in their book, *Tyranny of the Minority*. The Constitution is supposed to safeguard democracy, they noted, but many of the founders who created it were suspicious of popular democracy. In modern times, the constitutional framework allows partisan minorities to thwart majorities and sometimes even govern them.[216]

In recent decades extremists in the GOP gained enormous political leverage through inequities in the constitutional system. They elected U.S. senators in lightly populated rural states who exerted as much authority as a senator from heavily populated California or New York. Republican candidates for the U.S. Senate and House in southern states and in some western and midwestern states needed only to appear more radical than their competitors in primary elections to win the party's nomination. After receiving the GOP's support, they easily secured a seat in the national government in Republican-leaning districts.

Republican extremists strengthened their grip on local and national politics by establishing rules that disenfranchised Democratic voters. President Donald Trump and conservative justices on the Supreme Court undermined reforms achieved by the Voting Rights Act. The radicals' influence in state governments enabled Republicans to gerrymander electoral districts. Manipulation of district maps ensured GOP dominance, even in states where Democrats received more popular votes than Republicans.

The most striking example of "tyranny of the minority" was in elections for President of the United States. Republicans won the popular vote in only one of eight presidential elections between 1992 and 2020. The GOP benefited from the Electoral College's peculiarities. Despite Republicans' failure to achieve a popular mandate for bold action, they acted like their victories through the Electoral College demonstrated they were clear favorites of the American people. Republican politicians demanded huge adjustments in governmental affairs after winning the electoral count but losing the popular vote. During years under presidents George W. Bush and Donald Trump, Republicans implemented radical economic, social, political, and foreign policy changes, and they established ultra-conservative dominance at the Supreme Court.

The Republican Party, strengthened by constitutional advantages, has been reshaping American life for several decades, but it could eventually face a crisis. A growing majority of American voters is disgusted with the behavior of far-right flame-throwers. The radicals' prominence in the GOP could become a major liability. Electoral demographics are changing. Many young voters are appalled by extremism.

It is long past time for disillusioned Republicans to speak out against their party's excesses loudly and forcefully. The United States needs a responsible, mainstream, center-right party, not the ultra-right version that is dividing American society and undermining democracy. Representative Jim McGovern, a Democrat from Massachusetts, identified the need for courage across the aisle when he said, "There are a lot of Republicans who are rational human beings who are horrified by this, but they don't seem to have the guts to stand up to it and push back." McGovern's description relates to recent U.S. political history, but it need not apply to the future. Republicans that are "rational human beings" can serve their party and their country admirably by resisting extremism.[217]

Bringing the GOP back to the political mainstream seems like a pipe dream in view of the Republican Party's current excesses. Nevertheless, it is worthwhile discussing changes that would be helpful in shifting the party's direction. Even though a sweeping transformation would be a daunting task and seems unlikely to occur soon, it is helpful if *some* "rational human beings" *start* to demand changes.

What are the most fundamental problems in Republican politicking that need attention?

Three improvements would be particularly helpful. All three relate to the language of politics. Modifying Republican rhetoric constitutes an important first step toward directing GOP politics back to the mainstream.

1. Recognize Government's Value

Republican messaging about the role of government in American society needs major adjustment. Back in the time when Dwight D. Eisenhower was the principal face of modern Republicanism, the public's attitudes about the federal government's role in American society were generally positive. Those affirmative perspectives are now in short supply. Recent opinion surveys reveal a substantial decline in the American people's impressions about government.[218] Republicans' negative characterizations, promoted over several decades, contributed to the changing views.

In 1958 approximately three out of four American respondents indicated they trusted the government to do the right thing almost always or most of the time. A survey released in September 2023 showed less than 20% of Americans trusted the government in those terms (25% of Democrats registered trust and only 8% of Republicans). There are many reasons for the shift from positive to negative impressions. The public's growing concern about dysfunction in Congress is a significant factor. Yet the long-term denigration of the government in the Right's communications played a significant role.

Ronald Reagan's statements affected the shift. In his inaugural presidential address Reagan asserted "Government is not the answer to our problem; government is the problem." At a press conference, he joked, "The nine most terrifying words in the English language are: I'm from the Government, and I'm here to help." Through eight years of leadership at the White House, the Reagan administration put these ideas into action. It diminished the size, reach, and influence of Washington. In the decades after Reagan retired from politics, Republican leaders often expressed suspicion of federal power. Reagan was not fully responsible for the negativity, but his impact was significant.

Donald Trump, more than any Republican leader in the twenty-first century, accentuated that hostility. After Trump lost the 2020 presidential election and prepared to make another run for the White House, his references were frequently hostile. Trump promised to "obliterate" the "deep state" in a second term. "Either the deep state destroys America, or we destroy the deep state," he declared at a rally. Speaking to another crowd, Donald Trump promised to bring revolutionary change after a second inauguration. "We will expel the warmongers from our government," he announced. "We will drive out the globalists. We will cast out the communists, Marxists, and fascists. And we will throw off the sick political class that hates our country."[219]

The adjustments Trump sought had been under consideration by some conservative strategists for decades. During and after Ronald Reagan's presidency, theorists at rightwing think tanks crafted rationales for undermining the authority of Washington's regulatory agencies. In the 2020s, they pointed to Article 2 of the Constitution and claimed a president had broad control over the executive branch. They found inspiration in ideas developed by Reagan administration lawyers that supported deregulation. Those conservative theorists said a president had the authority to rein in "unelected" heads of the government agencies.

This interpretation of the Constitution gave the chief executive authority to block federal offices from creating rules for consumer protection, the safety of air, water, and food, the regulation of banks and financial markets, and much more. Kevin D. Roberts, president of the conservative Heritage Foundation, said contributors to Project 2025, a plan for presidential transition framed with Trump in mind, aimed to dismantle "the rogue administrative state."[220]

Many responsible conservatives in the Republican Party reject this vision of unbridled presidential power. They recognize the danger of letting a wannabe dictator like Trump bend the federal government at his will. They should recognize, however, that conservative politics is part of the problem. Rather than endorse "traditional conservatism," which Edmund Burke famously described as "a disposition to preserve and an ability to improve, taken together," many Republicans championed extreme applications of the ideology. Their purist versions of laissez-faire became prominent in Republican communications. Leaders on the right demanded that government "bureaucrats" keep their hands off the economy. The Republican case for deregulation and government downsizing became a matter of faith. GOP politicians sounded like free-market fundamentalists.

Barry Goldwater articulated ultra-conservative economic theories when he campaigned for the presidency in 1964. Ronald Reagan treated the government as a threat to freedom in numerous public statements. George H. W. Bush promised to carry the torch for Reagan-style conservatism (he backtracked somewhat by supporting tax increases to avert a fiscal crisis). George W. Bush appointed numerous enthusiasts of laissez faire-style economics to positions in the federal government. Donald Trump amplified Republican resistance to the "deep state."

The GOP's stands on economic issues turned rigid. On each major policy issue, Republican leaders made predictable judgments. In one form or another, they endorsed Reagan's perspective. Government was not the answer to America's problem, they asserted. Government *was* the problem.

When Democrats supported reform measures to address shortcomings in health care, threats from climate change, risks of financial meltdown, and other challenges, the GOP's response resembled a mantra. Let private enterprise handle the situation, Republicans argued. An activist federal government would make the situation worse, they asserted.

Traditional Conservatives that want to bring the Republican Party back into the political mainstream will need to adjust their negative and absolutist messaging about the role of government in American society. They, too, will sound like extremists if they continue treating "government" as the enemy of the American people. Government is not an alien force that must be crushed. The government is us. Its purpose is to deal with problems that cannot be solved individually or through the local community.

If Republicans continue to insist that government is the enemy of progress, they will have little to offer when addressing the nation's problems. This void was evident on September 27, 2023, when seven Republican candidates participated in a presidential debate at the Reagan Library. Throughout the evening, the contenders blamed "government" principally for the nation's troubles. By villainizing the federal government, they evaded consideration of pragmatic solutions to current problems. They offered only platitudinous statements about making big, vague changes on "day one" of their presidency.

Those candidates knew Republican voters would be suspicious if they proposed specific policies. Policymaking, after all, is the responsibility of governmental leaders. Mitt Romney identified the situation directly when announcing that he would not seek reelection to the U.S. Senate. Romney complained that far-right Republicans had little interest in policy. They focused on "resentment and settling scores and revisiting the 2020 election."[221]

Republican politicians are out of step with the American people. While it is true that opinion polls reveal public trust in the federal government hovered near record lows in recent years, Americans have also expressed positive views of the federal government's performance in several specific areas. After surveying 11,001 adults in the USA, the Pew Research Center reported in 2020 that "majorities *want* the government to play a major role on everything from keeping the country safe from terrorism to ensuring access to health care and alleviating poverty." Majorities said the government did a very good or somewhat good job responding to natural disasters (62%), strengthening the economy (54%), and maintaining infrastructure (53%). [222]

Pew found that large majorities of Democrats (about three quarters) said government should play an influential role, while Republicans were less enthusiastically supportive of a significant role for the government. Nevertheless, one half or more of Republicans said the government should play a major role in 9 of the 10 topics Pew surveyed. Of course, the judgments of Democrats and Republicans are affected to some degree by the person who occupies the White House at the time of polling. Donald Trump was president in 2020, and his position may have given Republicans a more sanguine impression of government's value at the time. Nevertheless, overall, Pew reported finding common ground for both parties "in views of the role government *should* play."

The problem of Republican extremism in modern American society is not simply related to Donald Trump's outrages, the antics of GOP radicals that created dysfunction in Congress, and the unsubstantiated beliefs of culture warriors that traffic in conspiracy theories. It is a problem created by sober, thoughtful, traditional Republicans that communicate grossly negative judgments about the role of the federal government in national affairs.

Conservatism need not imply fierce resistance to governmental efforts to improve the economy and the lives of the American people. An important first step for Republicans that want to return the GOP to the mainstream is to adjust their party's messaging about the federal government.

2. Reject Falsehood; Affirm Truth

Truth took a beating when extremist rhetoric ran amok. Disseminating fallacious statements became a rewarding strategy for building a successful career in GOP affairs. By making outrageous claims, far-right politicians raked in financial contributions, drew attention in the news and opinion media, and achieved victories in primary and general elections. Treating untruths as facts became normative in GOP rhetoric.

This was particularly evident in recent years when some Republican candidates and officials vigorously presented rationales for voter suppression. They showed no remorse about undermining fundamental American democratic traditions. Numerous Republicans asserted that Joe Biden had been elected president through fraud, and claimed Donald Trump was the true winner. Some Republicans didn't back conspiracy theories about a stolen election directly, but they treated the phony accusations generously. They claimed to have "questions" and "concerns" about voting irregularities.

Republicans often promoted grossly false accusations about prominent Democrats. Donald Trump repeated a lie that President Barack Obama lacked an authentic U.S. birth certificate. Rather than criticize Trump's deceit, many Republicans mentioned the claim or refused to denounce it. They suggested Democrat Hillary Clinton was guilty of horrendous decision-making in connection with the Benghazi tragedy in Libya. It didn't matter that years of GOP-led investigations failed to produce evidence of Mrs. Clinton's culpability. The purpose was evident: to damage Hillary Clinton's reputation.

Lies and misrepresentations in Republican communications frequently involved the dissemination of scare words. The speakers' object was to frighten voters. This practice was on vivid display at the 2020 Republican National Convention. One orator after another characterized the Democrats as "socialists" even though very few Democrats identify with the ideology. At the RNC event Kimberly Guilfoyle asserted Joe Biden, Kamala Harris "and their socialist comrades will fundamentally change this nation." Nikki Haley said the Democrat's "vision for America is socialism." RNC Chairperson Ronna McDaniel declared, "Democrats have chosen to go down the road to socialism."[223]

For years following the 2020 tumult related to George Floyd's death and protests by Black Lives Matter, GOP politicians repeated another falsehood that grossly misrepresented the opposing party's' goals. They claimed Democrats wanted to "defund the police." A few obscure figures that demanded racial justice uttered those words, but they did not speak for the Democratic Party. Yet Republicans repeated the charge often, aiming to arouse fear among voters and improve opportunities for their party's candidates in local and national elections.

Republican politicians that were uncomfortable with these fabrications and innuendos remained silent. Despite the GOP's abundant use of false and dangerous rhetoric, politicians went along to get along. They heard party members undermine democracy by asserting that the press was the "enemy of the people," yet they did not denounce the claim. When Donald Trump appeared to justify political violence, most Republican leaders did not respond critically. When GOP officials throughout the country sanctioned book banning, Republican politicos did not object vigorously. When GOP militants in Congress attempted to shut down the government, Republican leaders refused to accuse the radicals of endangering the U.S. and global economy and the livelihood of millions of Americans. When the MAGA movement threatened to undermine America's fundamental commitments to democracy, many Republican leaders did not express concern.

Perhaps most astounding, when the *Washington Post's* fact checkers reported that Donald Trump made 30,573 false and misleading claims when he was President of the United States, most Republicans ignored the evidence.[224]

What could they say? They had not called out the falsehoods during Trump's four years in the White House. They allowed the demagogue to spin bogus claims with impunity. Republican communications operated in a post-truth political environment. Misrepresentation of the facts became a common feature in their political rhetoric.

A broad-based and vigorous commitment to truth-telling is essential for reversing the party's extremist direction. The Republican Party cannot effectively return to mainstream politics if its public figures continue to circulate lies or refuse to challenge them. Changing this dishonest political culture will be difficult, but the process needs to begin. If GOP rhetoric remains unmoored from the facts, efforts to reform the party will fail.

3. Abandon Vicious Personal Attacks

In recent years, the right's language became extraordinarily harsh. To excite voters' anger, GOP politicians ramped up attacks. They vilified prominent leaders of the opposition, including President Barack Obama, presidential candidate Hillary Clinton, and House Speaker Nancy Pelosi.

Even though politicians and strategists in both parties engage in personal attacks, Republicans have been much more inclined to depict their opponents as irredeemable monsters. They've engaged frequently in character assassination. Democrats criticized opponents, too, but their reproach focused more on political decision-making. They often joked about President George W. Bush's inarticulateness, for instance, but their *principal criticism* related to Bush's economic policies and the war and occupation in Iraq.

Partisans on the right demonized public figures that were not politicians, as well. They treated distinguished public servants as dangerous individuals, grossly distorting their public records. This practice was strikingly evident in Republicans' scornful references to George Soros and Anthony Fauci.

Soros had long been a favorite target of the right. George Soros's principal crime in Republicans' eyes was providing financial support to Democratic causes and candidates. Wealthy donors that favored conservative politics gave *much more money* to favored causes and politicians. Propagandists on the right ignored that evidence.

George Soros made outstanding contributions in 120 countries through his philanthropy. Soros's Open Society Foundation promoted education, democratic governance, freedom of expression, and respect for individual rights. Among other things, it helped millions of people in eastern Europe improve their lives after the collapse of communism. What did Soros's detractors do to benefit humanity?

Anthony Fauci, who long served the U.S. government as a top infectious disease expert, was another favorite target. Republicans hurled a variety of insults, calling him a "Democratic operative," claiming he gave presidents Trump and Biden incorrect advice about the coronavirus, and arguing that

Fauci supported dangerous research at China's Wuhan laboratory. Mentioning Fauci's name in a negative context became a surefire way for rightwing operatives to excite partisans' disgust.[225]

Anthony Fauci, through almost forty years of research and leadership as an infectious disease adviser, saved countless lives from the ravages of HIV/AIDS, Ebola, and SARS-CoV-2. How many lives did Fauci's ferocious right-wing critics save?

Decades ago, Newt Gingrich contributed to the growth of scurrilous charges in GOP messaging. He advised Republican candidates to be "nasty." Gingrich urged the new generation of Republicans to "raise hell" and stop being "nice." Politics was, above all, a cutthroat "war for power," he argued. To fight and win, Republicans needed to insult opponents. Call Democrats pro-communist, radical, un-American, anti-flag, traitors, tyrannical, sick, pathetic, and corrupt, he recommended. Numerous GOP candidates learned to "speak like Newt."

Angry political language can affect behavior. Donald Trump criticized Vice President Mike Pence for not supporting his efforts to overturn the 2020 election, and on January 6, 2021, Trump told a huge crowd of followers, "We fight like hell. And if you don't fight like hell, you're not going to have a country anymore." Minutes later, hundreds of his supporters moved to the Capitol, broke through barriers, attacked police, and entered the halls of Congress. Some of the invaders shouted, "Hang Mike Pence!" Others sounded like they aimed to harm Nancy Pelosi, Speaker of the House.

When Donald Trump came under several indictments in 2023, elected officials, prosecutors, judges, even members of the FBI. received threats of physical harm or death. Some public servants needed around-the-clock protection by armed security guards. Fear of violence troubled Republican senators, too. Senator Mitt Romney revealed that many of his GOP colleagues worried they would be attacked if they criticized Donald Trump. Some of them believed Trump deserved to be impeached in the second Senate trial, Romney indicated, but they did not dare vote to convict. They feared for their own safety and that of family members.[226]

Many Republicans were disturbed by the uptick in vicious language and threats of physical harm against public figures, but they were reluctant to express their concern publicly. The silence of GOP leaders facilitated the escalation of dangerous rhetoric.

The third opportunity to challenge extremist politics is clear. Modulation of hateful rhetoric is long-past due.

How can Republicans change their party's negative judgments about government, its promotion of untruths, and its engagement in vicious name-calling?

Acting alone will produce almost certain defeat. Individual Republicans that criticized the GOP's excesses such as Liz Cheney, Adam Kinzinger, Jeff Flake, and Mitt Romney made little impact. But if *numerous* leaders in the party act *collectively* to resist extremism, they might launch a successful correction. They would discover they have allies, including Democrats, independents, and commentators in the national media. Broad-based calls for change could undermine the militants' cause and begin to steer the party away from hyper-partisan, extremist politics.

Some encouraging signs of growing Republican resistance have appeared. One impressive example among many occurred in late 2023 when three prominent conservative lawyers, George Conway, J. Michael Luttig, and Barbara Comstock, described their work with the Society for the Rule of Law Institute. That organization aimed to mobilize conservative law professionals in defense of democracy. Conway, Luttig, and Comstock complained that numerous people in the conservative legal movement acquiesced when Donald Trump campaigned for a second presidency and seemed likely to circumvent laws and norms if he won another term at the White House.[227]

Conway, Luttig, and Comstock criticized the influential Federalist Society, too. That organization, well-funded by millionaires and billionaires, had long promoted a far-right, libertarian agenda. All of President Donald Trump's nominees for the Supreme Court were current or former members of the Federalist Society, and many of Trump's lower court nominees were as well. The three reformers complained that leaders in the Federalist Society "conspicuously declined to speak out against the constitutional and other excesses of Mr. Trump and his administration."

Conway, Luttig, and Comstock directed their appeal to conservatives in the legal profession, but the broader implication of their plea was obvious. Not just conservatism needed reform. The favored political party of conservatives also needed to change.

By urging colleagues on the right to speak up against extremism, these prominent conservatives addressed a problem that is described throughout this book: the absence of strong protest from the right when major threats to democracy became manifest. The Republican Party responded weakly and ineptly when an incompetent, corrupt, and destructive individual acquired enormous influence in GOP affairs. Donald Trump's ascension was surprisingly easy, because Republicans failed to speak out boldly years before -- when GOP extremism began to take shape.

Donald Trump's influence was not simply a product of his drive and personality. Since the 1950s, pressures for fidelity and unity intensified in the party. Leaders enabled the shift toward extremist politics. They stifled disagreements about policy and candidates, purged dissenters, and promoted ideological uniformity. By fostering an undemocratic political culture, they contributed significantly to the GOP's problems and the nation's crisis as well.

An early example of acquiescence, conformity and opportunism occurred in 1950, when Republican senator Joseph McCarthy achieved fame and power by making numerous false accusations. McCarthy engaged in brutal character assassination. His behavior undermined the nation's democratic traditions and practices.

The Republican Party's response to McCarthy's excesses was timid, as Senator Margaret Chase Smith's experience revealed. Smith asked GOP colleagues to endorse a Declaration of Conscience that defended the Constitution. Americans should not uphold a party that favored "political exploitation" at the expense of "national interest," she argued. Employing language that is now venerated in the history books, Smith said, "I don't want to see the Republican Party ride to political victory on the four horsemen of calumny – fear, ignorance, bigotry, and smear."[228]

Unfortunately, Margaret Chase Smith's Republican colleagues did not back her eloquent appeal. They were caught in a dilemma. Many of them feared McCarthy but benefited from his popularity (it produced victories for Republican candidates in local and state elections). They chose to run with the benefits. Some GOP senators defended McCarthy outright; others remained silent. Only six Republicans endorsed Smith's "Declaration of Conscience." Soon five removed their names.

Approximately three-quarters of a century later, the GOP was in a related quandary. Another unhinged demagogue held vast sway in the party. Again, Republican leaders could not muster the courage to challenge him vigorously and successfully. Many were disgusted with Donald Trump's behavior, yet they sensed resistance would damage their political careers and harm Republican candidates' fortunes in subsequent elections. They acquiesced.

Will this pattern change? Can the Republican Party initiate a process of reform that moves its politics into the mainstream? A shift seems likely – sooner or later.

The Republican Party has moved so far away from the American people's preference for moderate, centrist politics that it is risking a major backlash. In recent years Republican strategists managed to delay a reckoning by weaponizing the politics of fear. Negative campaigning often produced victories. In the long run, however, that negativity has limitations. Disgust is growing over the party's long and sorry record of partisan excess, dysfunctional leadership, and failure to deal with American society's problems. The modern GOP has an embarrassingly trivial record of legislative accomplishments. Its anti-government agenda leaves many voters wondering: where's the beef?

The efforts of Conway, Luttig, and Comstock represent just one small example of frustrated reformers attempting to jump-start changes in conservatism and Republicanism. The Society for the Rule of Law Institute cannot alone make a significant difference. If numerous Republican politicians, intellectuals, strategists, donors, and voters demand adjustments, however, they might ignite a revolution.

The culture of silence and conformity has prevailed far too long in the right's political affairs. As Conway, Luttig, and Comstock announced in their appeal, it is time for Republicans to "speak out as vocally and forthrightly as is necessary to meet the urgency that this moment requires."

NOTES

Chapter One

1. David Corn traces the long-term rise of extremism in the party and finds roots well-before the 1950s in *American Psychosis: A Historical Investigation of how the Republican Party went Crazy* (New York: Twelve, 2022).

2. A useful analysis of Arthur Larson's ideas can be found in David Stebenne, *Modern Republican: Arthur Larson and the Eisenhower Years* (Bloomington: Indiana University Press, 2006).

3. David M. Oshinsky, *A Conspiracy so Immense: The World of Joseph McCarthy* (New York: The Free Press, 1983), 103-114.

4. Rick Perlstein, *Before the Storm: Barry Goldwater and the Unmaking of American Consensus* ((New York, Bold Type Books, 2001), 383-385.

5. Nicole Hemmer, *Partisans: The Conservative Revolutionaries Who Remade American Politics in the 1990s* (New York: Basic Books, 2022), 209-229.

6. Julian E. Zelizer provides an excellent discussion of Newt Gingrich's influence in *Burning Down the House: Newt Gingrich, the Fall of a Speaker, and the Rise of the New Republican Party* (New York: Penguin Press, 2020).

7. Geoffrey Kabaservice provides an insightful analysis of these changes in *Rule and Ruin: The Downfall of Moderation and the Destruction of the Republican Party: From Eisenhower to the Tea Party* (New York: Oxford University Press, 2012), and Matthew Continetti shows how radicals betrayed the conservative intellectual movement in *The Right: The Hundred-Year War for American Conservatism* (New York: Basic Books, 2022).

8. Thomas Frank, *What's the Matter with Kansas? How Conservatives Won the Heart of America* (New York: Metropolitan Books, 2004), 7.

9. Dana Milbank, *The Destructionists: The Twenty-Five Year Crack-Up of the Republican Party* (New York: Doubleday, 2022), 146-158, 170-181; E. J. Dionne, Jr., *Why the Right Went Wrong* (New York: Simon & Schuster, 2016), 236-260.

10. Tim Alberta offers a detailed overview of these developments in *American Carnage: On the Front Lines of the Republican Civil War and the Rise of President Trump* ((New York: Harper Collins, 2019).

11. https://www.nytimes.com/2015/10/13/opinion/the-republicans-incompetence-caucus.html

12. https://www.theatlantic.com/magazine/archive/2022/01/brooks-true-conservatism-dead-fox-news-voter-suppression/620853/

13. https://archive.nytimes.com/krugman.blogs.nytimes.com/2015/10/13/everett-dirksen-doesnt-live-here-anymore/?module=BlogPost-Title&version=Blog%2520Main&contentCollection=Opinion&action=Click&pgtype=Blogs&region=Body&_r=0

14. https://newdemocratcoalition.house.gov/media-center/press-releases/new-dems-meet-with-president-obama

15. https://www.politico.com/story/2009/03/obama-i-am-a-new-democrat-019862

16. https://news.gallup.com/poll/245462/democrats-favor-moderate-party-gop-conservative.aspx

17. https://www.brookings.edu/articles/have-democrats-become-a-party-of-the-left/

18. https://www.washingtonpost.com/politics/2023/10/04/mccarthy-speaker-ouster-analysis/

Chapter Two

19. https://www.youtube.com/watch?v=3_4r6sZOHDM

20. https://highways.dot.gov/highway-history/general-highway-history/president-franklin-d-roosevelt-and-excess-condemnation

21. https://www.army.mil/article/198095/dwight_d_eisenhower_and_the_birth_of_the_interstate_highway_system#:~:text=His%20motivations%20for%20a%20highway,hydrogen%20bomb%2C%20which%20instigated%20a

22. https://www.richmondfed.org/publications/research/econ_focus/2021/q2-3/economic_history

23. https://www.washingtonpost.com/us-policy/2020/10/18/trump-biden-infrastructure-2020/

24. https://www.americanyawp.com/reader/25-the-cold-war/senator-margaret-chase-smiths-declaration-of-conscience-1950/

25. https://www.washingtonpost.com/politics/cheney-trump-mccarthy-vote/2021/05/11/1bb8fa56-b2a9-11eb-ab43-bebddc5a0f65_story.html

26. https://thehill.com/homenews/house/553105-kinzinger-on-cheney-ouster-history-will-call-this-low-point-of-the-republican/

27. https://www.senate.gov/about/origins-foundations/electing-appointing-senators/contested-senate-elections/130Tydings_Butler.htm

28. https://www.washingtonpost.com/investigations/former-mccarthy-aide-showed-trump-how-to-exploit-power-and-draw-attention/2016/06/16/e9f44f20-2bf3-11e6-9b37-42985f6a265c_story.html

Chapter Three

29. https://www.vanityfair.com/news/2004/10/florida-election-2000

30. https://www.washingtonpost.com/history/2018/11/15/its-insanity-how-brooks-brothers-riot-killed-recount-miami/

31. https://content.time.com/time/nation/article/0,8599,89450,00.html

32. https://www.tallahassee.com/story/opinion/2019/02/03/ion-sancho-roger-stones-dirty-tricks-helped-sway-2000-florida-recount/2742713002/

33. https://www.miamiherald.com/news/politics-government/article221722465.html

34. https://www.theatlantic.com/politics/archive/2020/08/bush-gore-florida-recount-oral-history/614404/

35. https://www.washingtonpost.com/history/2018/11/15/its-insanity-how-brooks-brothers-riot-killed-recount-miami/

36. https://www.politifact.com/article/2022/jun/14/most-republicans-falsely-believe-trumps-stolen-ele/

37. https://www.presidency.ucsb.edu/documents/address-conceding-the-2000-presidential-election

38. https://www.americanrhetoric.com/speeches/algore2000concession-speech.html

39. https://www.npr.org/2012/08/30/160358091/transcript-clint-eastwoods-convention-remarks

40. https://www.politico.com/story/2012/10/how-obamas-debate-strategy-bombed-082037#:~:text=DENVER%20%E2%80%94%20A%20stunned%20Obama%20campaign,Obama%20looking%20timid%20and%20disengaged.

41. https://www.dispatch.com/story/news/politics/2012/01/31/debate-coach-seems-to-have/23337988007/

42. https://www.wvxu.org/politics/2020-07-30/watching-an-american-presidency-go-down-the-chute-in-cleveland

43. https://www.cbsnews.com/news/let-detroit-go-bankrupt-column-dogs-romney-in-michigan/

44. https://www.cnn.com/2012/11/07/politics/why-romney-lost/index.html

45. https://thehill.com/homenews/news/386392-mccain-i-regret-picking-palin-as-my-vice-presidential-nominee/

46. https://www.theguardian.com/media/2003/feb/17/mondaymediasection.iraq

47. https://www.nytimes.com/2017/12/23/business/media/murdoch-trump-relationship.html

48. https://www.npr.org/2024/04/26/1247352050/trump-hush-money-trial-david-pecker

49. https://www.nbcnews.com/think/opinion/comey-s-october-surprise-shook-america-four-years-ago-today-ncna1245018

50. https://www.nbcnews.com/think/opinion/comey-s-october-surprise-shook-america-four-years-ago-today-ncna1245018

51. https://en.wikipedia.org/wiki/Gallup%27s_most_admired_man_and_woman_poll#:~:text=Clinton%20topped%20the%20list%20in,most%20admired%20woman%2013%20times.

52. https://www.washingtonpost.com/news/the-fix/wp/2016/08/31/a-record-number-of-americans-now-dislike-hillary-clinton/

Chapter Four

53. https://www.npr.org/2022/09/29/1125462240/inflation-1970s-volcker-nixon-carter-interest-rates-fed

54. Alan Brinkley, *American History: A Survey* (Boston McGraw Hill, 2007), 668.

55. Maury Klein, *Rainbow's End: The Crash of 1929* (New York: Oxford University Press, 2001), 242.

56. https://www.investopedia.com/terms/s/sl-crisis.asp

57. https://www.nytimes.com/2011/01/26/business/economy/26inquiry.html

58. *The Financial Crisis Inquiry Report* (Public Affairs: New York, 2011), xvii-xviii.

Chapter Five

59. https://www.washingtonpost.com/archive/opinions/1996/01/07/the-nixon-inside-stones-head/2bfdb46b-1115-4119-be71-0ba43620ae39/

60. For a fuller discussion of President Richard Nixon's interest in the movie, *Patton*, see Robert Brent Toplin, History by Hollywood (Urbana & Chicago: University of Illinois Press, 2009), 172-175.

61. Richard Nixon quoted in Stephen E. Ambrose, *Nixon: The Triumph of a Politician, 1962-1972*, 322-345, vol 2 of Nixon, 3 vols. (New York, 1989).

62. William Rogers quoted in Hugh Sidney, "The Presidency: Anybody See Patton?" clipping in the Academy of Motion Pictures Arts and Sciences archives, Los Angeles.

63. For a fuller discussion of the political impact of *Fahrenheit 9/11*, see Robert Brent Toplin, *Michael Moore's Fahrenheit 9/11: How One Film Divided a Nation* (Lawrence, Ks: University Press of Kansas, 2006).

64. https://www.cbsnews.com/news/reagan-miniseries-irks-rnc-chair/

65. https://www.theguardian.com/world/2013/aug/05/rnc-boycott-threat-cnn-nbc-hillary-clinton

66. https://www.nytimes.com/2013/08/07/opinion/dowd-reince-is-right.html

67. https://www.youtube.com/watch?v=ndKtBfBwLGM

Chapter Six

68. https://www.washingtonpost.com/opinions/elitism-wont-defeat-trump-ism/2016/08/07/ca4971b6-5b67-11e6-831d-0324760ca856_story.html

69. Geoffrey Kabaservice, *Rule and Ruin: The Downfall of Moderation and the Destruction of the Republican Party* (New York: Oxford University Press, 2012), xv-xviii.

70. Robert Reich, *Reason: Why Liberals Will Win the Battle for America* (New York: Alfred A Knopf, 2004), 113.

71. A fuller discussion of this topic can be found in Robert Brent Toplin, *Radical Conservatism: The Right's Political Religion* (Lawrence, Ks., University Press of Kansas, 2006).

72. Thomas Frank, *What's the Matter with Kansas? How Conservatives Won the Heart of America* (New York: Henry Holt, 2004)122. 172, 175, 221, 226.

73. Thomas Frank, *What's the Matter with Kansas? How Conservatives Won the Heart of America* (New York: Henry Holt, 2004)122. 172, 175, 221, 226.

74. Fareed Zakaria, *The Future of Freedom: Illiberal Democracy at Home and Abroad* (New York: W. W. Norton, 203), 142.

75. Michael Lind, *Up from Conservatism: Why the Right is Wrong for America* (New York, Free Press, 1996), 252.

76. David Brock, *Blinded by the Right: The Conscience of an Ex-Conservative* (New York: Crown, 2002), 285.

77. Daniel J. Balz and Ronald Brownstein, *Storming the Gates: Protest Politics and the Republican Revival* (Boston: Little Brown, 1995), 52.

78. Sidney Blumenthal, *The Rise of the Counter-Establishment: From Conservative Ideology to Political Power* (New York: Times Books, 1986), 328-329.

79. https://www.theatlantic.com/ideas/archive/2020/08/party-no-content/615607/

80. https://janda.org/politxts/PartyPlatforms/Republican/rep.956.html

Chapter Seven

81. Brandy X Lee, ed., *The Dangerous Case of Donald Trump: 27 Psychiatrists and Mental Health Experts Assess a President* (New York, Thomas Dunne Books, 2017).

82. Mary Trump, *Too Much and Never Enough: How My Family Created the World's Most Dangerous Man* (New York, Simon and Schuster, 2020).

83. https://www.huffpost.com/entry/seth-meyers-donald-trump-white-house-correspondents-dinner_n_5ae70cb6e4b055fd7fcde4b0

84. https://www.theatlantic.com/politics/archive/2020/01/trump-iran-decision/604687/

85. Leon Festinger, Henry W. Riecken, Stanley Schachter, *When Prophesy Fails: A Social Psychological Study of a Modern Group that Predicted the Destruction of the World* (New York: HarperCollins College Division, 1964).

86. Stanley Milgram, *Obedience to Authority: An Experimental View* (New York: HarperCollins, 1974).

Chapter Eight

87. https://www.adweek.com/tvnewser/october-2018-ratings-fox-news-channel-averaged-more-viewers-than-cnn-and-msnbc-combined/

88. For a broad view of controversies about Fox News see Brian Stelter, *Hoax: Donald Trump, Fox News, and the Dangerous Distortion of Truth* (New York: Atria/One Signal Publishers, 2020); Brian Stelter, *Network of Lies: The Epic Saga of Fox News, Donald Trump, and the Battle for American Democracy* (New York: Atria/One Signal Publishers, 2023).

89. https://www.washingtonpost.com/lifestyle/media/fox-news-hosts-go-mum-on-hydroxychloroquine-the-covid-19-drug-they-spent-weeks-promoting/2020/04/22/eeaf90c2-84ac-11ea-ae26-989cfce1c7c7_story.html

90. https://www.pgpf.org/blog/2023/04/healthcare-spending-in-the-united-states-remains-high

91. https://www.nbcnews.com/health/health-news/1-3-americans-worry-about-being-able-afford-health-care-n1144426

92. https://www.pbs.org/newshour/health/november-19-1945-harry-truman-calls-national-health-insurance-program

93. https://www.washingtonpost.com/world/national-security/trump-obamacare-supreme-court/2020/05/06/4a53ba54-8fe1-11ea-9e23-6914ee-410a5f_story.html

94. https://www.commonwealthfund.org/publications/issue-briefs/2023/jan/us-health-care-global-perspective-2022#:~:text=Yet%20the%20U.S.%20is%20the,among%20the%20highest%20suicide%20rates.

95. https://www.washingtonpost.com/opinions/2020/03/25/lets-make-sure-this-crisis-doesnt-go-waste/

96. https://www.newsweek.com/donald-trump-operation-warp-speed-vacci-nations-joe-biden-1575597

97. https://www.newsweek.com/donald-trump-operation-warp-speed-vacci-nations-joe-biden-1575597

98. https://www.pbs.org/newshour/health/years-of-research-laid-ground-work-for-speedy-covid-19-vaccines

99. https://www.scientificamerican.com/article/for-billion-dollar-covid-vac-cines-basic-government-funded-science-laid-the-groundwork/

Chapter Nine

100. https://www.nbcnews.com/politics/donald-trump/trump-administra-tion-s-lack-unified-coronavirus-strategy-will-cost-lives-n1175126

101. An excellent overview of responses to the Covid crisis can be found in The Covid Crisis Group, *Lessons from the Covid War: An Investigative Report* (New York: Public Affairs, 2023).

102. https://www.ncbi.nlm.nih.gov/pmc/articles/PMC5468112/; https://enviro-datagov.org/an-embattled-landscape-series-part-2a-coronavirus-and-the-three-year-trump-quest-to-slash-science-at-the-cdc/

103. https://avalon.law.yale.edu/20th_century/froos1.asp

104. https://www.latimes.com/world-nation/story/2020-03-29/federal-social-distancing-guidelines-to-be-extended-to-april-30-trump-says

105. https://www.nytimes.com/2021/05/29/opinion/wuhan-lab-leak-theory-covid.html

106. https://www.nytimes.com/2021/05/31/opinion/media-lab-leak-theory.html

107. https://www.cnn.com/2020/03/25/politics/trump-coronavirus-china/index.html

108. https://www.washingtonpost.com/opinions/2020/04/14/state-depart-ment-cables-warned-safety-issues-wuhan-lab-studying-bat-coronavirus-es/

109. https://www.nytimes.com/2021/03/04/health/covid-virus-origins.html?action=click&module=RelatedLinks&pgtype=Article

110. https://www.nbcnews.com/politics/joe-biden/china-s-stonewall-covid-origin-probe-pushed-biden-reveal-latest-n1268875

111. https://www.cbsnews.com/news/covid-19-wuhan-origins-60-minutes-2021-06-06/

112. https://www.nytimes.com/interactive/2021/04/17/us/vaccine-hesitancy-politics.html

113. https://www.nytimes.com/2021/07/11/business/media/vaccines-fox-news-hosts.html?action=click&module=Top%20Stories&pgtype=Homepage

114. https://www.ncbi.nlm.nih.gov/pmc/articles/PMC5922215/

115. https://www.sacbee.com/news/politics-government/article130205484.html

116. https://en.wikipedia.org/wiki/The_Republican_War_on_Science

117. https://www.theguardian.com/politics/2009/jan/16/greenpolitics-george-bush

118. https://en.wikipedia.org/wiki/Trump_administration_political_interference_with_science_agenciesng

119. https://www.cnn.com/videos/health/2021/04/18/republicans-vaccine-hesitancy-dr-anthony-fauci-sotu-bash-vpx.cnn

120. https://www.newsweek.com/anthony-fauci-says-get-over-this-political-statement-get-vaccinated-covid-rates-spike-1607764

121. https://www.google.com/books/edition/Pox_Americana/EnauK-2PI_9sC?hl=en&gbpv=1&printsec=frontcover

122. https://ask.loc.gov/science/faq/362358

123. https://www.battlefields.org/learn/articles/washington-inoculates-army

124. https://www.nytimes.com/2021/04/14/us/politics/republicans-covid-vaccines.html

125. https://www.nytimes.com/2021/04/14/us/politics/republicans-covid-vaccines.html?searchResultPosition=1

126. https://www.tennessean.com/story/news/health/2021/04/18/survey-white-rural-republicans-reject-covid-19-vaccines/7166086002/

127. https://www.npr.org/sections/health-shots/2021/04/07/984697573/vaccine-refusal-may-put-herd-immunity-at-risk-researchers-warn

128. https://www.nytimes.com/2021/04/30/health/covid-vaccine-hesitancy-white-republican

Chapter Ten

129. https://www.pewresearch.org/short-reads/2023/07/21/favorable-views-of-supreme-court-fall-to-historic-low/#:~:text=The%20court's%20favorable%20rating%20has,significantly%20more%20negative%20than%20positive.

130. William E. Leuchtenburg, *Franklin D. Roosevelt and the New Deal*, 1932-1940 (New York: Harper & Row), 1963, 231-238.

Chapter Eleven

131. https://news.gallup.com/poll/388988/political-ideology-steady-conservatives-moderates-tie.aspx

132. https://www.theatlantic.com/politics/archive/2012/11/the-coalition-of-transformation-vs-the-coalition-of-restoration/265512/

133. https://www.pewresearch.org/politics/2011/04/08/civil-war-at-150-still-relevant-still-divisive/

134. https://www.battlefields.org/learn/primary-sources/cornerstone-speech

135. https://www.nytimes.com/2004/11/04/politics/campaign/samesex-marriage-issue-key-to-some-gop-races.html

136. https://abcnews.go.com/WNT/story?id=230634&page=1

137. https://www.newyorker.com/news/annals-of-inquiry/how-a-conservative-activist-invented-the-conflict-over-critical-race-theory

138. https://www.newyorker.com/news/annals-of-inquiry/how-a-conservative-activist-invented-the-conflict-over-critical-race-theory

139. https://newrepublic.com/article/162737/critical-race-theory-conservative-scam

140. https://www.washingtonpost.com/politics/2021/06/15/scholar-strategy-how-critical-race-theory-alarms-could-convert-racial-anxiety-into-political-energy/

141. https://www.mediamatters.org/diversity-discrimination/nbc-news-reporter-explains-how-right-wing-organizations-and-media-are

142. https://www.theatlantic.com/national/archive/2013/08/the-most-powerful-dissent-in-american-history/278503/

143. https://www.nytimes.com/2021/06/29/magazine/memory-laws.html

144. https://www.tennessean.com/story/news/politics/2021/05/05/tennessee-bans-critical-race-theory-schools-withhold-funding/4948306001/

Chapter Twelve

145. https://www.bradyunited.org/key-statistics

146. https://www.nbcnews.com/storyline/las-vegas-shooting/more-americans-killed-guns-1968-all-u-s-wars-combined-n807156   https://www.nbcnews.com/storyline/las-vegas-shooting/more-americans-killed-guns-1968-all-u-s-wars-combined-n807156

147. Robert Brent Toplin, *Unchallenged Violence: An American Ordeal* (Westport, Conn. Greenwood Press, 1076), 216-228.

148. https://www.nytimes.com/2022/05/25/world/europe/gun-laws-australia-britain.html

149. https://www.npr.org/sections/goatsandsoda/2021/03/24/980838151/gun-violence-deaths-how-the-u-s-compares-to-the-rest-of-the-world

150. https://www.washingtonpost.com/history/2019/08/09/they-were-killers-with-machine-guns-then-president-went-after-their-weapons/

151. https://www.atf.gov/rules-and-regulations/national-firearms-act

152. https://www.vox.com/policy-and-politics/2017/9/5/16255380/sessions-trump-administration-decision-end-daca

153. https://www.khou.com/article/news/local/texas/in-texas-undocumented-immigrants-have-no-shortage-of-work/285-373024063

154. https://www.ilctr.org/entrepreneur-hof/sergey-brin/

155. https://www.brookings.edu/articles/why-the-trump-administrations-anti-immigration-policies-are-the-united-states-loss-and-the-rest-of-the-worlds-gain/

156. https://www.businessinsider.com/immigrants-have-a-huge-role-in-founding-american-startups-2019-8

157. https://www.nytimes.com/2018/08/23/business/trump-immigration-business-leaders-economy.html

158. https://www.forbes.com/sites/stuartanderson/2021/04/01/evidence-mounts-that-reducing-immigration-harms-americas-economy/?sh=4f858fd7202c

159. https://www.brookings.edu/articles/why-the-trump-administrations-anti-immigration-policies-are-the-united-states-loss-and-the-rest-of-the-worlds-gain/

160. https://www.cnbc.com/2022/03/29/there-are-now-a-record-5-million-more-job-openings-than-unemployed-people-in-the-us.html#:~:text=watchlive-,There%20are%20now%20a%20record%205%20million%20more%20job,unemployed%20people%20in%20the%20U.S.&text=Job%20openings%20edged%20lower%20to,the%20level%20of%20unemployed%20workers.

161. https://www.washingtonpost.com/opinions/2022/04/05/fixing-legal-im-migration-help-worker-shortages/

162. https://www.nytimes.com/2022/04/05/opinion/great-resignation-employment.html

163. https://www.investopedia.com/articles/investing/123015/3-economic-challenges-japan-faces-2016.asp

164. https://www.bloomberg.com/news/articles/2023-03-20/un-science-report-to-provide-stark-climate-warning

165. https://nymag.com/movies/reviews/17092/

166. https://medium.com/@ptknight/innovation-for-sufficiency-and-sustainability-1b6029b5abb0

167. https://www.latimes.com/archives/la-xpm-2006-may-23-na-bushgore23-story.html

168. https://abcnews.go.com/Politics/story?id=122640&page=1

169. https://archive.thinkprogress.org/sen-inhofe-compares-people-who-believe-in-global-warming-to-the-third-reich-e48c05f89608/

170. https://www.govinfo.gov/content/pkg/CHRG-115hhrg25098/html/CHRG-115hhrg25098.htm

171. https://www.americanprogress.org/article/climate-deniers-117th-congress/

172. https://www.nytimes.com/2008/05/13/us/politics/12cnd-mccain.html

173. https://www.globalcitizen.org/es/content/miamis-streets-are-flooding-now-climate-change-isn/

174. https://www.usatoday.com/story/news/politics/2021/03/08/republican-led-states-sue-president-joe-biden-over-climate-change-order/4635600001/

175. https://www.newyorker.com/magazine/2006/04/24/ozone-man

176. https://abc30.com/archive/8338801/

Chapter Thirteen

177. Francis Fukuyama, *The End of History and the Last Man* (New York: Harper Perennial, 1993).

178. https://www.google.com/search?q=Michael+Moore%27s+speech+when+-accepting+academy+award+for+Bowling+for+Columbine&rlz=1C-1CHBD_enUS791US791&oq=Michael+Moore%27s+speech+when+accepting+academy+award+for+Bowling+for+Columbine&gs_lcrp=EgZ-jaHJvbWUyBggAEEUYOdIBCTM3NDM5ajBqNKgCCLACAQ&sourceid=chrome&ie=UTF-8#fpstate=ive&vld=cid:cd54040e,vid:M7Is43K6l-rg,st:0

179. Robert Draper, *To Start a War: How the Bush Administration Took America into Iraq* (New York: Penguin Random House, 2021).

180. https://www.washingtonpost.com/news/post-politics/wp/2014/06/05/hillary-clinton-on-iraq-vote-i-still-got-it-wrong-plain-and-simple/

181. https://www.google.com/search?q=Michael+Moore%27s+speech+when+-accepting+academy+award+for+Bowling+for+Columbine&rlz=1C-1CHBD_enUS791US791&oq=Michael+Moore%27s+speech+when+accepting+academy+award+for+Bowling+for+Columbine&gs_lcrp=EgZjaHJvbWUyBggAEEUYODlBCTM3NDM5ajBqNKgCCLACAQ&sourceid=chrome&ie=UTF-8#fpstate=ive&vld=cid:cd54040e,vid:M7Is43K6lrg,st:0

182. https://www.washingtonpost.com/politics/2022/04/06/house-gop-nato-support/

183. https://carnegieendowment.org/2003/09/30/russia-s-transition-to-democracy-and-u.s.-russia-relations-unfinished-business-pub-1363

184. https://www.washingtonpost.com/opinions/2022/03/16/why-west-must-boost-military-supplies-to-ukraine/

185. https://www.bloomberg.com/opinion/articles/2022-08-15/why-did-trump-take-classified-documents-to-mar-a-lago

186. https://abcnews.go.com/Politics/year-republicans-biden-white-house-argue-afghanistan-withdrawal/story?id=88401631

187. https://www.whitehouse.gov/briefing-room/speeches-remarks/2021/07/08/remarks-by-president-biden-on-the-drawdown-of-u-s-forces-in-afghanistan/

188. https://theindependent.ca/commentary/the-nonagenarians-notebook/why-is-the-united-states-always-fighting-a-war-somewhere/

189. https://freakonometrics.hypotheses.org/50473

190. https://www.politico.com/magazine/story/2015/06/us-military-bases-around-the-world-119321/#:~:text=Despite%20recently%20closing%20hundreds%20of,about%2030%20foreign%20bases%20combined.

191. https://foreignpolicy.com/2011/04/04/is-america-addicted-to-war/

192. https://www.pgpf.org/blog/2023/04/the-united-states-spends-more-on-defense-than-the-next-10-countries-combined

193. https://www.whitehouse.gov/briefing-room/speeches-remarks/2021/05/28/remarks-by-president-biden-addressing-service-members-and-their-families/

194. Craig Whitlock, *The Afghanistan Papers: A Secret History of the War* (New York: Simon and Schuster, 2021).

195. https://www.youtube.com/watch?v=rH6C7bYfiVs

196. Allison Graham, *Destined for War: Can America and China Escape Thucydides' Trap?* (Boston: Houghton Mifflin Harcourt, 2017).

197. https://www.theatlantic.com/international/archive/2015/09/united-states-china-war-thucydides-trap/406756/

198. https://www.bloomberg.com/news/articles/2019-11-21/kissinger-says-u-s-and-china-in-foothills-of-a-cold-war

199. https://www.nytimes.com/2023/08/31/opinion/republican-candidates-china-russia.html

200. https://www.cnbc.com/2020/07/18/op-ed-the-cold-war-between-us-and-china-just-got-a-lot-hotter.html

201. https://www.ft.com/content/0f423616-d9f2-4ca6-8d3b-a04d467ed6f8

202. https://www.foreignaffairs.com/print/node/1126494

203. https://www.foreignaffairs.com/articles/united-states/2021-02-05/kevin-rudd-usa-chinese-confrontation-short-of-war

204. https://www.theguardian.com/world/2020/may/17/donald-trump-and-xi-jinping-meet-the-new-cold-warriors

205. https://thehill.com/policy/international/508769-pompeo-urges-nations-to-pressure-chinas-communist-party-to-change/; https://www.washingtonpost.com/world/national-security/at-nixon-library-pompeo-declares-china-engagement-a-failure/2020/07/23/c4b073f2-cd29-11ea-99b0-8426e26d203b_story.html

206. https://apnews.com/article/donald-trump-alaska-antony-blinken-yang-jiechi-wang-yi-fc23cd2b23332fa8dd2d781bd3f7c178

207. https://www.washingtonpost.com/us-policy/2022/10/09/inflation-economy-biden-covid/

208. https://www.pewresearch.org/short-reads/2022/06/15/in-the-u-s-and-around-the-world-inflation-is-high-and-getting-higher/

209. https://www.reuters.com/world/us/republicans-blame-biden-inflation-are-they-right-2021-11-01/

210. https://www.cnn.com/2021/08/06/politics/inflation-gop-fact-check/index.html

211. https://www.nbcnews.com/politics/politics-news/republicans-target-biden-democrats-over-inflation-what-would-they-do-n1284839

212. https://www.nytimes.com/2024/02/16/opinion/ezra-klein-biden-audio-essay.html

213. https://www.cnn.com/2024/05/10/opinions/us-election-isnt-playing-out-how-i-thought-zakaria/index.html

214. https://www.npr.org/2023/08/07/1192432628/conservatives-mull-how-2nd-trump-presidency-could-reshape-the-federal-government

215. https://www.nytimes.com/2023/07/17/us/politics/trump-plans-2025.html

Epilogue

216. Steven Levitsky and Daniel Ziblatt, *Tyranny of the Minority: Why American Democracy Reached the Breaking Point* (New York: Crown, 2023, 10.

217. https://www.nytimes.com/2023/09/23/us/republicans-congress-free-dom-caucus.html

218. https://www.pewresearch.org/politics/2023/09/19/public-trust-in-govern-ment-1958-2023/frnld

219. https://www.npr.org/2023/08/07/1192432628/conserva-tives-mull-how-2nd-trump-presidency-could-reshape-the-federal-gov-ernment

220. https://www.nytimes.com/2023/07/17/us/politics/trump-plans-2025.html

221. https://www.nytimes.com/2023/09/13/us/politics/mitt-romney-retire-ment.html

222. https://www.pewresearch.org/politics/2020/09/14/americans-views-of-government-low-trust-but-some-positive-performance-ratings/

223. https://www.npr.org/2020/08/25/905895428/republicans-blast-demo-crats-as-socialists-heres-what-socialism-is

224. https://www.washingtonpost.com/politics/2021/01/24/trumps-false-or-misleading-claims-total-30573-over-four-years/

225. https://thehill.com/homenews/senate/583716-gop-anger-with-fauci-rises/

226. https://www.washingtonpost.com/politics/2023/09/14/romney-politi-cal-violence-republicans/

227. https://www.nytimes.com/2023/11/21/opinion/trump-lawyers-constitu-tion-democracy.html

228. https://www.americanyawp.com/reader/25-the-cold-war/senator-marga-ret-chase-smiths-declaration-of-conscience-1950/

INDEX

Abortion, 14
Abu Ghraib, 184
Access Hollywood, 55
Acheson, Dean, 9
Affordable Care Act, 21-22, 48, 96, 102, 120
The Afghan Papers, 194
Afghanistan, 177, 190-96
al Qaeda, 80
Alito, Jr., Samuel, 141-42, 145
All the President's Men (movie), 76-78
Allison, Graham, 196, 199
Ambrose, Stephen E., 71-72
American Recovery and Reinvestment Act, 97, 174
American Rescue Plan, 201
The Art of the Deal, 89
Army-McCarthy Hearings, 3
Atlas, Scott, 135
Atwater, Lee, 148

Bachmann, Michele, 51
Baker, James, 38
Balz, Daniel J., 22, 93.
Barrett, Amy Coney, 141-42, 145
Bell, Derrick, 154
Benghazi, 58, 155, 222
Bentsen, Lloyd, 50
Bernanke, Ben, 67
Bernstein, Carl, 76
Bernstein, Jared, 205
Beschloss, Michael, 3
Biden, Joe, 28, 31, 40, 50, 115, 121-31, 137,182-188, 190-193, 198, 201-14, 222
Black Lives Matter, 146
Blinken, Anthony, 199
Blow, Charles M., 161

Blumenthal, Sidney, 94
Bowling for Columbine (movie), 82, 184
Bremer, Paul, 184
Brinkley, Alan, 64
Brinkley, Douglas, 72
Bongino, Dan, 111-13
Bork, Robert, 141-2
Brezinski, Mika, 86
Bright, Dr. Rick, 115-116
Brin, Sergey, 167
Brock, David, 93
Brooks Brothers Riot, 37-40
Brownstein, Ronald, 94, 149
Buchanan, Patrick, 11-12
Buckley, William F., 27
Burford, Anne Gorsuch, 133
Burke, Edmund, 18-19
Bush, George H.W., 11, 45, 49, 141-142, 148, 182.
Bush, George W., 12-13, 37-40, 45, 48, 50, 67, 80-82, 86, 133-135,141, 143, 153, 171-3, 178, 180-185, 216, 219
Bush, Jeb, 41
Bush, Laura, 58
Butterfield, Alexander, 72
Byrd, Robert, 182

CIA, 75, 78, 180
The Caine Mutiny, 87-90
Canada, 136, 161, 168
The Candidate (movie), 77
Capito, Shelley Moore, 203
Carlson, Tucker, 111-12, 114, 116,154, 196
Carson, Ben, 51
Carter, Jimmy, 2, 60-3, 79
Carville, James, 60
CBS, 83, 85, 110, 131-2

Celebrity Apprentice, 199
Centers for Disease Control and Prevention, 124, 134
Changan, 173-4
Chasing Shadows, 72
Cheney, Dick, 38, 50-1,134
Cheney, Liz, 2, 31-3, 225
China, 16, 78, 102, 168, 172-3, 175, 196-200, 20
Chips and Science Act, 201, 204
CIA, 75, 78, 180
Citizen Kane (movie), 70
Citizens United, 82
Civil Rights Act, 147
Civil War, 146, 150-2, 192, 202
Climate change, 97, 112, 134, 169-176
Clinton, Bill, 20, 23-4, 93, 135, 166, 213
Clinton, Hillary, 21, 52-9, 82, 85-7, 101, 155, 180-2, 189, 222, 224
CNN, 85-6, 110, 162, 166
cognitive dissonance, 103
Colbert, Stephen, 82
Confederacy, 150-1
Conservative Political Action Conference, 134
Conservatism, 11, 14, 20, 91-8
Constitution, 218-19
Consumer Financial Protection Bureau, 96
Conway, George, 225-7
Council of Economic Advisers, 62
Covid, 17,114-7, 204, 206, 212
Crenshaw, Kimberle, 154
Critical Race Theory, 15. 146, 153-56, 158
Cruz, Ted, 150
Cuban Missile Crisis, 177
Culture warriors, 14-15, 17

The Dangerous Case of Donald Trump, 99
Daschle, Tom, 181-2
David, Laurie, 170
Declaration of Conscience, 8, 31-2, 228
Defense Intelligence Agency, 75
Deferred Action for Childhood Arrivals (DACA), 165-166
Democratic Party, 4,10,18-24, 40-2, 44-6, 49, 57-9, 61-2, 64-8, 94-6, 149, 180, 205, 209-13, 222, 224
Democrats, 4,10,18-24, 40-2, 44-6, 49, 57-9, 61-2, 64-8, 94-6, 149, 180, 205, 209-13, 222, 224

Department of Health and Human Services, 125
Department of Homeland Security, 125, 183
Deregulation, 15-6, 50, 63-8
Destined for War, 196
Dirkson, Everett, 23
District of Columbia v. Heller, 164
Dodd-Frank Wall Street Reform and Consumer Protection Act, 64, 97
Draper, Robert, 178
Dog Whistle Politics, 147-9
Douthat, Ross, 130
Dowd, Maureen, 86
Dred Scott decision, 150
Dukakis, Michael, 148

Earth in the Balance, 170
Eastwood, Clint, 42-43
Edelstein, David, 170
Edwards, John, 50
Eisenhower, Dwight D., 3, 7-8, 25-31, 98, 192
Eisenhower Highway Act, 25, 28
Election (1960), 213
Election (1964), 9-10, 219
Election (1972), 20
Election (1976), 76-80
Election (1980), 10-11, 20
Election (1984), 20
Election (1992), 11-12, 216
Election (1996), 12
Election (1980), 60-63
Election (1992), 11-12, 216
Election (2000), 37-42
Election (2008), 20, 50-51
Election (2012), 14, 42-51
Election (2016), 51-59, 87-90
Election (2020), 213-14, 216, 222
Election (2024), 207-214
Emanuel, Rahm, 121
Environmental Protection Agency, 133, 171
Europe, 118-9, 206
E-Verify, 166

Facebook, 55-6
Fahrenheit 9/11, 80-83
Fair Deal, 120
Fallon, George, 29

Fauci, Dr. Anthony, 127, 134-5, 224-5
FBI, 56, 75, 78, 187-8
Federal-Aid Highway Act, 30
Federal Reserve, 20, 62-3, 67
Feingold, Russ, 182
Feinstein, Diane, 182
Felt, Mark, 77
FEMA, 39, 128
Festinger, Leon, 103-4
Financial Times, 196
Florina, Carly, 51
Floyd, George, 146, 150, 222
Ford, Gerald, 61, 77-9
Fox News, 53-4, 103, 107, 110-16,130, 132,
  154, 196
Frank, Thomas, 15, 92-3
Freakonomics, 192
Fukuyama, Francis, 177

Gallagher, Trace, 116
Gallup poll, 22, 57, 78, 140
Galston, William, 22
Gates, Robert, 186
Geller, Joe, 39
Gephardt, Dick, 181
Geithner, Timothy, 67
Gillespie, Ed, 83, 85
Gingrich, Newt, 12, 45,51, 225
Goldwater, 2,9,147, 219
Google, 167
Gore, Al, Jr. 37-42, 50, 169-73, 182
Gorsuch, Neil, 141-5
Graham, Dr. Barney, 122
Graham, Lindsay, 111
Great Depression, 4, 26, 28, 63, 129,205
Great Recession, 60, 63-7, 97, 174
Greenberg, David, 71-2
Green New Deal, 202
Guilfoyle, Kimberly, 222
Guns, 97, 159-165
Guterres, Antonio, 170

Halbrook, Hal, 77
Haldeman, Bob, 75
Haley, Nikki, 210, 222
Hannity, Sean, 54, 111, 113, 115-6
Heritage Foundation, 21
Heuvel, William Vander, 79
Hillary: The Movie, 82
Hiss, Alger, 8

Hofstadter, Richard, 9
Holmes, Jr., Oliver Wendell, 156-8
Homestead Act, 202
Hoover, Herbert, 64, 125-128
Hopkins, Anthony, 70
House Republican Conference, 206
Huntsman, Jon, 51
Hurricane Katrina, 39
Hussein, Saddam, 12, 80, 113, 178, 181-3
Huston, Tom, 75
Hydroxychloroquine, 114-15, 134

Immigration, 11-15-16, 48-9, 96, 112-3,
  168-9
Immigration Reform Control Act, 166
An Inconvenient Truth (movie), 169-173
Ingraham, Laura, 112, 114
Inflation Reduction Act, 204
Inhofe, Jim, 171
Iran, 100-2
Iraq, 12-3, 80, 112, 177-185, 192-3
Inflation, 20, 61-3, 204-7, 212-3
Inside Job (movie), 82, 86
Intergovernmental Panel on Climate
  Change, 170-1
Infrastructure, 97, 202-4
ISIS, 104
Issa, Darell, 174

Japan, 89, 152, 168-9
Jefferson, Thomas, 84
Jinping, Xi, 173-4
Jobs, Steve, 167
John Birch Society, 9-10
John Brown's raid, 151
Johns Hopkins Center for Health Security,
  137
Johnson, Lyndon, 10, 20, 72, 147
Justice Department, 78

Kabaservice, Geoffrey, 91
Kagan, Elena, 145
Kagan, Robert, 89
Kahn, Khizr, 101
Kalmoe, Nathan, 140-1
Kamarck, Elaine, 22
Kariko, Katalin, 122
Kasich, John, 51
Kavanaugh, Brett, 141-5
Kennan, George, 185

Kennedy, Edward, 182
Kennedy, John F., 20, 44, 72, 178, 213
Kennedy, Paul, 191-2
Kent State, 74
Kerry, John, 182
Kinzinger, Adam, 2, 226
Klain, Ron, 124-5
Klein, Ezra, 208-9
Korean War, 34, 192
Krauthammer, Charles, 89
Kristol, William, 50
Krugman, Paul, 19-21
Kushner, Jarod, 54
Kutler, Stanley, 72
Kyoto Protocol, 134, 170

Laden, Osama bin, 178
Larson, Arthur, 7, 25-28
The Last of the President's Men, 72
Lazio, Rick, 58
Lehman Brothers, 67
Levitsky, Steven, 215
Libya, 58, 222
Lieberman, Joe, 50
Lincoln, Abraham, 98, 151-2, 202-4
Lind, Michael, 93
Luttig, J. Micharl, 225-7

MacCallum, Martha, 111-2
Maddow, Rachel, 3
MAGA, 4, 17, 105-8, 223
Maher, Bill, 82
Mahomes, Patrick, 135
Mattis, Jim, 111, 113
McEnany, Kayleigh, 122
McCain, John, 50, 88, 101, 171
McCain-Feingold Act, 82
McCarthy, Joseph, 2, 7-9, 25, 31, 33, 157, 227
McCarthy, Kevin, 122
McConnell, Mitch,95, 111, 202-7
McDaniel, Ronna, 222
McFaul, Michael, 186
McGovern, Jim, 217
McPherson, James, 150
Meachem, Jon, 3
Mellon, Andrew, 65
Meyers, Seth, 100-1
Michel, Bob, 2

Middle East, 89, 93, 181-3, 191
Migration Policy Institute, 166
Miller, Diane Disney, 71
Milgram, Stanley, 105-8
Minimum wage, 97
Mississippi, 146-53
Mitchell, John, 75
Mondale, Walter, 46
Moderna, 111-2
Morning Joe, 86-7
Moody's Analytics, 205
Moore, Michael, 58-9, 80-83, 183-4
Morrill Act, 202
Morse, Wayne, 32
Movies, 69-90
mRNA vaccine, 121-2, 137
Murdoch, Rupert, 53-4
Murphy, Chris, 212
Murtha, John, 184
Murrow, Edward R., 35
Musk, Elon, 167

Obama, Barack, 16, 20-1 44-9, 55, 59, 67, 80-1, 99-103, 124, 135, 146, 148, 150, 154, 166, 171,-4, 182, 186, 205, 213, 222, 224
Obamacare, 21, 48, 120, 154 (also, see Affordable Care Act)
Obedience to Authority, 106-8
Obergefell v. Hodges, 142
One Hell of a Gamble, 178
One Man Against the World, 72
O'Reilly, Bill, 113
Operation Desert Storm, 192
Operation Warp Speed, 121-2
Organization of Petroleum Exporting Countries (OPEC), 61-2
Oswald, Lee Harvey, 160

Naftali, Timothy, 177-80
National Cancer Institute, 134
National Commission on the Causes of the Financial and Economic Crisis in the United States, 67
National Firearms Act, 163-4
National Institutes of Health, 122
National Republican Senatorial Committee, 206
National Review, 27
National Rifle Association, 164-5

Native Americans, 152
Negative Partisanship, 52
Neither Liberal nor Conservative, 140
New Deal, 29, 66, 129, 140
New Democrat Coalition, 20
New York City, 128, 144
New York State, 144-5, 215
New York Times, 19, 86, 110, 130,154, 161, 183, 211
Newsom, Gavin, 212
Nicholas, Peter, 101-2
Nixon (movie), 70
The Nixon Tapes, 72
Nixon, Richard, 38, 61, 69-80, 147
No Labels, 18
Norquist, Grover, 13, 95

Page, Larry, 167
Palin, Sarah, 50
Patton (Movie), 73-6
Patton, George S., 73-6
Pecker, David, 54
Pelosi, Nancy, 101, 115, 224-5
Pennsylvania, 52, 56, 211, 214
Pense, Mike, 225
Perot, Ross, 45
Perry, Rick, 51
Perry, William J., 186
Peterson, Christopher, 103
Pew Research Center, 139, 150, 220-1
Pfizer-BioNTech, 121-2
Phillips, Dean, 212
Priebus, Reince, 85-6
Podesta, John, 55
Pompeo, Mike, 198, 130
Powell, Colin, 180
President's Council on Bioethics, 134
Price, Ray, 71
Public Citizen, 72
Putin, Vladimir, 55-6, 185-88

Quayle, Dan, 49-50

Reagan, Nancy, 84-5
Reagan, Ronald, 7, 10-1, 14-5, 19, 22, 45-8, 60-2, 66, 79, 84-5, 95, 133, 141-2, 147-8, 218-9
The Reagans (movie), 83-5
Reason, 91
Redford, Robert, 76-7, 80

Reich, Robert, 91
Reid, Harry, 182
Relman, Dr. David A., 131
A Republican Looks at His Party, 26-7
Republican National Convention, 11, 96, 222
Richardson, Heather Cox, 3
Religulous, (movie), 82
The Rise and Fall of the Great Powers, 191
Roberts, John, 142
Roberts, Kevin D., 219
Robinson, Eugene, 89
Rockefeller, Jay, 182
Rockefeller, Nelson, 2, 10
Roger & Me (movie), 82
Roosevelt, Franklin D., 28, 66, 120, 125-6, 129, 140, 163-4
Rubenstein, David, 23
Rufo, Christopher, 154-5
Rule and Ruin. 91
Rogers, William, 75
Romney, Mitt, 13-14, 21, 23, 42-49, 148, 220, 225
Rosenstein, Rod, 112
Rumsfeld, Donald, 184
Russia, 55-6, 89, 102, 112, 177, 185-190, 206, 213
The Russia Hoax, 112
Russians, 55, 110
Ryan, Paul, 48, 88

Sanders, Bernie, 21
Santorum, Rick, 51
Saudi Arabia, 62, 81
Savings and Loan Crisis, 66
Scalia, Antonin, 141-2
Schiff, Adam, 101
Schultze, Charles, 62
Schwartz, Tony, 89
Scott, George C., 73-5
Second Amendment, 163-4
Securities and Exchange Commission, 66
Slouching Toward Gomorrah, 141
Subprime Mortgages, 67
Sicko (movie), 82
Silver, Nate, 56
Smallpox, 136-7
Smith, Margaret Chase, 8, 31-3, 227-8
Snyder, Timothy, 156-7
Social Security, 26

Spotlight (movie), 76
1619 Project, 54, 156
Soviet Union, 78
Spurlock, Morgan, 82
Stalin, Joseph, 35, 156
States' Rights, 151
Stephens, Bret, 130
Stevens, John Paul, 41
Stewart, Jon, 82
Stone, Roger, 38
Stone, Oliver, 70-3
Supply Side Economics, 19
Supreme Court, 39-42, 48, 82, 85-6, 112,
    120, 151, 162-3
Syria, 110, 113

Taliban, 144
Texas, 50
Thucydides's Trap, 196-8
Trump, Donald, 3-4, 6, 13, 16-8, 22, 25,
    30-7, 49-58, 87-90, 100-117, 120-1, 146,
    150, 165-6, 169, 175, 185-90, 196, 198m
    207-8, 211-227

Ukraine, 85, 185-6, 188, 206, 213
United Kingdom, 102, 119, 161, 206
United Nations, 170, 180, 199
United States v. Miller, 164
Uvalde, 159

Vaccine Research Center, 122
Vietnam War, 71-5, 192, 196
Volcker, Paul, 62-3
Voting Rights Act, 141, 147, 216

Wall Street Journal, 65
Washington, George, 135-8
Washington Post, 22, 32, 55, 58, 76, 110,
    223
Watergate, 76-80
What's the Matter with Kansas?, 15, 92-3
Whitlock, Craig, 194
White House Correspondents' Dinner, 102
Whitman, Charles, 160
Weiner, Tim, 72
Welles, Orson, 70
Whitmer, Gretchen, 212
WikiLeaks, 55
Winfrey, Oprah, 135
Woodward, Bob, 72, 76, 78

World Health Organization, 130-1, 134
Wuhan Institute of Virology, 129-32
Wellstone, Paul, 62

YouTube, 184

Zakaria, Fareed, 93, 208-9
Ziblatt, Daniel, 215
Zandi, Mark, 205
Zedong, Mao, 34